Language Arts Activities
for Children

Language Arts Activities for Children

Donna E. Norton

Texas A & M University

Charles E. Merrill Publishing Company
A Bell & Howell Company
Columbus   Toronto   London   Sydney

Published by Charles E. Merrill Publishing Co.
A Bell & Howell Company
Columbus, Ohio 43216

This book was set in Oracle and Souvenir
Cover Design Coordination: Will Chenoweth
Production Coordination: Linda Hillis Bayma

Photo Credits: Bradley Norton, 279; *Resource Teaching* (Charles E. Merrill, 1977), 87; Dan Unkefer, 1, 21, 137; *Values in the Classroom* (Charles E. Merrill, 1977), 179; Cynda Williams, 241, 327.

Library of Congress Catalog Card Number: 79-92667

International Standard Book Number: 0-675-08134-3

1 2 3 4 5 6 7 8 9 10—85 84 83 82 81 80

Printed in the United States of America

Preface

Bringing effective language arts activities into the classroom is an exciting experience for both the children and the teacher. Stimulating activities add sparkle to the environment and enrich children's learning experiences. We are, however, living in a time when educators are facing criticism about the effectiveness of instruction, the development of language arts competencies in the classroom, and the ability of schools to meet the needs of a diverse school population. Unfortunately, adding stimulation and enrichment to the environment and effectively meeting competency needs in language arts may be considered opposing goals. It is the purpose of this activities book to illustrate how the classroom can have both effective teaching that builds skills and a stimulating, enriched environment.

This is a very practical book. All activities in the book are developed in a lesson plan format. To my knowledge, this is the only language arts activity book in which lesson plans are fully developed. This format was developed through work in inservice education and teacher education. We found that effective teaching required a model for lesson plan development, clearly stipulated objectives, and a step-by-step development of the lesson. We also discovered that peer teaching, student teaching, and inservice classroom teaching improved when the application of methods stressed in language arts classes was demonstrated through lesson plan development. These plans can be used directly by the teacher, modified for individual needs, or used as a model for additional activities.

This book would not be possible without interaction with children, teachers, and undergraduate students. I wish to thank all of the excellent teachers who have provided inspiration and ideas; the school systems which have provided opportunities for consultation, inservice, and workshops; the undergraduate students who enthusiastically tried ideas; and the children who provided the final evaluation. I sincerely hope you, the teacher or future teacher, will have equally exciting teaching experiences when you use the activities developed in this book.

Contents

Contents

1 Creative Language Arts

Motivation—stimulation—creativity—enriched environments—effective lesson plans—effective teaching techniques! Do these terms mean anything in the development of an effective language arts curriculum? The answer is yes—and all these factors should be visible in the elementary classroom environment. We should see their effects on how children develop communication skills, and we should see their influence in what children produce during language arts instruction. We should see positive changes in children's attitudes toward communication skills, and we should see their effects in the teaching strategies the classroom teacher uses.

Imagine a classroom that ignores these powerful educational tools. If we were to walk into that classroom, we would probably find ourselves in a sterile environment—the room would contain no colorful bulletin boards showing children's creative writing, and there would be no learning centers or library corners for stimulating children's creative thinking and individual growth. In this sterile environment, the teacher would lead no motivational periods or stimulating discussions before assigning tasks. Students would not be stimulated by the thoughts of others, and would have few opportunities for oral language growth, creative written expression, or for developing a love for books. The materials used in this sterile classroom would reflect lack of creativity, motivation, and attention to individual needs. Numerous ditto sheets might require children to answer factual questions with little prior motivation or group discussion to clarify and extend ideas. The teacher would not interact with the children as they wrote; would not provide opportunities for children to listen to and read a variety of stories; would not motivate oral and written expression; would not use knowledge of children's needs to develop instructional tasks; and would not organize the classroom to make use of individual, small-group and large-group activities.

In contrast, the classroom that uses these powerful tools is a rich environment for learning. There are many opportunities for children to experience the environment, work at stimulating learning centers, and interact purposefully with classmates and teacher. Children's interests are considered in helping them select literature. Their interests are also used to stimulate other children by providing opportunities for children to share their reading interests with others in a recreational reading group or a literature learning center. Interests are considered for assignments using research, interest, and ability groups. Motivational periods provide vital stimulation before children are asked to write; teacher–student interaction is important while students write. The teacher helps clarify ideas and provides instruction when necessary. Children's interests in the media may be used to motivate reading, writing, critical evaluation, and creative oral expression. The teacher in this environment understands the need to read and tell stories to children everyday, to stimulate a love for literature as well as appreciative listening skills. The teacher understands the scope and sequence of the language arts curriculum and provides opportunities for children to develop all the communication skills.

Teachers as well as children require stimulating instruction. It is not an easy task to develop the enriched environment and instructional tasks that stimulate and motivate effective communications skills. Creative activities require time for preparation and planning, and finding this extra time is often difficult in teachers' busy schedules. It is the purpose of this book to provide ideas and complete lesson plans for the preservice and inservice teacher to use as suggested, to adapt for individual needs, or to use the ideas for developing additional activities.

CONSIDERATIONS IN ORGANIZING LANGUAGE ARTS INSTRUCTION

Before discussing how to use the activities in this book, let us review some of the considerations for effective and efficient classroom organization and instruction. Effective language arts instruction should provide for individual needs. Providing for the individual needs of a whole classroom, however, requires considerable instructional, organizational, and management ability. First, the students' language arts abilities need to be evaluated so instruction can be geared toward their actual needs. After evaluation, the teacher must provide instruction that meets the discovered needs. Flexible grouping practices are the most efficient way to meet the language arts needs of all the students. Without flexible groupings, the language arts teacher has an almost impossible task. At one extreme is complete individualization of instruction for all students; at the other extreme is identical instruction for the whole class. Neither of these alternatives allows for the best use of instructional time. Besides, these alternatives would not meet the special requirements of the various language arts. Development of many of the oral language skills would be inconceivable on an individual basis. Can you imagine a one-person discussion or a one-person creative dramatization? To meet both the children's needs and the requirements of the various language arts, the classroom must provide opportunities for children to work individually, in pairs, in small groups, and with the whole class.

The following checklist will help the teacher evaluate effective and efficient instructional practices. Are each of the following factors included in language arts planning, instruction, and classroom organization?

Questions to Answer for Planning Effective and Efficient Language Arts Instruction

	Always	Sometimes	No
1. Do I evaluate students' language arts abilities?	_____	_____	_____
2. Do I provide opportunities for children to work in appropriate groupings?	_____	_____	_____
a. individual instruction?	_____	_____	_____
b. assignments that can be completed individually?	_____	_____	_____
c. assignments that can be completed in pairs?	_____	_____	_____
d. small-group instruction?	_____	_____	_____
interest groups?	_____	_____	_____
research groups?	_____	_____	_____
ability groups?	_____	_____	_____
special needs groups?	_____	_____	_____
e. whole-class instruction where appropriate?	_____	_____	_____
3. Do I provide students opportunities to work in motivating learning centers?	_____	_____	_____
4. Do I provide adequate instructional time for all of the language arts skills?	_____	_____	_____
a. oral communications?	_____	_____	_____
b. written communications?	_____	_____	_____
c. listening?	_____	_____	_____
d. reading?	_____	_____	_____
e. spelling?	_____	_____	_____
f. literature?	_____	_____	_____
g. grammar, usage?	_____	_____	_____
h. handwriting?	_____	_____	_____
i. media?	_____	_____	_____
5. Do I balance the language arts subjects so listening, creative writing, literature, oral expression, and media are all emphasized?	_____	_____	_____
6. Do I use both formal and informal methods for learning?	_____	_____	_____
7. Do I have a balance between oral and written work?	_____	_____	_____
8. Do I consider motivation and stimulation in language arts lesson planning?	_____	_____	_____

9. Do I use flexible room arrangements
    so students can work in groups, pairs,
    and individually?   _____ _____ _____

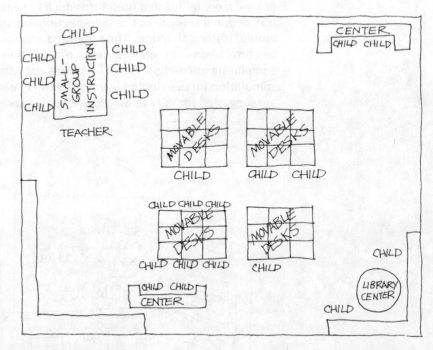

AREAS OF THE LANGUAGE ARTS
DEVELOPED IN THIS TEXT

Effective instruction should balance all areas of the language arts. For this reason, the activities in this text include oral language, listening, language experience, writing, media, grammar, usage, spelling, handwriting, punctuation, and literature. Because language arts skills are interrelated, many of the activities are designed to improve more than one language arts skill.

Besides covering a wide variety of areas, the activities also demonstrate diversity for grouping practices. Many of the activities are easily adaptable for whole-class, group, or individual instruction. For example, many of the writing activities suggest motivational periods for stimulating whole classes or large groups. These motivational periods are then followed by individual writing sessions during which the teacher interacts with each student.

To help the teacher provide motivating learning centers, the text includes activities for use with a learning-center format. The listening section, for example, includes several "Listening Post" activities, complete with suggestions for taped listening lessons and self-correcting activity cards.

To provide greater flexibility of instruction, some of the activities can be completed in a short instructional period, while others are the components of whole units of study. As an example of this flexibility, the literature section contains activities developed around story telling and literature which are easily completed in one instructional session. In the same section is a unit of study developed around historical fiction. The suggested activities in this unit could be correlated with social studies to provide several weeks of stimulating instruction. Since literature also offers marvelous stimulation for developing learning centers, learning center activities are suggested for fairy tales, picture books, and historical fiction.

HOW ARE THE ACTIVITIES PRESENTED?

Each activity in this text is designed for maximum usefulness to the teacher. The purposes of the activity are listed first, stating the various language arts skills that will be developed by the activity. Without an understanding of the activity's purpose the teacher cannot decide whether children need the activity or whether they have actually benefited from instruction once it is completed. In addition, since communication skills are interrelated, many activities are designed to develop several language arts skills at once. Let us consider, for example, the language experience activity 2 in section 4 titled "Sammy Circle's Colors." The purposes for this activity are:

1. To involve students in a motivational activity resulting in oral discussion and a dictated story.
2. To identify colors illustrated in a rebus chart story.
3. To match colors on cardboard circles with colors on a rebus chart story.

These purposes relate to the skills and objectives that are stated in most language arts scope and sequence charts for early elementary grades. If children can already identify colors by both concrete color example and printed words, they will not need to spend time on this activity.

Each activity is also coded according to the **type** of activity and the **term** of the activity. Both effective classroom management and effective teaching require instructional activities that allow the teacher to work with the whole class, smaller groups, and individual children. Many of the activities in the text may be adapted for each of these groupings. In our example, "Sammy Circle's Colors," the teacher can use the activity with the whole class, if the total class needs reinforcement in color identification or the reading of color labels. If, however, only a small group requires this instruction or review, the activity may be used with that group or even an individual child. The additional reinforcement activities listed for the activity also suggest other group and individual activities designed to strengthen color identification. The second coding of each activity refers to the time required to complete the activity: STA means the activity is a short-term activity which can be completed in one or two instructional sessions; LTA means the activity is a longer term activity which can be developed over several sessions or even weeks; LC indicates that the activity is developed in learning center format. The activity "Sammy Circle's Colors" is coded as a short-term activity since it can be completed in one session although follow-up reinforcement activities may require additional time.

After these stated purposes for the activity, there is a list of materials necessary to complete it. These materials are specific, including the names of books, references, suggestions for pictures, motivational activities, media, charts, or stipulations for art or other supplies. All suggestions for charts, paragraphs, games, etc., are developed fully in the procedural section of the activity. In our example, "Sammy Circle's Colors," the materials include:

Sammy Circle drawn in each of the basic colors; chart story, "Sammy Circle's Colors"; chart paper for dictated story; art supplies for individual pictures.

In this activity the motivational chart story is developed as follows:

Each activity designates the approximate grade-level range appropriate for the activity (lower elementary, middle elementary, upper elementary, middle school) rather than a specific grade. Approximations are more useful since children's needs, interests, and abilities vary greatly. Many of the activities may be easily adapted to the needs of younger or older students by rewording the directions and changing the motivating activity. Our example, "Sammy Circle's Colors," has a grade designation of kindergarten, first grade. While this is the grade level at which colors are usually taught, the activity may be used with older students requiring remedial assistance.

Finally, each activity gives step-by-step procedures for developing the activity with children. If the activity demands reading a literature selection, background information about the book is provided. If the activity requires a motivational chart, paragraph, or game to share with children, the chart is developed, the paragraph is included, or the game board is illustrated and directions included. The procedures in our example, "Sammy Circle's Colors," include:

1. Lead an oral discussion about Sammy Circle and his problems with colors. Begin the discussion by introducing "Sammy Circle." Draw Sammy on a card or sheet, but do not color in the circle. Explain that Sammy Circle is unhappy because he wants to be colorful, but cannot decide which color he wants to be. He wants the children to "read" the chart story "Sammy Circle's Colors" that describes his problems. After they "read" the story along with their teacher, he wants them to draw a picture illustrating the solution to his problem, and dictate a short story telling about the picture.
2. Introduce the story "Sammy Circle's Colors," which has been printed on large sheets of tagboard or newsprint. Encourage children to follow along as you read. Allow children to "read" the rebus pictures. Read the story a second time, encouraging children to "read" with you.
3. Discuss the color choices Sammy Circle has for his coat. Encourage the children to discuss advantages and disadvantages for choosing each color. Which color did they choose? Why? What would they feel like if they were wearing a brown, purple, or yellow coat? What would they do after they chose their coat?
4. Have the students dictate a language experience chart story which solves Sammy's problem.

Since the purpose for this activity is the reinforcement of color identification, as well as oral language and written language, this activity includes five activities designed to provide additional practice with color identification. These include:

1. Have the students match the Sammy Circles drawn on colored paper with the appropriate rebus drawing on the chart story.
2. Randomly name colors depicted on the chart story. Have children point to the appropriate color on the chart.
3. Ask students to draw a picture illustrating "Sammy Circle's Colors," for Sammy's coat and the activities he would do after he dressed in his coat. Encourage them to dictate individual stories after they finish their pictures.
4. Match colored felt circles on the flannel board.
5. Have children who are ready match the printed word with the corresponding color circle.

USING THE ACTIVITIES

The way the language arts activities in this text will be used depends upon the teacher's purpose. The text can be effectively used by several different groups of preservice and inservice teachers. At the undergraduate level, the activities may be used to supplement the main text in the language arts methods course. Since this activities book covers the major areas of the language arts, it can be used as a supplementary text for any of the language arts methods texts. (A list of these methods texts is presented at the end of this introduction.) As a supplementary text, this activities book illustrates, through the complete development of lesson plans, the research findings and methods presented in the main methods book used in the course. The activities are completely developed for use as stipulated by college students during practicum sessions, student-teaching experiences, or peer-teaching experiences. The materials may also be adapted for individual needs, or used to stimulate the development of other language arts activities. The activities also represent a file of ideas and lessons that will be useful throughout one's teaching career.

Inservice teachers who have already covered the language arts research and methods will be able to use this activities book immediately as a source of ideas and lesson plans with their students. Again, the activities may be used directly from the book, or they may be changed to meet the individual needs of the classroom teacher. It is also hoped that the ideas presented will stimulate the development of other language arts activities in the classroom.

Language arts curriculum specialists will find many uses for this activity book. The text illustrates effective language arts methods for inservice teachers; inservice teachers may participate in the activities during inservice or workshop presentations, then apply the activities in their own classrooms. The book can also be used as a guide to help inservice teachers prepare additional language arts instructional plans.

The activities in this text have been used with all of the above groups of preservice and inservice teachers. They have been used to teach children, and to demonstrate effective instructional procedures to preservice and inservice teachers and to curriculum specialists. I developed and used the activities during my experiences as a classroom teacher, a language arts curriculum specialist for public schools, a director for a university language arts/reading clinic, and as a university professor. I hope the activities will stimulate both children and teachers in the areas of the language arts.

Let us now assume that you have evaluated the needs of your class and wish to provide language arts instruction using these activities. How should you approach this task? First, look at the way the activities are grouped in this book. There are sections for oral language, listening, language experience, writing, media, mechanics of language, and literature activities. Read the activities you are considering. What is the stated purpose of each activity? Does that purpose correspond with the instructional needs of your students? Check the recommended materials. Do you have the materials? Are there any materials, such as a chart or tape, that you must prepare before you begin the lesson? Look at the grade levels given for the activity. Do you need to make any adaptations for your students? Read the step-by-step procedures for the activity. Do you want to use the activity with a large group, small group, or with an individual child? Do you need to make any modifications for your grouping? Do you want a short-term activity that can be completed in one session, or do you want a longer term activity that may take several sessions to complete? Do you want to develop a whole unit of study? Do you want to develop a learning center dealing with that subject? Do you need to make any modifications because of these requirements? (Many short-term activities can be developed into learning-center or unit activities. Likewise, many of the activities listed under learning centers can be used as short-term activities without developing a total unit or learning center.)

The following chart lists each activity by number and name; whether the activity can be used by the whole class, a group, or by individuals; and whether it is a short-term activity (STA), a longer term activity (LTA), or learning center (LC) activity:

Oral Language Activities

	Activity	Instructional Organization	Term
2-1	My Time of Wonder	class, group	STA
2-2	Pictures Stimulate Discussion	class, group, individual	STA
2-3	Talking About the Familiar	individual, pairs	STA
2-4	The Telephone	pairs, group	STA
2-5	Gussie the Puppet	class, group	STA
2-6	Story Telling from Lost and Found Advertisements	class motivation, group	STA
2-7	Oral Questioning	class, group, individual	STA
2-8	A Woman Can Be...	class, group, individual	STA
2-9	Category Detectives	group, individual	STA
2-10	Campbell's 59'ers	class, group	LTA
2-11	Solving Problems with Role Playing	class, group	STA

Oral Language Activities *(cont.)*

	Activity	Instructional Organization	Term
2-12	Interviewing	class, group, pairs	LTA
2-13	In the Round	class, group	STA
2-14	Pat-si-oo-ree-oo-ree-ay	class, group	STA
2-15	Low Bridge, Everybody Down	class, group	STA
2-16	Yankee Doodle	class, group	STA
2-17	The Old Chisholm Trail	class, group	STA
2-18	What's It Like to Be a Rag Doll	class, group	STA
2-19	A Walk through Imagination	class, group	STA
2-20	A Softball Game without a Ball	class, group	STA
2-21	Communicating with Indian Sign Language	class, group	LTA
2-22	A Television Production Staff*	class, group	LTA
2-23	Putting On Our Own T V Show—Part I*	class, group	LTA
2-24	Putting On Our Own T V Show—Part II*	class, group	LTA

Listening Activities

	Activity	Instructional Organization	Term
3-1	Using Sounds to Learn about the World	class, group	STA
3-2	Listening for Different Purposes—Why and How	class, group	STA
3-3	Listening Times	class, group	LTA
3-4	The Listening Post	individual	LC
3-5	Listening for Directions	individual	LC
3-6	The Class Crier	class, group	STA
3-7	Listening for Main Ideas and Supporting Details	group, individual	STA

*Activities 2-22, 2-23, and 2-24 may be used together to develop a creative dramatization.

	Activity	Instructional Organization	Term
3-8	Were Pilgrims Dull?	class, group, individual	STA
3-9	The Mystery of the Kidnapped Chemist	individual	LC
3-10	Poor Richard	class, group,	STA
3-11	Playing Detective with Fairy Tale Heroes	individuals	LC
3-12	Playing Detective with Famous Americans	individual	LC
3-13	Fools and Foolishness in Folktales	class, group	STA
3-14	Radios Days of Old	class, group	LTA

Language Experience Activities

	Activity	Instructional Organization	Term
4-1	Sammy Circle's Discovery	class, group, individual	STA
4-2	Sammy Circle's Colors	class, group, individual	STA
4-3	Rhyming Rebus Games	group, individual	STA
4-4	Jill, Bill, and Will on Sampson's Hill	group, individual	STA
4-5	Rhyming Picture Stories	group, individual	STA
4-6	Increasing Sight Word Knowledge	group, individual	STA
4-7	Reinforcing Phonic Instruction	group, individual	STA
4-8	The Disappearing Pineapple	group, individual	STA
4-9	Making Butter	group, individual	STA
4-10	Our Book of Opposites	group, individual	STA
4-11	Mapping Our Classroom	group, individual	STA
4-12	Magic Waves	group, individual	STA
4-13	Planning My Vacation	group, individual	STA
4-14	Golden Fleece Award	group	STA

Writing Activities

	Activity	Instructional Organization	Term
5-1	Myself and My Family	class or group motivation, individual writing	LTA
5-2	My Lovable Dirty Old Bear	class or group motivation, individual writing	STA
5-3	My Favorite Possession	class or group motivation, individual writing	STA
5-4	Hats Change My Identity	class or group motivation, individual writing	STA
5-5	My First 100 Years	class or group motivation, individual writing	STA
5-6	The Wonderful Miracle	class or group motivation, individual writing	STA
5-7	Wow! I Just Won $100	class or group motivation, individual writing	STA
5-8	American Indian Names	class or group motivation, individual writing	STA
5-9	My Nature Name	class or group motivation, individual writing	STA
5-10	Indian Symbols	class or group motivation, individual writing	STA
5-11	My Own Totem Pole	class or group motivation, individual writing	STA
5-12	School is . . .	class or group motivation, individual writing	STA
5-13	Haiku	class or group motivation, individual writing	STA
5-14	Typographical Tricks with Poetry	class or group motivation, individual writing	STA
5-15	Develping Imagery with Similes	class or group motivation individual writing	STA
5-16	Developing Imagery with Metaphors	class or group motivation, individual writing	STA
5-17	Space Words	class or group motivation, individual writing	STA
5-18	Knowing My Audience and My Purpose	class, group	STA
5-19	Writing Letters	class, group	STA
5-20	Writing Invitations	class, group	STA
5-21	Writing for My Own Enjoyment and Remembrance	class, group	STA
5-22	Writing a News Story	class, group	STA

	Activity	Instructional Organization	Term
5-23	The Controlling Idea in a Paragraph	class, group	STA
5-24	Organization Using —Chronological Order	class, group	LTA
5-25	Organization Using Questions and Answers	class, group	LTA
5-26	Organization Using Spatial Concepts or Physical Details	class, group	LTA
5-27	Organization Using Problem, Cause and Solution Format	class, group	LTA

Activities for the Mechanics of Language

	Activity	Instructional Organization	Term
6-1	The Comedie of Errors	whole class, group	STA
6-2	CB Slang	whole class, group	STA
6-3	The Beginning of the English Language	whole class, group	LTA
6-4	The English Language in the United States	whole class, group	LTA
6-5	Building Sentence Patterns	whole class, group, individual	STA
6-6	Sentence Expansion	whole class, group, individual	STA
6-7	Holiday Jumble	whole class, group, individual	STA
6-8	Playing Sentence Detective	group, individual	STA
6-9	Who, Whose, Whom, and Which	group, individual	STA
6-10	Past, Present, and Future	group	STA
6-11	Ride the Amtrak Line	group	STA
6-12	Tic-Tac-Toe	group	STA
6-13	Synonym Concentration Game	group	STA
6-14	Relating Meaning and Spelling	group	STA

Activities for the Mechanics of Language *(cont.)*

	Activity	Instructional Organization	Term
6-15	Alphabetical Sentences	class, group, individual	STA
6-16	Personal Learning Centers for Writing	class	LC

Literature Activities

	Activity	Instructional Organization	Term
7-1	Investigating Children's Interests	individual	STA
7-2	The Fantasy of Mother Goose	class	STA
7-3	Mother Goose Is Alive in Upper Elementary	class, group	LTA
7-4	Rabbit Hill (Newbery Award, 1945)	group	STA
7-5	Sylvester and the Magic Pebble (Caldecott Award, 1970)	group	STA
7-6	Sam, Bangs, and Moonshine	class, group, individual	STA
7-7	Shadow of a Bull	individual	STA
7-8	The Bronze Bow	group, individual	STA
7-9	The Little House	group, individual	STA
7-10	Finder Keepers	class, group, individual	STA
7-11	The Egg Tree	class, group, individual	STA
7-12	The 21 Balloons	individual	STA
7-13	Maurice Sendak and His Literature—An Interest Center	individual	LC
7-14	Hans Christian Anderson—A Fairy Tale Interest Center	group, individual	LC
7-15	Carol Ryrie Brink's Caddie Woodlawn— An Interest Center for Historical Fiction	group, individual	LC

	Activity	*Instructional Organization*	*Term*
7-16	The Salem Witch Hunts—A Historical Fiction Unit	class, group	LTA
7-17	Storytelling	class, group	STA

Media Activities

	Activity	*Instructional Organization*	*Term*
8-1	Investigating Viewing Interests and Habits	class	STA
8-2	Survey of Time Spent Watching Television and Programs Watched	class	LTA
8-3	Using a T.V. Guide for Selective Viewing	class	LTA
8-4	Using Television to Motivate Reading—Part I	class, group	LTA
8-5	Fantasy and Fact on Television and in Television-related Books	class, group	LTA
8-6	Using Television to Motivate Reading—Part II	class, group	LTA
8-7	Identifying Commercials on Children's Shows	class, group	STA
8-8	The Power of Persuasion—A Unit of Study	class, group	LTA
8-9	Identifying Persuasive Techniques	class, group	STA
8-10	Fantasia: A Walt Disney Unit	class	LTA
8-11	Categorizing Newspaper Ads—Part I	group, individual	STA
8-12	Categorizing Newspaper Ads—Part II	group, individual	STA
8-13	The Parts of a Newspaper	class, group	STA

	Activity	Instructional Organization	Term
8-14	Significance of Newspaper and Periodical Names	class, group	STA
8-15	Relating Parts of a Newspaper to a Book or Story	class, group, individual	LTA
8-16	Headlines Show the Main Idea	group, individual	STA
8-17	Newspapers Help Us Shop for Food	group	STA
8-18	Newspapers Help Us Do More Shopping	group	STA
8-19	Advertisers Try to Appeal to a Specific Population	group	STA
8-20	Critical Reading— Fact vs. Fiction	group	LTA
8-21	Critical Reading— Fact vs. Opinion	group	LTA
8-22	Newspaper and Magazine Reading Habits	group	LTA

LANGUAGE ARTS TEXTBOOKS

Burns, Paul C., and Broman, Betty L. *The Language Arts in Childhood Education*. Chicago: Rand McNally College Publishing Co., 1979.

Hennings, Dorothy Grant. *Communication in Action*. Chicago: Rand McNally College Publishing Co., 1978.

Kean, John M., and Personke, Carl. *The Language Arts*. New York: St. Martin's Press, 1976.

Lundsteen, Sara W. *Children Learn to Communicate*. Englewood Cliffs, N.J.: Prentice-Hall, 1976.

Norton, Donna E. *The Effective Teaching of Language Arts*. Columbus, Ohio: Charles E. Merrill Publishing Co., 1980.

Petty, Walter; Cross, Marion E.; and Skeen, Elvis M. *Developing Language Skills in the Elementary Schools*. Boston: Allyn & Bacon, 1975.

Rubin, Dorothy. *Teaching Elementary Language Arts*. New York: Holt, Rinehart & Winston, 1975.

Tiedt, Iris M., and Tiedt, Sidney. *Contemporary English in the Elementary School*. Englewood Cliffs, N.J.: Prentice-Hall, 1975.

2 Oral Language
Activities

The development of oral language skills is one of the most crucial and exciting parts of the language arts curriculum. Instruction in oral language is exciting because it includes the development of creative thinking and interpretation through creative drama, puppetry, pantomime, and group discussion. Oral language instruction is crucial; a child's oral skills are essential for success in every part of life, both at school and at home.

Work such as the longitudinal study by Loban[1] points out the need for oral language instruction that helps each child organize ideas and illustrate complex generalizations.* The teacher needs to include instructional activities that help children develop discussion skills, questioning techniques, and creative thinking.

The activities in this section offer numerous stimuli for oral language development. The activities begin with those that use sensory experiences, familiar objects, and pictures to motivate oral discussion and story telling. The activities suggest ways to develop oral questioning strategies through focusing, extending, and raising. Several activities expand language and organizational abilities by identifying multiple labels for pictures and categorizing pictures or words into groups.

Group discussion skills that help children organize ideas and do creative problem solving can best be developed through brainstorming discussion groups and role playing activities. Role playing also helps children learn and refine interviewing skills.

Choral reading and speaking are a major form of stimulating oral language activity. Choral reading and speaking choirs were used by the ancient Greeks, and minstrels and churchmen used choral speaking choirs during the Middle Ages and the Renaissance. This oral language technique is as useful and enjoyable today as it was long ago. Children enjoy choral activities which allow them to participate in groups and cooperatively develop an enjoyable rendition of a poem, story, or song. Through choral exercises, children who may be hesitant in individual oral reading have an opportunity to practice speaking and reading skills in a nonthreatening environment.

Because dramatization and story acting are enhanced by body action and gesture, pantomime activities are included. Using actions alone, the pantomimist presents to an audience the ideas and emotions that would normally be conveyed by the spoken word. The pantomime activities presented in this section follow the sequence recommended by Fran Tanner:[2] loosening up, developing believable action, and developing observational skills.

The section concludes with a series of activities that utilize the study of television production to stimulate development of dramatizations.

*Full citations of works referred to in the text are listed at the end of the book.

ACTIVITY 2-1:
MY TIME OF WONDER

TYPE		TERM	
CLASS	☑	STA	☑
GROUP	☑	LTA	☐
IND	☐	LC	☐

Purpose:

1. To develop sensory awareness
2. To stimulate creative thinking and oral language
3. To expand descriptive vocabularies

Materials:

Time of Wonder, a picture story book by Robert McCloskey

Grade level:

Lower and middle elementary

Procedures:

1. To stimulate sensory awareness, read Robert McCloskey's *Time of Wonder,* a story about a family's summer vacation on an island. The story describes the many animals, plants, shells, and sailboats that make the island a place of wonder. One day a hurricane changes the island by uprooting trees and uncovering shells. The family goes exploring to discover the changes in their island.

2. After you read *Time of Wonder,* have the children describe the wonderful things the family experienced on the island.

3. Ask the children if they have ever had their own experiences with a time or place of wonder. Have them describe their place. Suggest to the students that we can experience many times of wonder if we use our senses to smell, see, feel, and hear what is around us. Tell the students they are going on a trip of wonder to try to see, smell, feel, and hear things they may not have noticed before. Prepare them to use their senses and, if feasible, ask them to make a collection of items they find. (Ask them, however, not to pick wildflowers or disturb other endangered plant life.) Some "Time of Wonder" trips include:

    A trip to a field near your school
    A walk in the woods
    A trip to the zoo

A walk along a beach
A walk in the neighborhood
A trip through a grocery store
An exploration of the foods and spices in the kitchen
A trip to a vegetable garden
A trip to a fruit orchard
A trip to a fabric store
A trip to a department store

4. Have the students describe their own "Time of Wonder" experiences. Encourage them to extend their experiences through questioning that invites them to describe their experiences fully.

5. Encourage children to experience a "Time of Wonder" with their own families. Have them set up displays and describe the things they experience.

ACTIVITY 2-2:
PICTURES STIMULATE DISCUSSION

TYPE		TERM	
CLASS	☑	STA	☑
GROUP	☑	LTA	☐
IND	☑	LC	☐

Purpose:
1. To stimulate oral discussion
2. To stimulate creative thinking
3. To develop oral descriptive skills

Materials:
File of pictures illustrating variety of subjects that suggest vivid descriptions and topics for creative stories

Grade level:
Lower and middle elementary

Procedures:
1. This activity can be repeated many times using a variety of pictures. The pictures may be used to stimulate large-group, small-group, or individual discussion and oral stories. For example:
a. A picture of a mother bear in a clearing with two baby cubs at the edge of the woods could stimulate an oral story.

"My father and I were out in the woods hunting all day. My dad wanted a bear skin to put on the floor of his den. We came upon a clearing and we saw a huge bear right in the middle of the meadow. My dad started to raise his gun when I saw something move. I yelled, "Don't shoot.""

Have the students look at the picture, tell why the boy asked his dad not to shoot, and then suggest endings for the story.

b. Flower pictures encourage children to describe the colors, shapes, sizes, textures, and emotions suggested by flowers. A child might pretend he is one of the flowers, starting as a seed warming in the soil, sprouting through the earth, then growing and stretching until he is a rose, daisy, thistle, etc.

c. Pictures of old deserted buildings suggest many stories. Who lived in the house? What did they do when they lived there? Why did they leave? Pretend you are going for a walk and come upon a deserted house. Do you go in? What happens if you do?

d. Using pictures of musical instruments, have each student select a musical instrument, pretend to be a musical instrument salesman and try to convince the class that this instrument is the best one to buy. Have older students research the musical instrument they choose and give an oral report to the class. Ask each student to pretend he is one of the instruments in the picture file and describe what it would be like to be that instrument, what it feels like to be part of an orchestra or band, and the music he likes to play. Have him tell about his most interesting experience as an instrument. Have the student pantomime his instrument while others in the class guess its identity.

e. With nature pictures, divide the students into pairs, and give one child a picture of a tree, etc. Have this child describe the picture to a second child, who draws the picture from the other's description without being told the identity of the picture. Have the students compare the pictures and drawings. For another activity, have the students pretend the picture is a setting for a story or movie. Ask them to describe the setting, suggest a title for the story, and tell the story that might take place there. A third activity could require children to compare the descriptions of grass, leaves, stones, twigs, bark, trees, etc.,

that would be developed from a picture, with the descriptions of the same items as developed from real life.

f. Using pictures of people, have each student choose a picture, describe the person in the picture, choose a name for that person, and tell a story about what he thinks might be happening to the person. Divide the students into small groups and give each student in the group a picture of a person. Have the group create an oral story using all the characters in the pictures.

g. With pictures of recreational sports, divide the class into pairs, allow each pair of children to select a recreational picture, and have one student pretend to be a sportscaster while the other is being interviewed for a TV show. Allow each child to select a picture and describe how he feels when he is doing the activity. Divide into two teams and use the pictures to stimulate the activities for a game of charades. The first player draws a picture from the recreation file and acts out the sport for his own team. His team is allowed one minute to guess what he is doing.

ACTIVITY 2-3:
TALKING ABOUT THE FAMILIAR

TYPE		TERM	
CLASS	☐	STA	☑
GROUP	☐	LTA	☐
IND	☑	LC	☐

Purpose:
1. To stimulate conversational skills after experimenting and discovering
2. To stimulate creativity

Materials: Clay, crayons, finger paints, blocks, trips, etc.

Grade level: Early elementary

Procedures:
1. The young elementary child needs many opportunities to experiment with and discover the world around him. The environment that allows him to experiment should also allow him to talk about his experiences. Oral communication should be with his peers and the teacher. Many children who are normally too shy to talk become quite expressive when describing an experience they have actually had. As possibilities:

    a. Provide children with play dough or clay. Encourage them to squeeze it, smell it, roll it, pull it, shape it, and build it into real and imaginary forms. Have them tell you their experiences informally as they experiment. Ask them questions about their sensory experiences. For a "Show and Tell" session, ask each child to make his favorite zoo animal, pet, friend, or imaginary animal. Have each one tell about his creation during "Show and Tell."

b. Have children experiment with blocks or Lincoln logs. As they are making their creations, have them tell you about them. What shapes can they create? What can they do in their imaginary creations? How can they make them taller, smaller, wider, flatter, etc.?

ACTIVITY 2-4:
THE TELEPHONE

TYPE		TERM	
CLASS	☐	STA	☑
GROUP	☑	LTA	☐
IND	☐	LC	☐

Purpose:

1. To make a play telephone and have a conversation with someone
2. To practice conversational skills

Materials:

Two paper cups, long strings, nail, two buttons for each child-made phone; toy phones or walkie-talkies

Grade level:

Early elementary

Procedures:

1. Ask the children whether they enjoy talking on the telephone. Discuss the purpose of the telephone with them, and have them list reasons for talking on the telephone. Tell the children they are going to make their own phones, and will have a chance to talk to their friends on their phones.
2. You may make one phone for the group to share, a phone for every two children, or have each child make his own phone so each will have one to take home. Directions for making the phones are as follows:

   Carefully poke a hole in the bottom of each paper cup. Put a long piece of string through the hole and tie a button onto the end of the string inside the cup. Attach the string in the same way to the second cup. Stretch the two cups apart so the string is tight. Have one partner hold the cup to his ears, while the other speaks into his cup. Use the child-made phones for conversations.

3. Provide toy telephones and allow children to practice talking on the phone. Some suggested roles include:

Talking to a friend about things that happened in school
Calling your mother or father to ask for a ride home because
  it's raining
Calling a friend to ask if the friend may stay overnight
Calling a friend to ask if the friend may accompany your
  family to the zoo, a museum, or other outing
Calling the police in an emergency
Calling the fire department in an emergency
Calling mother's or father's office or home to ask one of them
  to pick you up from school because you are sick

ACTIVITY 2-5:
GUSSIE THE PUPPET

TYPE		TERM	
CLASS	☑	STA	☑
GROUP	☑	LTA	☐
IND	☐	LC	☐

Purpose:
1. To create a puppet production
2. To develop oral language and stimulate creative dramatics

Materials:
Louie, a picture story book by Ezra Jack Keats

Grade level:
Lower elementary

Procedures:
1. To motivate a puppet presentation, read Ezra Jack Keats's *Louie.*
   Louie, the hero of this story, is a very quiet boy. He attends a puppet show and is attracted to Gussie, a puppet. After the show, Louie meets Gussie, then dreams about her. When Louie awakes, he follows a green string and finds Gussie waiting for him.
2. After reading the story, have the students suggest stories that they would like to see Gussie and her puppeteers (your class) perform.
3. After the class chooses a story, have them develop simple puppets and present the story as a puppet show. Directions for making puppets and developing a puppet production may be found in Donna Norton's *The Effective Teaching of Language Arts* (Columbus, Ohio: Charles E. Merrill Publishing Co., 1980).

ACTIVITY 2-6:
STORY TELLING FROM LOST-AND-FOUND ADVERTISEMENTS

TYPE		TERM	
CLASS	☑	STA	☑
GROUP	☑	LTA	☐
IND	☐	LC	☐

Purpose:

1. To stimulate oral discussion

2. To tell a creative story motivated by humorous or unusual lost-and-found advertisements

Materials:

Collection of humorous or unusual lost-and-found advertisements; newspapers containing lost-and-found advertisements

Grade level:

All grades; lost-and-found advertisements can be read to younger children

Procedures:

1. Search the lost-and-found advertisements and select thought-provoking ads.

2. Introduce lost-and-found ads to the children by discussing the kinds of things people might lose and how they might try to get the items back. Ask the group if any of them has ever lost anything, why the items were lost, and how they tried to find them.

3. Talk about the newspaper's lost-and-found section. Show it to the group, explaining that people often lose items. Read aloud some of the ads and allow students to speculate about how the item was lost, what happened when it was lost, who found the item, whether there was a reward offered, how the owner would try to find the item, and what the students would do with a reward if they earned it.

4. Allow children to select a specific lost-and-found ad and develop a creative story related to that ad. Some examples include:

Lost: Two male Dobermans in vicinity of the University campus. Answer to the names of Ringo and Savage.	Lost: Northgate Cinema, man's wedding ring. Gold with 3 small diamonds. Sentimental value, substantial reward.
Found: Black cat, about 12 months old, wearing flea collar, front paw in cast.	Lost: Boy's 20″ Sear motorcross bike, black and yellow. Reward from unhappy boy.
$500 REWARD For return of information on 20-ft camper last seen in Westgate Mall Shopping Center.	

5. Divide class into smaller groups and allow students to tell their stories to their own groups.

6. Design a "Lost and Found" bulletin board. Put the lost-and-found ads and the illustrations of the stories on the bulletin board.

7. Lost-and-found ads may easily be used to motivate creative writing.

ACTIVITY 2-7:
ORAL QUESTIONING

TYPE		TERM	
CLASS	☑	STA	☑
GROUP	☑	LTA	☐
IND	☑	LC	☐

Purpose:

1. To stimulate and increase children's comprehension levels during oral interaction
2. To use four questioning strategies effective in improving children's ability to comprehend: focusing, extending, clarifying, and raising.[3]

Materials:

These questioning strategies can accompany any oral discussion activity, and can relate to a story, film, picture, guest speaker, experiment, or content area subject.

Grade level:

All grades; questions can be designed for any level of cognitive development

Procedures:

The examples after each procedure pertain to a literature selection that has been read to the group; the procedures are equally effective with any other subject for discussion.

1. Focusing: After the children have listened to a story, read a story, watched a film, listened to a guest speaker, or done a science experiment, ask a question that focuses their attention on the purpose for listening to or reading the story, listening to the speaker, etc. This focusing question provides the mental set for the oral discussion that follows. The same sequence of questioning may be used several times with different focus questions. For example:

Following the teacher's oral reading of *Bill Cosby: Look Back in Laughter* by James T. Olsen, the following question could be asked to focus attention on the factual information in the story:

Bill Cosby is now a famous comedian, but how do you know that he did not always have an easy life when he was growing up? (He lived in an inner-city ghetto area; he had his first job when he was six; his father left home; he gave the money he earned in a grocery store to his mother.)

2. Extending: If the students have not answered the question as fully as they can, ask an extending question which requires additional information at the same level of comprehension. For example:

> Who could give us another idea about Bill Cosby's life when he was growing up? Could you tell us more about Bill's job in the grocery store? Tell us more about Bill's experience in school.

3. Clarifying: Encourage students to provide clear answers by asking clarifying questions. These questions encourage children to return to a previous comment in order to explain or redefine. For example:

> Could you explain in more detail what happened after Bill Cosby's father left home?

4. Raising: Finally, ask students questions that obtain information on the same subject but at a higher level of comprehension. Questions can be asked that raise thinking from the factual to the evaluative level. For example:

> Do you think Bill Cosby should have given all the eight dollars he made at the grocery store to his mother? Why or why not?

Questions can raise thinking from the factual to the appreciative level. For example: If you were Bill Cosby as a child, would you feel sorry for yourself? Why or why not? Do you think Bill Cosby felt sorry for himself? Why or why not?

ACTIVITY 2-8:
A WOMAN CAN BE...

TYPE		TERM	
CLASS	☑	STA	☑
GROUP	☑	LTA	☐
IND	☑	LC	☐

Purpose:

1. To recognize the possibility of multiple labels for pictures
2. To expand vocabulary through an oral language activity
3. To look for picture clues that suggest labels

Materials:

Pictures that suggest multiple labels and descriptive identifications; pictures that contain clues to more specific identification

Grade level:

Early elementary

Procedures:

1. Explain to the students that a picture, an object, or a person, can often be identified by different labels. Use one of the children as an example. Ask the rest of the group how many different labels they can think of to identify this child. Examples are: Jonathan is a boy; Jonathan is a first grader; he is Sharon's brother; he is Mr. and Mrs. Alton's son, etc. Discuss with the children what each label means and when they think it would be appropriate to use each label.

2. Provide pictures which suggest multiple labels. Discuss the different labels appropriate for each picture. Have the students give reasons for their labels. (This activity also expands occupational awareness. For example, a woman can have many different labels and occupational choices besides "Mother" or "housewife." She can be a doctor, lawyer, teacher, or engineer. Similarly, a man can also have many different labels and occupational choices.)

    Pictures of the following will suggest multiple labels: a man; a woman; a boy; a girl; a dog; a horse; a car; a plate of food; a tall building; a tree.

Some of the labels might be: "She is a woman and someone's daughter. She could be a wife, mother, niece, aunt, teacher, secretary, doctor, artist, mechanic, nurse, actress, etc." Or, "It is a tall, seven-story building. It could be an apartment house, a department store, an office building, a medical center, a museum, an art gallery, etc."

Discuss when each label would or would not be appropriate. Encourage each student to choose the label he likes for the picture and to tell an oral story about the person or object with that label.

3. Provide a series of pictures showing the same subject matter but providing more clues to the identity of the person or object. Tell the students that this time the pictures provide more information about the person or object. They are to become picture detectives and look for clues in the pictures which will help them label more accurately. For example, show pictures of women in many circumstances, such as a ballerina, a woman teaching a classroom of children, a woman in a family setting, a woman doctor in a hospital or clinic, a woman engineer, a woman painting a picture, etc. Discuss the labels that now may be used. What do they know about the person? How do they know this? What do they still not know about the person? How could they find this additional information?

ACTIVITY 2-9:
CATEGORY DETECTIVES

TYPE		TERM	
CLASS	☐	STA	☑
GROUP	☑	LTA	☐
IND	☑	LC	☐

Purpose:

1. To expand oral vocabulary

2. To develop critical thinking

3. To identify the relationship among several objects or pictures, select the object that does not belong to the group, name other objects that belong to the category, and tell why objects do or do not belong to the category

---

Materials:

Objects or pictures of objects that can be categorized

Grade level:

Many grades; the objects for grouping can be selected according to the children's ability levels and needs

---

Procedures:

1. Provide a collection of concrete items, pictures of items, or lists of words that can be categorized into ever-narrowing categories. (Use concrete items with younger children so they can visualize the items being grouped and discussed.) Explain to the students that you have grouped items into categories of things that are alike, but that each group contains an object that does not belong to the group. The students will play "category detectives" by trying to figure out the final definition of the category. The following objects may be used:

   a. Final Category: Fruits that Grow on Trees

      (1) Category: Things to Eat

| orange | apple | peach | ball | plum |

What do the items have in common? Which item does not belong with the other items? Why? Describe each item. Look at the next group of items. Do you still think your category is correct?

(2) Category: Fruits

orange   apple   peach   plum   stringbean

Now what item does not belong? Why? What do the other items have in common? What would you call this group in order to exclude the item that does not belong? Look at the next group. Are you right?

(3) Category: Fruits that Grow on Trees

orange   blueberries   apple   peach   plum

Proceed with the same questioning and discussion strategy until students have identified the category.

(4) Ask the students to suggest other items that could be placed in the final category.

b. Final Category: Clothes Worn by Girls
   (1) Category: Things to Wear
       shoes, slacks, *camera,* coat, stockings
   (2) Category: Things to Wear (excluding accessories)
       ring, shoes, slacks, coat, stockings
   (3) Category: Clothes Worn by Girls
       shoes, slacks, coat, stockings, dress

c. Final Category: Wooden Furniture in the Bedroom
   (1) Category: Furniture
       chair, table, desk, *doll,* stool
   (2) Category: Furniture Made from Wood
       chair, table, desk, stool, *sofa*
   (3) Category: Furniture Made from Wood and Found in the Bedroom
       chair, table, desk, stool, bed

d. Final Category: Dangerous Jungle Animals
   (1) Category: Animals
       lion, snake, *boy,* tiger, elephant
   (2) Category: Jungle Animals
       lion, snake, tiger, elephant, *sheep*
   (3) Category: Jungle Animals that can be Dangerous to Man
       lion, snake, tiger, elephant, crocodile

CAMPBELL'S 59'ERS

TYPE		TERM	
CLASS	☑	STA	☐
GROUP	☑	LTA	☑
IND	☐	LC	☐

Purpose:

1. To interact orally with a group and find workable answers to a problem
2. To develop creative thinking skills
3. To identify the responsibilities of each member of a discussion group
4. To develop respect for other students' opinions

Materials: Suggested topics for discussion and problem solving; newspaper articles that suggest problems requiring solutions

Grade level: Middle and upper elementary, middle school

Procedures:

1. Explain to the students that groups often need a number of ideas or must solve problems in creative ways. One way to gather a lot of ideas before groups try to solve a problem is a "buzz session." During a buzz session, everyone quickly presents ideas and suggestions. All ideas are written down; none are criticized or judged appropriate or inappropriate. (The ideas will be considered in greater detail later, when several may be chosen for investigation and discussion leading to a workable solution to the problem.) The whole class may form a large buzz session with the teacher acting as secretary and moderator, or the class may be divided into smaller groups which are allowed a limited time to generate ideas and suggestions before reporting back to the larger group. (The choice depends on the children's experience and ability.) In this latter type of buzz session, known as the "Phillips 66 Buzz Session," students are divided into groups of 6 and allowed to generate ideas rapidly for 6 minutes. The teacher may choose any combination of numbers and minutes. For example, buzz sessions carried on in Anthony Campbell's fifth-grade room might group 5 students and discuss rapidly for 9 minutes; the class might name itself "Campbell's 59'ers." If the teacher is not the secretary for the

whole group, each group should appoint someone to write down the ideas.

2. Present a problem to the groups that will stimulate their thinking. The problem should be important to the group and one they can empathize with. It should also be phrased in such a way that the solution is not limited by the wording of the problem. Students may suggest problems they feel strongly about, or the teacher can use some of the following problems:

How can we eliminate the long time spent in the school cafeteria?

How can we earn money to go on a class trip at the end of the year?

How can we make our school grounds more attractive?

How can we make the playground more useable and fun at recess?

How can we make the streets safer when we walk or bike to school?

How can we improve our school newspaper?

How can we show our parents what we've learned when they come to open house?

How can we get the "mini-courses" we want and how can we get the teachers for them?

3. After children's ideas have been stimulated in the buzz session, tell them they will have an opportunity to try to really solve the problem through a longer problem-solving discussion session. Tell them that every person in the discussion group, however, has a responsibility to solve the problem. Ask the students to suggest responsibilities they believe would be necessary for solving the problem. List these responsibilities; for example:

IN A PROBLEM-SOLVING DISCUSSION GROUP, EVERY MEMBER HAS RESPONSIBILITIES

1. Know the problem.
2. Collect the facts you need to know so you can contribute to the discussion.
3. Understand the causes of the problem and any characteristics the solution must have.
4. Participate in the discussion.
5. Be a good listener to other peoples' ideas.
6. Keep your mind open for other peoples' viewpoints.
7. Show respect for all ideas.
8. Keep in mind that your main purpose is to find the best solution to the problem, not to sell your idea.

---

4. Allow the students an opportunity to gather facts on the problem, then divide the class into smaller discussion groups. Choose a chairman or discussion leader for each group. Prepare the discussion leaders for their responsibilities:[4]
   a. Study the problem.
   b. Prepare a series of questions that stimulate thinking: what, why, who, how?
   c. Open the discussion by explaining the purpose of the group.
   d. Guide the thinking of the group by asking questions and summarizing points.
   e. Ask for examples and support for ideas and suggestions.
   f. Get everyone involved in the discussion.
   g. Summarize ideas.
   Allow the groups to meet, providing guidance when necessary.

5. Provide an opportunity for all discussion groups to share their solutions with the whole class. Discuss the recommendations and try to reach a joint agreement.

6. The newspaper is another source of topics for problem-solving discussion groups. Find examples of stories related to local, state, national, or world problems, and have discussion groups tackle the problems. Advice columns such as "Ann Landers" also provide topics for problem-solving discussions.

ACTIVITY 2-11:
SOLVING PROBLEMS
THROUGH ROLE PLAYING

TYPE		TERM	
CLASS	☑	STA	☑
GROUP	☑	LTA	☐
IND	☐	LC	☐

Purpose:
1. To solve real problems through role playing
2. To develop oral communication skills through a spontaneous activity
3. To develop tolerance for others' viewpoints and feelings

Materials: Conflict situations that are important to the group

Grade level: All grades; determining factor is subject matter of the role-playing problem

Procedures: General procedures for use with all levels of role playing will be presented first. These general procedures will be followed by some specific role-playing conflicts for different grade levels.

1. Present a situation involving conflict that is important to the students. You may tell it in story format, and end the story when the conflict is clearly stated. At that point, ask the group what they would do in the situation described.

2. Encourage a short discussion of the problem. Ask for volunteers to role play the parts. The group may role play the situation several times with different volunteers. Prepare the listeners for the activity so they can take part in the discussion after the role playing or will be ready to be actors in the next activity.

3. Have the group act out the role spontaneously without any staging or other props. The emphasis is on resolving the problem, not on the acting.

4. The group evaluates their role playing experience. The teacher asks questions to clarify the ideas and solutions. Was the problem solved? Would the solution cause any other problems? Are there any other ways to solve the problem?

Examples:

<u>Lower Elementary</u>

a. New crayons have been taken from a child's desk—Jennifer is a first-grade child who is very excited because she has a brand new box of crayons. Her first box of eight crayons had all broken, and her mom had bought her the biggest box in the store. The box even had a crayon sharpener! Jennifer liked the gold and silver colors, and showed the class the beautiful pictures she could make. After recess, Jennifer opened her desk to take out her new box of crayons, and they were gone. Jennifer looked around the room and saw that Jackie was coloring with crayons that looked just like Jennifer's. When Jennifer asked Jackie about the crayons, Jackie said they belonged to her. Jennifer did not believe Jackie and was sure the crayons were the new ones she had brought that morning. How should they solve this problem? What should Jennifer do? What should Jackie do? What should the teacher do?

b. Sharing on the playground (this can be developed into many role playing situations since there are numerous items on a playground that cause conflict)—For example: There are only three swings, and the same three children always run to the swings and stay on them all recess, not allowing anyone else to swing; there is only one jump rope, and several students refuse to share it; one child always pushes ahead in the line and takes several turns on the slide before the rest of the waiting children get their turns.

<u>Middle-Upper Elementary</u>

a. Sharing responsibility in group work—A class has been divided into groups to do reports on Indians, countries, animals, weather, etc., depending on the subject in that grade. Jim, Sandy, Christie, and Greg are doing a report together. They must present their findings to the class on Friday. They have planned to show slides that one of the children's parents took while on vacation and talk about the slides, demonstrate a Mexican folk dance, show a map of the country and talk about its physical characteristics, and show a piñata and other hand-crafted items from that country. Sandy, Christie, and Greg have done all the work, but Jim wants to take most of the credit by showing and talking about the slides. How should they solve this problem? What should they say to Jim? What should they have him do? Should they talk to the teacher? If they do, what should the teacher say and do?

b. Cliques, ostracizing a friend—Several girls have a slumber party, but decide not to invite Vickie's best friend because Susie doesn't like her. Both Vickie and her best friend feel hurt and angry. How would you solve this problem?

c. Have students suggest role playing situations that are meaningful to them.

ACTIVITY 2-12:
INTERVIEWING

TYPE		TERM	
CLASS	☑	STA	☐
GROUP	☑	LTA	☑
IND	☐	LC	☐

Purpose:

1. To identify the purpose and audience for an oral interview

2. To develop and practice interviewing skills through role playing

3. To obtain information from another person using interviewing techniques

Materials:

Lists of role playing suggestions for interviewing; newspaper help-wanted ads that can be used to motivate an interviewing session. References containing directions for interviewing may be included for older children.

Grade level:

This activity can be adapted to almost all levels. Lower-elementary students can interview teachers, parents, brothers, and sisters. Interviewing can become more sophisticated in the upper grades, and students can interview various professional people as well as practice interviewing skills that will benefit them throughout their lives.

Procedures:

1. Show the words "conversation" and "interview" to the students. Suggest that both words describe a means of oral communication; however, the purposes and methods of these two types of communication are quite different. Ask students if they know the difference between having a conversation with someone and having an interview. Lead the students into the conclusion that a conversation is an informal talk or exchange of ideas in which the topics may include anything that interests the people talking. In contrast, an interview has a predetermined goal, and the interviewer asks for specific information, avoiding many topics he may consider unimportant.

2. Develop a list of purposes or needs for interviewing. For example:

PEOPLE INTERVIEW

1. Doctors interview patients to find out why the patients are sick.
2. Managers interview job applicants to decide whom they will hire.
3. Reporters interview people to gather information for a newspaper story.
4. Authors interview people to acquire information for a book or story.
5. Teachers interview students about problems in school.
6. Teachers interview parents about student's problems or work at home.
7. Parents interview teachers about their children's work at school.
8. Lawyers interview clients to learn details to help the clients.
9. College admission people interview high school students to decide if they should be admitted or receive a scholarship.
10. Police interview suspected criminals to learn about their actions.
11. Detectives interview people to learn facts for an investigation.
12. Television newsmen interview people for the TV news.
13. Talk-show hosts interview famous people to learn about their lives.
14. High school students interview different professionals to learn about careers.
15. Company managers interview employees to learn about problems or to decide if the employee should be promoted.

3. Discuss the different purposes for interviewing and the definite goals of the interviews as suggested by the purpose. Ask students if they believe interviewing skills are important to both the interviewer and the interviewee. Have them explain why.

4. Develop a list of " Interviewing Do's and Don'ts." Older students may refer to management references to gain some tips suggested by people who frequently interview personnel.[5]

INTERVIEWING

Do	Don't
1. Prepare for the interview, know what you want to ask or anticipate what you'll be asked	1. Ramble off the topic
2. Encourage the interviewee to talk	2. Criticize the interviewer or interviewee
3. Have a friendly facial expression	3. Argue with the interviewer or interviewee
4. Be a careful listener	4. Show nervousnous or discourtesy by tapping the table or chewing gum
5. Keep the interview on the subject	5. Ask closed questions that have a single yes or no answer
6. Ask open questions that allow interviewee to respond with sufficient information	6. Dress sloppily
7. Be polite	
8. Keep interview within the pre-set time limits	
9. Dress attractively	

5. Divide the students into small groups so they can role play different interviewing circumstances. Have the groups suggest questions they would like to have answered or topics covered for some of the purposes identified for interviewing. For example, a newspaper reporter interviewing the winner of a gold medal at the Olympics might ask:

> Why did you decide to enter the Olympics?
> What kind of training did you do to become a winner?
> How did you feel when you knew you had won?
> What other athletic events do you participate in?
> Do you eat anything special like they show on TV? If you do, what do you eat?
> What advice could you give other young people who also want to be winners in sports?
> What do you want to do when you get back home?

Have the students in the small groups role play several different interviews. Have other students in the group observe the effectiveness of the interview and suggest changes. Allow all students in each small group to play the part of both the interviewer and the interviewee. Then have them discuss their experiences in both capacities. Did they feel differently when they were being interviewed than when they were the one doing the interviewing? If so, why was there a difference?

6. Find "Help Wanted" ads or stories from the newspaper and have students pretend they want a job or want to learn more about a subject. Divide the class into small groups and have them role play both the interviewer and the interviewee. For some subjects, both interviewer and interviewee will need to do some reference work to prepare for the interview. For example:

Help Wanted

Help Wanted: Teenager to baby sit with 6-year-old after school, 5 days a week. Must be reliable, apply in person.

Help Wanted: Fast food restaurant needs summer help. We will train you for the position.

Join Our Team
We are hiring men and women sales representatives. We offer you a demonstration car, insurance plan, paid vacation, and opportunity for advancement. Call Friendly Car Company for top-paying job in car sales.

We Are Looking for Engineers
Major oil company in Arabia seeks petro-chemical engineers. Excellent fringe benefits, high pay for high risk job. Send résumé to Desert Oil representative, Oil Tower, Houston, Texas.

Stories in the News

Fireman Wins Medal For Saving Child

Five-year-old Danny Delong owes his life to fireman Douglas Collins who risked his own life to pull Danny from the seventh floor of Park Tower Apartments.

Popular TV Stars To Appear At Auditorium

A special children's show involving the "Electric Company" cast will be presented Saturday afternoon at 2:00. Two lucky children will be chosen to have lunch with the stars before the show.

Camping Family Found After Four Nights on the Mountain

An early blizzard on Rabbit Ears Pass stranded a family on the mouintainside. Mr. and Mrs. Frankline, 10-year-old Amy, and 7-year-old Todd faced four nights in freezing cold after an early storm separated them from their camper.

7. Ask students to watch a TV talk show, identify the interviewing techniques they see, and plan a TV talk show of their own. Have them suggest the guests they wish to interview, the kinds of information they would like to know, and do reference work to find out about the guests. This activity can be developed around themes and related to subjects studied in content areas. For example:

> Phil Phox Presents the Greatest Scientists of Our Time
> Mike Monroe Interviews the First Astronauts on the Moon
> Walter Wallace Talks to Lewis and Clark
> Diana Dufflebag Brings You Cinderella, Snow White, Huck Finn, and Jack and the Beanstalk

8. After students have role played several situations, allow them to try their interviewing skills in real situations. A school newsaper, a study of occupations, a study of the school personnel, or a story of the neighborhood could all stimulate the need for an oral interview followed by a report back to the class. After the general subject for the interviewing has been selected, have the students list

the people they would like to interview and the questions they would like to ask each person. One interview topic might be People Who Run Our School, for which students might interview the principal, teachers, secretaries, coaches, librarians, janitors, cooks, the nurse, or bus drivers. Another topic might be Foods Liked and Disliked In the Cafeteria and Why, for which the students could interview other students, teachers, cooks, and anyone who eats in the cafeteria. The interviewer can compile charts showing what he has learned.

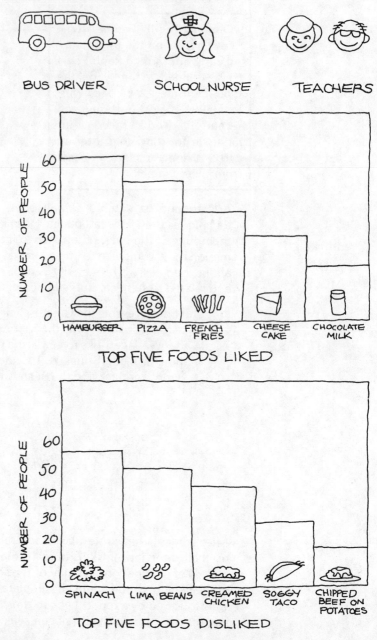

BUS DRIVER   SCHOOL NURSE   TEACHERS

TOP FIVE FOODS LIKED

TOP FIVE FOODS DISLIKED

IN THE ROUND

TYPE		TERM	
CLASS	☑	STA	☑
GROUP	☑	LTA	☐
IND	☐	LC	☐

Purpose:
1. To introduce children to the enjoyment of choral speaking
2. To divide into three speaking groups according to light, medium, and heavier voices, and develop cooperation in the round-choral speaking choir

Materials:
This introductory activity uses familiar verses known to the children; no reading materials are required

Grade level:
All grades

Procedures:
1. Have the students say or read a short piece or verse. Ask the class to listen carefully and help you divide the voices into light, medium, and heavy voices. Group the students according to voice quality.

2. Have the students try their voice choir using several verses they know. For example, try some familiar rounds in which the light voices begin, then the middle voices are added, then the heavy voices. The following verses in the round are enjoyable:

   a. Low Voices: Row, row, row your boat

      Low Voices: Gently down the stream
      Medium Voices: Row, row, row your boat

      Low Voices: Merrily, merrily, merrily, merrily
      Medium Voices: Gently down the stream
      Heavy Voices: Row, row, row your boat

      Low Voices: Life is but a dream
      Medium Voices: Merrily, merrily, merrily, merrily
      Heavy Voices: Gently down the stream

              (continued for three rounds)
   b. Three Blind Mice
   c. Frère Jacques

3. Try the same choral speaking groups but use familiar nursery rhymes.

ACTIVITY 2-14:
PAT-SI-OO-REE-OO-REE-AY

TYPE		TERM	
CLASS	☑	STA	☑
GROUP	☑	LTA	☐
IND	☐	LC	☐

Purpose:

1. To provide a linguistic experience in speaking, reading, interpreting, and listening
2. To develop cooperation through a group activity
3. To increase enjoyment in reading through a cumulative choral speaking verse
4. To interpret a piece of folk music written in the 1840s

Materials: Copies of the folk song "Pat-si-oo-ree-oo-ree-ay"

Grade level: Middle-to-upper elementary

Procedures:

1. Background information to share with students: In the 1840s, the first railroads were built in the United States. Much of the work was done by immigrants from Ireland who came to the United States because of the potato famines in their own country. The Irish workers used picks, shovels, and wheelbarrows to build the railbeds for the railroads. This folk song tells the tale of the hardworking railroad laborer.

2. Discuss the background of the song with the students. Talk about the Irish immigration to the United States, and the reasons many of the immigrants worked on the railroad. Ask the students if they think it would be an easy job to work on the railroad. Have them read the words of the folk song and decide what kind of a job working on a railroad would actually be. Ask the students to find sentences and phrases that support their ideas about the way the workers felt about their jobs.

3. Divide the class into seven groups. Read the folk song as a cumulative choral reading. In this type of choral group, the first stanza is read by group 1, the second is read by groups 1 and 2, etc., until the reading is completed. (Since this folk song is developed around a time sequence, voices are added to increase the volume

from the years 1841–1847.) This folk song may be divided in the following way:

Group 1:	In eighteen hundred and forty-one I put my corduroy breeches on. I put my corduroy breeches on To work upon the railroad.
Groups 1 & 2:	In eighteen hundred and forty-two I left the old world for the new. I left the old world for the new To work upon the railroad.
Groups 1, 2 & 3	In eighteen hundred and forty-three 'Twas then I met sweet Biddy Magee. An elegant wife she's been to me While working on the railroad.
Groups 1, 2, 3 & 4:	In eighteen hundred and forty-four I landed on Columbia's shore. I landed on Columbia's shore To work upon the railroad.
Groups 1, 2, 3, 4 & 5:	In eighteen hundred and forty-five I found myself more dead than alive. I found myself more dead than alive From working on the railroad.
Groups 1, 2, 3, 4, 5 & 6:	In eighteen hundred and forty-six I changed my trade to carrying bricks. I changed my trade to carrying bricks From working on the railroad.
Groups 1, 2, 3, 4, 5, 6 & 7:	In eighteen hundred and forty-seven Sweet Biddy Magee she went to heaven. If she left me one she left me eleven To work upon the railroad.
Groups 1, 2, 3, 4, 5, 6 & 7:	Pat-si-oo-ree-oo-ree-ay Pat-si-oo-ree-oo-ree-ay Pat-si-oo-ree-oo-ree-ay To work upon the railroad.

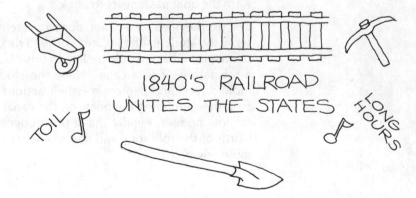

1840'S RAILROAD
UNITES THE STATES
TOIL
LONG HOURS

ACTIVITY 2-15:
LOW BRIDGE, EVERYBODY DOWN

TYPE		TERM	
CLASS	☑	STA	☑
GROUP	☑	LTA	☐
IND	☐	LC	☐

Purpose:

1. To provide a linguistic experience in speaking, reading, interpreting, and listening
2. To promote cooperation through a group activity
3. To increase enjoyment in reading, speaking and listening through a refrain choral arrangement
4. To interpret a piece of folk music written to depict the towpath and the workers who pulled boats along the Erie Canal

Materials:

Copies of words to the folk music "Low Bridge, Everybody Down"

Grade level:

All grades

Procedures:

1. Background information to share with students: In 1817, New York state started to build a canal to connect Albany with Buffalo, which was on the Great Lakes. The 340-mile canal was opened in 1825. By the year 1845, about 4,000 boats were carrying supplies on the canal. These boats were pulled along the canal by mules or horses, which traveled approximately three miles an hour. The mule driver had to watch out for low bridges over the canal, then warn the boat passengers to duck.

2. Discuss the need for a canal, due to western expansion. On a map, show the students the location of the Erie Canal. Ask the students to imagine what it would be like to drive boat-pulling mules along a towpath next to a canal. Have the students imagine they are mule drivers and pantomime their actions. Then have them pretend they are riding the boats on the canal and need to watch out for low bridges. Finally, have the students read or listen to the words of the folk song and describe what it would be like to be a mule driver.

3. Discuss how a refrain choral reading is accomplished. The teacher or another child may be the leader, and the students join in the chorus or refrain. For example:

Leader: I've got a mule and her name is Sal,
Fifteen miles on the Erie Canal.
She's a good old worker and a good old pal,
Fifteen miles on the Erie Canal.
We've hauled some barges in our day,
Filled with lumber, coal, and hay,
And we know every inch of the way
From Albany to Buffalo.

All: Low bridge! Everybody down!
Low bridge! We're coming to a town.
You'll always know your neighbor;
You'll always know your pal
If you've ever navigated on the Erie Canal.

Leader: We'd better get on our way, old pal!
Fifteen miles on the Erie Canal.
You can bet your life I'd never part with Sal,
Fifteen miles on the Erie Canal.
Get us there, Sal, here comes a lock;
We'll make Rome before six o'clock.
One more trip and back we'll go,
Right back home to Buffalo.

All: Low bridge! Everybody down!
Low bridge! We're coming to a town.
You'll always know your neighbor;
You'll always know your pal
If you've ever navigated on the Erie Canal.

ACTIVITY 2-16:
YANKEE DOODLE

TYPE		TERM	
CLASS	☑	STA	☑
GROUP	☑	LTA	☐
IND	☐	LC	☐

Purpose:

1. To provide a linguistic experience in speaking, reading, interpreting, and listening
2. To promote cooperation through a group activity
3. To increase enjoyment in reading, speaking, and listening through an antiphonal choral arrangement
4. To interpret a piece of folk music written in the 1700s, and descriptive of the Revolutionary War

Materials:

Copies of the folk song "Yankee Doodle"

Grade level:

All grades

Procedures:

1. Background information to share with students: The British brought the song "Yankee Doodle" to America. During the Revolutionary War, however, the colonial soldiers adopted the song as one of the symbols for the American struggle for independence.

2. Discuss the significance of the folk song "Yankee Doodle." Allow children to share their knowledge of the Revolutionary War period. Clarify any misconceptions. Have the students read the words to the song. Discuss such items as hasty pudding, Yankee Doodle Dandy, Captain Washington, slapping stallion, swamping gun, horn of powder, a nation louder, little keg, stabbing iron.

3. Divide the students into two groups. Boy and girl groupings work well for this, since the verses may pertain more to a boy's version of the war, while the chorus sounds as if it is a response to a masculine experience. Other groupings, such as high voices and low voices, however, are equally effective. This folk song may be divided in the following manner:

Boys, or Group 1:	Father and I went down to camp,
	Along with Captain Gooding;
	And there we saw the men and boys
	As thick as hasty budding.
Girls, or Group 2: (chorus)	Yankee Doodle keep it up,
	Yankee Doodle Dandy,
	Mind the music and the step,
	And with the girls be handy.
Boys, or Group 1:	And there we saw a thousand men,
	As rich as Squire David;
	And what they wasted every day,
	I wish it could be saved.
Girls, or Group 2:	*Repeat chorus*
Boys, or Group 1:	And there was Captain Washington
	Upon a slapping stallion,
	A giving orders to his men;
	I guess there was a million.
Girls, or Group 2:	*Repeat chorus*
Boys, or Group 1:	And then the feathers on his hat,
	The looked so very fine, ah!
	I wanted peskily to get
	To give to my Jermima.
Girls, or Group 2:	*Repeat chorus*
Boys, or Group 1:	And there I see a swamping gun,
	Large as a bag of maple,
	Upon a mighty little cart;
	A load for father's cattle.
Girls, or Group 2:	*Repeat chorus*
Boys, or Group 1:	And evertime they fired it off,
	It took a horn of powder;
	It made a noise like father's gun,
	Only a nation louder.
Girls, or Group 2:	*Repeat chorus*
Boys, or Group 1:	And there I saw a little keg.
	Its head all made of leather,
	They knocked upon it with little sticks,
	To call the folks together.
Girls, or Group 2:	*Repeat chorus*
Boys, or Group 1:	The troopers too, would gallop up
	And fire right in our faces;
	It scared me almost half to death
	To see them run such races.
Girls, or Group 2:	*Repeat chorus*
Boys, or Group 1:	It scared me so I hoofed it off,
	Nor stopped, as I remember,
	Nor turned about till I got home,
	Locked up in Mother's Chamber.
Girls, or Group 2:	*Repeat chorus*

ACTIVITY 2-17:
THE OLD CHISHOLM TRAIL

TYPE		TERM	
CLASS	☑	STA	☑
GROUP	☑	LTA	☐
IND	☐	LC	☐

Purpose:

1. To provide a linguistic experience in speaking, reading, interpreting, and listening

2. To develop cooperation through a group activity

3. To increase enjoyment in reading through the presentation of a line-a-child choral speaking arrangement

4. To interpret a piece of folk music written about the great age of the cowpuncher, during the 1870s to the 1890s.

Materials:

Copies of the folk song "The Old Chisholm Trail"

Grade level:

Middle-to-upper elementary

Procedures:

1. Background information to share with students: The Old Chisholm Trail of the late 1800s was used to move cattle from San Antonio, Texas to the railroad at Dodge City, Kansas, where some cattle were shipped to the eastern part of the United States. Other cattle continued on the trail to Cheyenne, Wyoming, or to Montana and the Dakotas. The rich pastures were used to fatten the cattle before they were sold. The trip up the Chisholm Trail often included several thousand cattle in one herd and required four or five months of horseback riding to manage the herd. The cowboy's life was hard; he encountered dust from the cattle, storms, long hours in the saddle, sleeping on the ground, and monotonous food. In order to overcome their boredom and to tell about their hardships, the cowboys sang songs like the "Old Chisholm Trail."

2. Discuss the background for the folksong. Have students find the location of the Chisholm Trail on a United States map. Ask them to pretend they are cowboys in the Old West. Do they think this would be an easy life? What would they like about it? What would be hard? After they have presented their ideas, have them read the words to "The Old Chisholm Trail." Have them look for support for their views in the words of the folk song.

3. Have the students read the selection using a line-a-child approach, with the chorus read by all students. Using a line-a-child method, each child reads a different line and all the children read the chorus. For example:

Child 1:	Come along boys and listen to my tale, And I'll tell you of my troubles on the . Old Chisholm Trail.
All:	Come a ti yi yippy yippy yi yippi yea, Come a ti yi yippy yippy yea.

Child 2:	With a ten-dollar horse and a forty-
	    dollar saddle
	I'm going down to Texas for to punch
	    them cattle.

All:	*Repeat chorus*
Child 3:	I woke up one morning on the old Chisholm Trail, A rope in my hand and a cow by the tail.
All:	*Repeat chorus*
Child 4:	I started up the trail October twenty-third I started up the trail with the 2-U Herd
All:	*Repeat chorus*
Child 5:	I'm in my saddle before daylight And before I sleep the moon shines bright.
All:	*Repeat chorus*
Child 6:	It's cloudy in the West, a-looking like rain, And my old slicker's in the wagon again.
All:	*Repeat chorus*

Child 7:	The wind began to blow, the rain began to
	    fall,
	It looked like we were going to lose them
	    all.

All:	*Repeat chorus*
Child 8:	I jumped in the saddle and grabbed hold the horn, Best cow puncher ever was born.
All:	*Repeat chorus*
Child 9:	Oh, it's bacon and beans most every day I'd as soon be eating prairie hay.
All:	*Repeat chorus*
Child 10:	There's a stray in the herd and the boss said kill it. So I shot him with the handle of a skillet.
All:	*Repeat chorus*
Child 11:	My feet in the stirrup and my hand on the horn, I'm the best cowboy ever was born.
All:	*Repeat chorus*

Child 12:	I went to the boss to draw my roll,
	He figured me out nine dollars in the
	hole.
All:	*Repeat chorus*
Child 13:	A-roping and a-trying and a-branding
	all day,
	I'm working mighty hard for mighty little
	pay.
All:	*Repeat chorus*
Child 14:	So I went to the boss and we had a little
	chat,
	And I hit him in the face with my big
	slouch hat.
All:	*Repeat chorus*
Child 15:	So the boss says to me, "Why, I'll fire
	you,
	Not only you, but the whole crew."
All:	*Repeat chorus*
Child 16:	So I rounded up the cowboys and we had
	a little meeting
	We all took a vote and the boss took a
	beating.
All:	*Repeat chorus*
Child 17:	So we organized a union and it's going
	mighty strong.
	The boss minds his business and we all
	get along.
All:	*Repeat chorus*
Child 18:	With my knees in the saddle and my seat
	in the sky,
	I'll quit punching cows in the sweet
	by and by.
All:	*Repeat chorus*

ACTIVITY 2-18:
WHAT IT'S LIKE TO BE A RAG DOLL

TYPE		TERM	
CLASS	☑	STA	☑
GROUP	☑	LTA	☐
IND	☐	LC	☐

Purpose:
1. To develop body control and communication
2. To relax the body and develop the ability to respond creatively to the environment

Materials:
Descriptions of warm-up activities. Teacher and student suggestions for warm-ups that allow students to loosen up their muscles. No props necessary, but space should be available so students can move freely.

Grade level:
All grades; vary complexity of the warm-up with the children's age level.

Procedures:

1. Discuss with students how an actor or any person shows actions, emotions, and feelings with the body. Let them try to talk with a partner without moving their hands or other parts of their bodies. Discuss how difficult this is. Introduce the term "pantomime," and tell the group that they will be trying some of the activities used by pantomimists such as Marcel Marceau. Tell the group that actors need warm-up periods just like athletes; body control is just as important to an actor as it is to a football or tennis player.

2. Have the students stand in a space that is free of obstacles so they can move freely; at this point, they are developing movement independently and not with other members of class.

3. Suggest that the students do loosening up exercises. For example:

   a. Stand with your feet apart and try to reach as high as you can; the sun is in the sky and you are trying to catch that beautiful yellow ball. Now look down at the ground; see that four leaf clover about three feet in front of your right foot; you want that clover but you can't move. Stretch way down and try to pick it. Oh look, a butterfly is flying by your left ear. The butterfly is just beyond your arm's length. Try to reach out gently and hold the butterfly.

b. How many of you have ever had a **Raggedy Ann** or **Raggedy Andy** doll? Pretend you are a rag doll and try to follow each suggestion: You are lying in the toy box and hoping someone will take you out and play with you. All of a sudden you hear a footstep; you try to listen very hard. The footsteps stop and a hand reaches into the toy box. The hand grabs you by the hair and pulls you straight up out of the toy box. You stop quickly when you are even with your owner's face. Your owner looks carefully at you and you stare back. What is going to happen to you? Your owner asks you if you would like to play in the apple tree in the back yard. You're excited and try to shake your head "yes." It's hard, though, because your owner is still holding you by the hair. Your owner makes a quick decision and lowers you rapidly. Your owner lets go of your hair and takes you by the arm. You can feel your head falling toward your side. The room looks funny from this view. Your owner is in a hurry and you can feel your body moving up and down as your owner runs down the stairs with you. Wow! that was a rough ride. At last you are out in the yard. Just feel that beautiful sunshine. It makes you feel good all over. Oh no, your owner is going to climb up into the apple tree and take you along. Bounce, bounce, bounce, you are hitting the trunk of the tree. That hurts! At last, you are sitting on a big tree limb. It feels good to be still. You look down and the ground looks like it's a long way away. You sit very still because you don't want to fall. After you have been there awhile, your owner starts to climb down. You realize you have been forgotten; you try to look down and get your owner's attention. Oh! you can feel yourself falling, down, down. All of a sudden you stop, but the stop didn't hurt you. Your owner caught you before you hit the ground. You are happy because your owner does love you and takes care of you. Your owner carries you carefully up the steps and puts you back in the toy box. You are happy to stay there for the rest of the day and think about what will happen tomorrow.

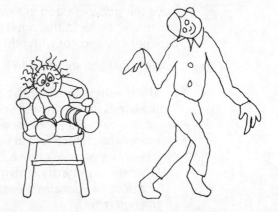

3. Have students suggest other exercises to use for warm-ups.

A WALK THROUGH IMAGINATION

TYPE		TERM	
CLASS	☑	STA	☑
GROUP	☑	LTA	☐
IND	☐	LC	☐

Purpose:

1. To interpret various actions and emotions through pantomime

2. To develop movement that corresponds with a musical presentation

3. To develop group interaction and cooperation through a group-developed pantomime

Materials:

Descriptions of actions for students to pantomime; records that suggest movements or a musical instrument, such as a piano, that can be used to suggest movement; folk stories to read to the group

Grade level:

All grades; vary complexity and subject matter to correspond with the students' grade levels

Procedures:

1. These activities may be done in various orders and on different days. Some of the activities are whole-group activities, in which children move independently from one another, and others are small-group activities, in which children must plan their movement cooperatively and then move as a group to express the action. These are examples of activities to help children develop believable actions.

a. This pantomime activity requires children to change actions on a walk, if the actions are to be believable. Your description might go like this:

"Today we are going to take an imaginary walk through a new attraction at Disney World (name any theme park that is known to the children). The attraction is called 'A Walk Through Imagination.' During this walk you will experience many different conditions that require you to walk or move in different ways. You must try to make your actions as believable as you can. Listen as I guide you through the attraction with my voice. Pretend you are actually going through 'A Walk Through Imagination' and move your body as if you were really there. Here you are at Disney World. You are excited about

ORAL LANGUAGE ACTIVITIES **65**

going into 'A Walk Through Imagination' and you hurry up to the ticket window. The ticket-taker tells you that you can enter in about ten minutes. You stand there waiting impatiently. As you stand there, you look at the other people who will be going in with you. Some are taller than you are, and some are shorter than you are. At last the ten minutes are up, and you hurry to the entrance. The entrance looks odd. Is that a tunnel? The only way to enter is to crawl on your hands and knees. As you go through the tunnel, a bat swoops down toward your head. You hurry faster because you see a room ahead. You're there. It feels good to stand up again. You stretch. All of a sudden, a high wind hits you, and you grab for the wall. The wall opens and you find yourself in a room of ice. You try to walk across the slippery, smooth ice. You think it would be fun to slide across the ice. You fall; the ice is cold. You're almost to the other side of the room, so you crawl to the door. The next room looks different. Could this be a dungeon? You look around. You'll need to be careful here. The path winds through a torture chamber. The first torture is a floor of very hot coals. You must walk across these hot, hot coals. You're across, but it looks like sand ahead. You carefully put your foot down. You hear a sucking noise as your foot goes down, down into the sand. You try to pull it out, because this must be quicksand. At last, you make it. You shake the sand off from your shoe and look at the sand. It's only about three feet wide. You know you can jump across. You move back and leap across the quicksand. To get out of the dungeon, you must walk across a narrow board over the moat. You look down and see crocodiles in the moat. You walk very, very carefully so you don't loose your balance. The next room has craters all over the surface. As you enter, you feel funny—as if you are floating in space. This must be the moon. You decide to experiment on the weightless surface. You leap in the air; you jump; you run. It is wonderful; you've never been able to move so easily. You're light as a feather. You're just about across the moon. The only way off the moon is to climb down a ladder. You go down, down, down. As you climb down, you see beautiful stars and moving comets. All of a sudden, you find yourself back on earth. You are in a beautiful green meadow. You want to skip through the grass and wildflowers. You see a lovely yellow buttercup and stop to smell it. The grass feels so good that you want to roll in the meadow. You roll toward the door, and see a pile of autumn leaves from last year. You jump up and decide to walk through them. It is fun to jump in the leaves and hear them crunching and crackling. The sun is out and the birds are singing. You finish your walk by enjoying this warm spring day. As you leave 'A Walk Through Imagination,' you are surprised. You didn't realize how many different ways your body could move."

b. Provide music, such as "The Nutcracker Suite," with different tempos and movements. Have the students sit on the floor in a gymnasium or other large space. Ask them to close their eyes and listen to the music and think about what the music is trying to say. Tell them they will be able to interpret the music any way they choose as long as the movement is believable when it is matched with the music. After they have listened to a selection, have them spread out in the space and listen to the music a second time while they move independently to the sound of the music. Allow them to talk about what each section of the music represented to them.

c. Folk stories and nursery rhymes also provide sound stimulation for developing believable actions. Select a folktale or nursery rhyme with both strong characterization and action. Have the students sit on the floor with their eyes closed. As you read a folktale to them, have them imagine the characters and actions that are taking place. Ask them to describe what they "see." Read the story a second time, allowing the students the opportunity to pantomime each character in the story. The following nursery rhymes are good for young children to pantomime:

> Jack be nimble,
> Jack be quick,
> Jack jumped over the candlestick.

Select a partner and pantomime:
> Jack and Jill went up the hill
> To fetch a pail of water.
> Jack fell down,
> And broke his crown,
> And Jill came tumbling after.

Divide into groups of four and pantomime:
> Three little kittens, they lost their mittens,
> And they began to cry,
> "Oh, mother dear, we sadly fear

That we have lost our mittens."
"What! lost your mittens, you naughty kittens!
Then you shall have no pie."
Mee-ow, mee-ow, mee-ow.
Then you shall have no pie.
The three little kittens, they found their mittens,
And they began to cry,
"Oh, mother dear, see here, see here,
For we have found our mittens."
"Put on your mittens, you silly kittens,
And you shall have some pie."
Purr-r, purr-r, purr-r
Oh, let us have some pie.

and:

Old Mother Hubbard
Went to the cupboard,
To fetch her poor dog a bone;
But when she got there
The cupboard was bare
And so the poor dog had none.

She took a clean dish
To get him some tripe;
But when she came back
He was smoking a pipe.

The dame made a curtsey,
The dog made a bow;
The dame said, "Your servant,"
The dog said, "Bow-wow."

She went to the tailor's
To buy him a coat;
But when she came back
He was riding a goat.

She went to the hatter's
To buy him a hat;
But when she came back
He was feeding the cat.

She went to the barber's
To buy him a wig;
But when she came back
He was dancing a jig.

Have the students choose a partner:

Little Miss Muffett
Sat on a tuffet
Eating her curds and whey;

Along came a spider,
And sat down beside her
And frightened Miss Muffett away.

The following folktales are enjoyable for pantomime: The
Three Little Pigs; The Three Billy Goats Gruff; Red Riding Hood;
and The Three Bears.

This pantomime activity may also be done as a guessing game.
Divide the students into smaller groups, and allow each group
to select a rhyme or story, practice doing it in pantomime, then
present it to the remainder of the students to guess the name
of the story or rhyme.

d. Provide children with opportunities to pantomime various feelings and emotions. This activity can be played as a game in
which children choose cards on which various emotions are
written, then portray the emotions in pantomime. The other
members of the group guess what emotion is being portrayed.
Vary the emotion words with the children's grade level. For
example:

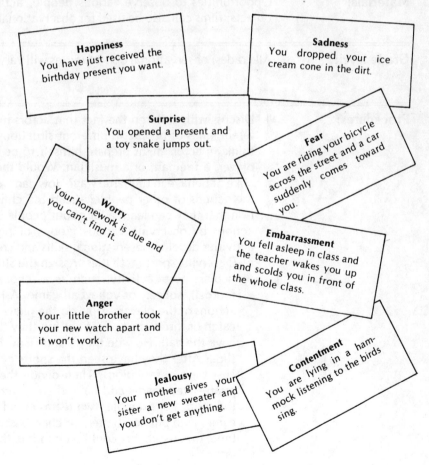

Happiness
You have just received the birthday present you want.

Sadness
You dropped your ice cream cone in the dirt.

Surprise
You opened a present and a toy snake jumps out.

Fear
You are riding your bicycle across the street and a car suddenly comes toward you.

Worry
Your homework is due and you can't find it.

Embarrassment
You fell asleep in class and the teacher wakes you up and scolds you in front of the whole class.

Anger
Your little brother took your new watch apart and it won't work.

Jealousy
Your mother gives your sister a new sweater and you don't get anything.

Contentment
You are lying in a hammock listening to the birds sing.

ACTIVITY 2-20:
A SOFTBALL GAME WITHOUT A BALL

TYPE		TERM	
CLASS	☑	STA	☑
GROUP	☑	LTA	☐
IND	☐	LC	☐

Purpose:

1. To observe various actions and emotions and interpret them through pantomime
2. To develop group interaction and cooperation through pantomime
3. To stimulate creative imagination and empathy

Materials:

Opportunities to observe various people, activities, and inanimate objects; films can also be used for observational purposes

Grade level:

All grades; observational opportunities will vary with grade level

Procedures:

1. Discuss with children the fact that actors must portray many different kinds of people in different situations. Ask them how they think an actor might prepare himself to be an old man, a tennis player, a fireman, or a musician. Would these four people move alike or behave in the same way? How can we find out more about the actions of other people? (Lead the children into the suggestion that they can learn a lot about people, their actions, and reactions by observing various groups of people.) The following activities develop observational skills and creative imagination.

   a. Observing sports activities: Assign the students to watch a particular sports activity, such as a school softball, basketball, football, soccer, or volleyball game. Ask them to observe the actions of the players. How do the players move? How do they catch or throw the ball? What are they doing when they don't have the ball? How do they stand? How do they run, jump, or slide? After they have seen the sports activity, have them discuss their observations. Then divide the students into appropriate-sized teams and have them pantomime the actions of the sport. For example, two teams could pantomime a softball game, with pitcher, batter, catcher, basemen, etc. At the same time, other students could pantomime the actions of the spectators.

b. Observing a musician, band, or orchestra: Assign the students to watch a particular musician, band, or orchestra. (Elementary students could watch the middle school or high school band or orchestra. Another alternative would be to ask several guest musicians to come to class so students can observe the actions of someone playing a wind instrument, a string instrument, or a percussion instrument.) After they have observed the musical activity, have them discuss the actions of each type of musician. How did they sit or stand? How did they hold their instruments? How did they play their instruments? What expressions did they show on their faces? How did the conductor act? How did they know he was the leader of the group? How did the conductor show pleasure or displeasure with the band or orchestra? Finally, divide the class into various segments of the band or orchestra, select a conductor, and pantomime a musical selection.

c. Observing chores completed by members of the family: Discuss with children the various chores that they and other members of the family perform. Using a brainstorming format (children rapidly provide oral suggestions), have the students list as many household chores as they can that require different bodily actions; for example; ironing a shirt, washing dishes, filling a dishwasher, vacuuming a rug, sewing on a button, dusting a table, mowing the lawn, baking a cake, painting a wall, cleaning a bathtub, watering plants, making a bed, setting the table, scrubbing a floor, sweeping a floor, washing windows, answering the telephone, feeding the dog, building a fire in the fireplace, frying hamburgers, hanging a picture, or switching on a light.

Assign the students the task of observing several of these chores and, if possible, actually trying them. Have them observe carefully all the required movements. After they have made their observations, have them pantomime their household chores in class while the rest of the group identifies and analyzes the chore and its corresponding movements.

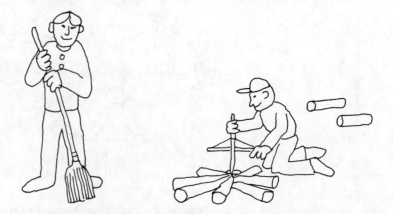

d. Observing hobbies and nonteam sports: Discuss with children the various hobbies and nonteam sports that people participate in. Using a brainstorming technique, have students list hobbies and sports that have distinctive movements that can be characterized through pantomime; for example, paddling a canoe, fishing, taking a picture, bicycling, changing a bicycle tire, hiking, boxing, tennis, swimming, bowling, golfing, or archery, wood carving, painting a picture, camping, weaving a rug, playing chess, or riding a horse.

Assign students to observe someone participating in a hobby or sport, then ask them to pantomime the hobby or sport for the rest of the group.

e. Observing inanimate objects: Show children various inanimate objects and discuss the characteristics of the objects. Have them explore the objects with their senses to describe the color, size, texture, weight, smell, sound, and use of the object. After they have observed various objects, have students pantomime an object for the group to guess. Assign students the task of observing inanimate objects outside the classroom, then pantomime the objects in class; for example, light bulb, vacuum cleaner, egg beater, tennis racket, clock, glass, a feather, balloon, rubber ball, mirror, chair, knife, candle, or driftwood.

f. Observing machines and in a group activity pantomiming the actions: Discuss with children that a machine usually has several moving parts that must work together. If the parts do not work together, the machine will not work correctly. Have the children observe several machines in class. Ask them to look at the moving parts and observe their location, sound, and rhythm. Examples of machines to observe in the school include a typewriter, car traveling by, telephone, electric mixer (in cafeteria), blender (in cafeteria), piano, bicycle, television, dishwasher (in cafeteria), or electric or gas stove (in cafeteria).

Divide the students into small groups, have them choose a machine, and cooperatively pantomime the machine for the rest of the class.

calendar (in cafeteria), piano, bicycle, television, dishwasher
(in cafeteria), or electric or gas stove (in cafeteria).
Divide the students into small groups; have them choose a
machine, and cooperatively pantomime the machine for the
rest of the class.

ACTIVITY 2-21:
COMMUNICATING WITH INDIAN SIGN LANGUAGE

TYPE		TERM	
CLASS	☑	STA	☐
GROUP	☑	LTA	☑
IND	☐	LC	☐

Purpose:

1. To develop an appreciation for oral language
2. To develop an understanding that we can communicate with body signs instead of words
3. To interpret the types of words that can be shown through sign language
4. To develop appreciation for a different culture

Materials:

Several foreign language records; references illustrating Indian sign language, such as Robert Hofsinde's *Indian Sign Language* (New York: William Morrow, 1956) or Hettie Jones's book of Indian poetry, *The Trees Stand Shining—Poetry of the North American Indians* (New York: The Dial Press, 1971).

Grade level:

Middle elementary

Procedures:

1. Demonstrate the problems related to communication between people who do not speak the same language. Play a tape or record of people talking in a language that is not understood by the class. Have the children hypothesize the conversation. Could they communicate with anyone who only spoke that language? What would they do if they needed to ask someone for a necessity such as food or water?

2. Direct the class to think about a sign language they could use to communicate with a non-English-speaking visitor in our own country. Divide the class into pairs, assigning one student to play the role of a foreign visitor asking directions or asking for a specific object in the classroom, while the second student gives the directions or provides the specific object. While performing this activity, they cannot use verbal language; they must use sign language. After the students have completed this activity, lead a

discussion in which children describe the problems encountered trying to communicate without oral language.

3. The Indians developed a "silent" or "sign" language so they could communicate with people whose language was different from their own. This sign language proved very effective. According to Benjamin Capps, "Though communication by gesture is probably older than speech itself, no system has ever proved more versatile and expressive than that developed by the Plains Indians." [6] Discuss with children the reasons that Indians would need a sign language. Why would Indians need to communicate with people who did not speak their own language? Do you think we can learn anything important about the Indian culture by studying their sign language?

4. Direct the students' attention to a reference book on sign language. Show pictures demonstrating the various signs. List the terms that are depicted in sign language. Why would these be important to the Indians?

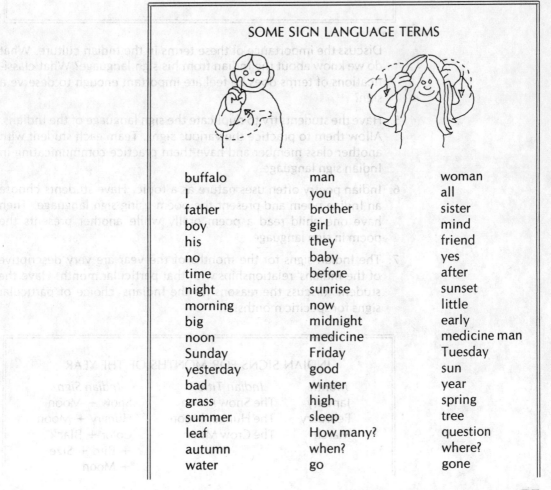

SOME SIGN LANGUAGE TERMS

buffalo	man	woman
I	you	all
father	brother	sister
boy	girl	mind
his	they	friend
no	baby	yes
time	before	after
night	sunrise	sunset
morning	now	little
big	midnight	early
noon	medicine	medicine man
Sunday	Friday	Tuesday
yesterday	good	sun
bad	winter	year
grass	high	spring
summer	sleep	tree
leaf	How many?	question
autumn	when?	where?
water	go	gone

make	work	do not
cat	dog	color
book	red	read
hunt	Apache	Pawnee
Indian	dance	sign language
name	house	crazy
angry	hot	want
stop	sick	eat
money	dollar	hungry
heart	January	February
March	April	May
June	July	August
September	October	November
December	snow	moon
bird	corn	rose
fire	laugh	good evening
good morning	horse	dog
bow	council	counting

Discuss the importance of these terms in the Indian culture. What do we know about the Indian from his sign language? What classifications of terms does he feel are important enough to deserve a sign?

5. Have the students try to duplicate the sign language of the Indians. Allow them to practice the various signs. Team each student with another class member and have them practice communicating in Indian sign language.

6. Indian poetry often uses nature as a topic. Have students choose an Indian poem and present the poem using sign language. Then have one child read a poem orally while another presents the poem in sign language.

7. The Indian signs for the months of the year are very descriptive of the Indians' relationships with that particular month. Have the students discuss the reasons for the Indians' choice of particular signs for specific months.

INDIAN SIGNS FOR MONTHS OF THE YEAR

Month	Indian Title	Indian Sign
January	The Snow Moon	Snow + Moon
February	The Hunger Moon	Hungry + Moon
March	The Crow Moon	Color + Black + Bird + Size + Moon

April	The Green Grass Moon	Color + Green + Grass + Moon
May	The Planting Moon	Corn + Make + Moon
June	The Rose Moon	Rose + Moon
July	The Thunder Moon	Bird + Fire + Moon
August	The Green Corn Moon	Color + Green + Corn + Moon
September	The Hunting Moon	Hunt + Moon
October	The Falling Leaf Moon	Leaf + Moon
November	The Mad Moon	Angry + Moon
December	The Long Night Moon	Night + Time + Moon

Divide the class into groups, allowing them to choose an Indian Month of the Year. Have them pretend they are living in an Indian village and develop a short, oral, creative drama depicting the happenings during that month. Ask each group to introduce their month using the Indian sign.

8. Play a game in which children choose the name of a month and depict that month using sign language.

9. The months of the year described by the Indian names reveal that the Indians who used them lived in a part of the United States that has four definite seasons of the year. Many children, however, live in locations that do not experience these same cycles. Suggest that children think about the months of the year in their section of the country, choose a descriptive title for their favorite month, write a story describing that month, develop an Indian sign for the month, and share their story and Indian sign orally with the class.

ACTIVITY 2-22:
A TELEVISION PRODUCTION STAFF

TYPE		TERM	
CLASS	☑	STA	☐
GROUP	☑	LTA	☑
IND	☐	LC	☐

Purpose:

1. To identify the production staff needed for a real television show
2. To identify the responsibilities of the production staff
3. To motivate the development of a classroom "television production"
4. To motivate creative expression through different types of television shows
5. To work effectively in a small group, research a subject, and orally present the subject

Materials:

References on television production, among which are:

Alkin, Glyn. *TV Sound Operations.* New York: Hastings House, 1975.

Bermingham, Alan, *et al. The Small TV Studio: Equipment and Facilities.* New York: Hastings House, 1975.

Millerson, Gerald. *The Technique of Television Production.* New York: Hastings House, 1972.

Sheriffs, Ronald E. *Television Lighting Handbook.* TAB Books, 1977.

Stasheff, Edward, *et al. The Television Program: Its Direction and Production.* New York: Hill and Wang, 1976.

The Videotape Book. New York: Bantam Books, 1975.

Zettle, Herbert. *Television Production Handbook.* Belmont, Calif.: Wadsworth, 1976.

Grade level:

Middle, upper, and middle school; younger children can receive a brief introduction to the television production staff as presented by the teacher, while older students could do independent research

Procedures:

1. Introduce the topic of television production by suggesting to students that they are going to try creative productions of some of their favorite kinds of television shows. But before they create

their own shows, they are going to learn about some of the people who are essential for a television show. Are the actors the only important people in the show? Why or why not? Ask them to suggest other staff members they feel are essential for a television show and to suggest the responsibilities of each staff member.

2. Provide references so students can locate information about people on a television production staff. Develop a chart showing the responsibilities of each staff member. For example:

STAFF FOR TELEVISION STUDIO

Producer: The person responsible for the staff and the content of the program

Director: The person who coordinates the activities of all the people in the program; supervises and manages the talent and other parts of the program; commands the camera operators

Artists, Actors, Performers: The people who perform in front of the camera—the actors in a play, the newsmen on a news program, the musicians in an orchestra

Camera Operators: The people who operate the television camera

Lighting Technicians: The people in charge of the studio lighting and special lighting effects

Set Designers: The people who design the studio sets or background for the programs

Graphic Designers: The people who design the visual aids

Audio Engineer: The person responsible for the musical backgrounds, sound effects, and sound levels of the performances

Video Engineer: The person responsible for the quality of the television pictures

Make Up: The people responsible for preparing the make up for the performers

Costume Designers: People responsible for designing the clothing worn by the actors

Script Writers: Write the dialogue for the show

---

3. Have the students choose one of the television staff members they would like to do further research about. Have them divide into small groups according to the television job they would like to research. Allow them an opportunity to research their topics and present their findings to the rest of the class. During their presenta-

tation, have them identify and describe the person's various responsibilities. Have them tell why or why not they would like to have that particular job at a television station.

4. If there is a television station near your school, this would be a logical time for students to go on a field trip to the station. Before they go, have them develop a list of questions they would like to ask and items or people they would like to see.

5. After they return from the station, have them compare and evaluate what they saw and heard with the information gained in their earlier research groups. Suggest that they will have a chance to experiment with some of the television jobs when the class puts on their own "television" shows.

PUTTING ON OUR OWN
TV SHOW—PART I

TYPE		TERM	
CLASS	☑	STA	☐
GROUP	☑	LTA	☑
IND	☐	LC	☐

Purpose:

1. To observe television shows and identify the kinds of shows that could be created in the classroom

2. To motivate oral language, stimulate creative imagination, and motivate creative dramatization

Materials:

No materials are necessary, although students should (with parental consent) observe the different types of shows so they can suggest classroom "television" programs they would like to produce

Grade level:

All grades; there is an adequate variety of formats for young children (especially educational T.V.) and older students

Procedures:

1. If this activity follows a study of television personnel, students are probably anxious to experiment with their own creative products. If students have not done the previous activity, suggest to them that the class is going to try something very exciting. They will have the opportunity to put on their own "TV" shows in class. (If video equipment is available you may explain to the group that they can actually see themselves on T.V.) Ask them to list the kinds of programs that are shown on T.V. Discuss what the students feel are different requirements for the programs.

2. Ask the students to observe the different kinds of programs on television, the format of the programs, and the requirements of the programs. Vary this assignment according to grade level; kindergarten and first-grade children might, for example, be asked to watch a segment of Sesame Street, The Electric Company, or Mr. Rogers' Neighborhood; to observe the actors in the program and what they do, to listen for sound effects, and the kinds of material that is presented. At the other extreme, upper elementary and middle school children might be asked to observe all types of programs; to identify specific requirements for each kind of program; to identify the type of material presented, to identify any

specific oral language requirements on the part of the actors and announcers; and to identify the format of the television presentation, including station breaks and commercials.

3. After they have watched various programs, have the children expand their original list of kinds of programs and discuss the nature of the programs, any special requirements, the purpose of the programs, and the audience for the programs. The discussion might cover the following:

Program	Purpose	Audience
Sesame Street	To educate and entertain	Children
Children's Classic	To entertain and develop enjoyment of books	Families
Story Telling Hour	To entertain and develop enjoyment of stories	Children
News, Weather	To inform people	Everyone
Cooking Show	To demonstrate a cooking skill	People interested in cooking
Nature or Animal Show	To inform and entertain	People interested in nature and animals
Game Show	To entertain	People who like game shows
Comedy Show	To entertain	Families
Variety Show	To entertain	Families
Consumer Programs	To inform	Adults
Dramas	To entertain	Adults

4. Discuss with the group the type or types of television shows they would like to create and perform. Discuss both the staff and performing requirements for each type of production. List the "TV" shows the class decides it would like to create.

ACTIVITY 2-24:
PUTTING ON OUR OWN
TV SHOW—PART II

Purpose:

1. To motivate oral language, stimulate creative imagination, and motivate creative dramatization
2. To create a group or class "TV" show and present the show to an audience
3. To develop cooperation by working with a group

Materials:

Sound effects, props, music, or other materials needed for the specific kind of TV show or shows the group chooses

Grade level:

All grades; change sophistication of presentation and format according to grade level

Procedures:

1. You have already prepared the background for this activity if your students have investigated the production staff for a television production; observed and discussed the characteristics of various types of programs; and discussed the type or types of TV shows they would like to create.

2. Divide the class into workable groups and help the groups plan a creative oral television presentation with appropriate staff responsibilities, performers, background music or sound effects and commercials or public service announcements (see media section). For example:

   a. Have a class of young children put on a "Sesame Street"- or "Electric Company"-format show. The whole class can work on the production, but smaller groups can each develop a creative presentation featuring puppets such as Big Bird, Ernie, and the Cookie Monster. Some groups can develop creative stories, while other groups think of creative jingles or dialogue to present facts they are learning in school. The "Sesame Street Show" should be presented several times so all children have opportunities to be both performers and technicians. This activity is also effective with older remedial-reading or special-education groups. These students can develop an "Electric Company" production that includes creative use of some of the skills they are learning, and present it to a group of younger children.

b. News, Weather, and Sports? We've Got Them All! Divide the class into groups to prepare the news, weather, and sports segments of the show. Have other groups work on the technical production, announcements, or advertisements. This TV show can present the news, weather, and sports that are of interest to the class. Students can use their interviewing skills (see Interviewing Activity in this section) to acquire information for the news broadcast; they can use science and map-reading skills to predict the weather; and they can use observational reporting skills to present the sports news.

c. The 40¢ Pyramid. A game-show format can be used with any grade level; the questions or tasks required of the students can be developed for any level. Divide the class into groups according to M.C., contestants, writers of questions or creators of stunts, judges for answers or evaluators of stunts, announcers, prize committee and technicians. Have the whole group choose a theme for their game show. Young children can prepare activities requiring physical coordination, knowledge of nursery rhymes, listening skills, knowledge of fairy tales, etc. Older children might choose to have questions about their content fields, questions about a topic that all the children would research, a musical answer game, a sports quiz. All the students should review the subject areas for the questions. Provide any necessary assistance for the writers of the questions or the developers of the stunts so they are appropriate for children of that ability level. This activity is also excellent for remedial-reading and many special-education groups. A great deal of learning takes place when children are researching information to develop questions for other children to answer, and children are usually very attentive if they know they are responsible for the information because another child will ask them questions about it.

PICK YOUR CATEGORY

A Literature	B Music	C Science
D Sports	E History	F Listening

d. How To? We Can Tell You! Using a brainstorming technique, have the children list their hobbies or other interests that could be demonstrated to an audience. Since many TV shows demonstrate how to cook fish, raise a garden, collect stamps, sew, etc., tell the students they will have an opportunity to demonstrate something they can do in a TV show format. Discuss the information they must include if they are going to show their audience how to do something. Act out two examples for the students, one in which the presentation is rapid and confused, and another in which the demonstration is clear, sequentially developed, and slow enough to follow. Paper-folding or kite-making activities are ideal for this purpose. Have the students try each activity as you demonstrate it, then discuss which demonstration was effective and why one was more effective than the other. Next, divide the class into groups according to hobbies or other skills they would like to demonstrate. Have each group prepare a "TV" demonstration to be shown to the rest of the class. Interact with the groups to provide necessary assistance and advice.

HOW TO?   WE CAN TELL YOU!

Announcer: Introduces program.

Station Break: Commercial message.

Announcer: Introduces first demonstration.

First Demonstration: How to make balloon animals.

Station Break: Commercial message.

Announcer: Introduces second demonstration.

Second demonstration: How to dance the Hokey Pokey.

Station Break: Commercial message.

Announcer: Introduces third demonstration.

Third demonstration: How to frost a cake.

Announcer: Thank audience for listening, sign off

---

e. **A Story! A Story!** Creative stories and interpretations of literature selections are presented in many different formats on television. Stories are read and told on such children's programs as
"Captain Kangaroo." Childrens classics like "Winnie the Pooh,"
"Pinnochio," and "Beauty and the Beast" are performed by puppetry, cartoons, and human actors. Both historical fiction and
nonfiction are presented in drama form. Discuss with students
the television program formats they enjoy when they watch
stories. Select several formats, divide into groups according to
the formats, and have each group develop a creative story or
oral interpretation of literature using that format. Present the
television "Story Hour" to the rest of the class or to a group of
younger children.

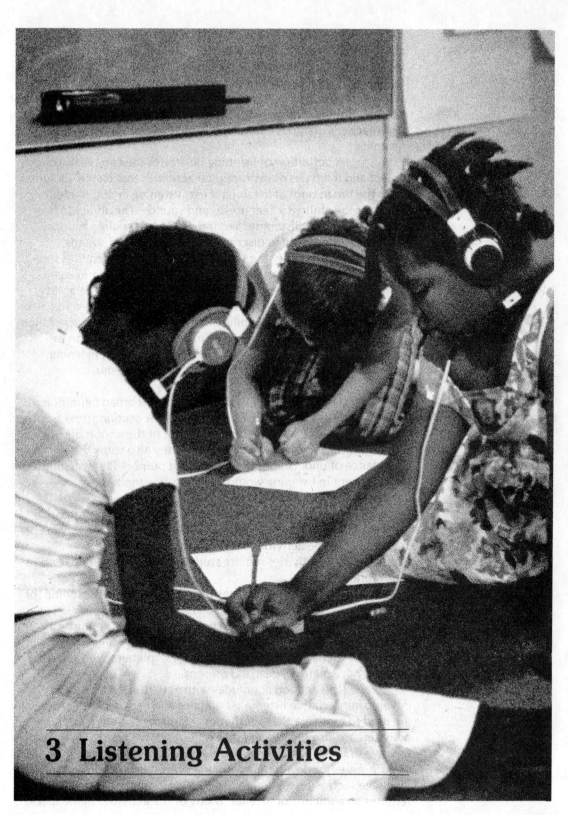

3 Listening Activities

Listening is probably the most frequently used communication skill. It has not been until recently, however, that listening instruction has become a major concern of elementary teachers and of researchers and methods instructors in language arts. While research indicates that both children and adults spend a major portion of their communication time listening, elementary textbooks and teacher's manuals contain few activities for instruction in listening.[1]

A definition of listening illustrates the complexity of the subject and the types of instructional activities that can be included under the broad term of listening. First, listening includes auditory acuity, or the ability to hear noises and sounds. The ability to hear is a prerequisite for listening. Second, listening requires auditory perception: the ability to discriminate sounds, blend sounds together, and remember the sounds. Third, listening requires the ability to attend to the sounds and concentrate on the message. Fourth, listening includes auditory comprehension, or the ability to get meaning from the listening experience. Getting meaning also suggests different listening abilities. These competencies may range from a factual understanding of the main idea of a selection to the ability to critically evaluate what is heard. Finally, listening includes appreciation of sounds, poetry, literature, music, drama, and media.

The activities in this section cover a broad definition of listening. The activities at the beginning of the section stress auditory awareness. They develop an understanding of the importance of listening and an awareness of listening. They also stress the importance of understanding the different purposes for listening. Improvement in listening would be difficult without this understanding.

A series of activities are designed to improve attentive listening. Some of these activities use a learning-center format; consequently, the activities are placed on tapes. These learning-center activities require students to identify sounds and follow oral directions.

Listening comprehension activities include listening for the main idea, supporting details, and sequence of events. There are also several activities designed to develop critical listening and thinking skills. Stimuli for critical listening activities include proverbs from "Poor Richard's Almanac," fairy tales, folktales, and famous heroes from America's past and present.

This section concludes with activities designed to develop appreciative listening. Folktales and early radio broadcasts are used to motivate these activities. Many appreciative listening activities are also located in other sections of this book. For example, creative drama, story telling, and the media provide many opportunities for developing listening skills. The activities in the oral language section also develop listening skills, since each oral activity requires an audience or listener. Many of the activities in the media section also develop listening skills through critical listening to television and radio commercials and other programs. Listening can be an exciting subject if the activities are stimulating to the child. The language arts curriculum can provide many such stimulating experiences.

ACTIVITY 3-1:
USING SOUNDS TO LEARN ABOUT THE WORLD

TYPE		TERM	
CLASS	☑	STA	☑
GROUP	☑	LTA	☐
IND	☐	LC	☐

Purpose:
1. To understand the importance of hearing
2. To identify sounds in the environment
3. To develop auditory awareness

Materials:
Literature: Ezra Jack Keats's *Apt. #3* (lower elementary) or Florence Heide's *Sound of Sunshine, Sound of Rain* (middle elementary); listening excursions in the classroom, school, school yard, and neighborhood

Grade level:
Lower and middle elementary

Procedures:
1. Two different selections of children's literature may be used to motivate an interest in this activity. For younger elementary children, use Ezra Jack Keats's *Apt. #3*. In this picture storybook, Sam and his brother hear music being played in a neighboring apartment and investigate its source. They discover that a blind harmonica player lives in the apartment. They are invited in for a visit, and are surprised to find that the blind man knows a great deal about them. He has learned this information by listening. For middle elementary children, use Florence Heide's *Sound of Sunshine, Sound of Rain*. In this book, Abram, a young blind black boy, learns to cope with the world about him. He learns to "see" with his hearing and discovers that he can experience the world around him.

2. Read one of the above selections to the class. Discuss with them what information they could learn about their environments if they had to both see and hear with their ears. What sounds could they hear? What would these sounds tell them? How important would their hearing become?

3. Explain to the class that they are going to experience the world with their hearing rather than their sight. In the classroom, have them cover their eyes and listen carefully to the sounds around them. After they have listened for several minutes, have them describe what they hear while still covering their eyes. Next, have them look around the room and visually identify the inside and outside sounds. Discuss the listening experience.

4. Take the class on listening excursions outside the classroom. Go to different locations in the school and listen for identifying sounds, describe the sounds and the listening experience. For example, a school cafeteria and kitchen have different sounds than the school library or gymnasium. Go on an excursion outside of the building and experience the sounds of the playground, a field, a neighborhood park, or a street near the school. If possible, take listening field trips to the zoo, a music store, a farm, a department store, a day care center, etc.

5. Go on a weather discovery excursion just outside the school building. Listen to the sounds of the weather during different weather conditions. What sounds characterize rain, snow, sunshine, sleet, wind, etc.? Develop a tape and chart illustrating the sounds of weather. The chart can be set up like this:

WEATHER	SOUNDS WE HEAR
Sunshine	
Rain	
Wind	
Sleet	

ACTIVITY 3-2:
LISTENING FOR DIFFERENT PURPOSES—WHY AND HOW

TYPE		TERM	
CLASS	☑	STA	☑
GROUP	☑	LTA	☐
IND	☐	LC	☐

Purpose:
1. To realize that we listen for different purposes
2. To identify purposes for listening
3. To describe personal requirements and responsibilities for different listening experiences

Materials:
A radio for passive listening; directions or announcements for attentive listening; a paragraph for directed listening; a commercial for critical evaluative listening; a story or record for appreciative listening

Grade level:
All grades; examples for the different types of listening should correspond with the students' ability and interest levels. (The examples in this activity are identified according to difficulty level. There are two examples for each part of the activity; one example is for use with lower elementary and the other with upper elementary.)

Procedures:
1. While students are involved in another activity, such as finishing art work or another assignment, turn on a radio at low volume. Do not attract the students' attention to the radio. After the radio has played for a few minutes and the other assignment is completed, ask the students if they can tell you what was on the radio broadcast. Ask them to be as specific as possible when relating the content of the radio program. Discuss why some students could report what was on the radio while others could not. (Most of the students will not be able to relate very much information unless a favorite personality or subject attracts their attention.) Ask the students to describe this type of listening. Are there other times when they "tune-out" what is heard for part of the time, but are able to remember a portion of what is heard? Tell the students this is called passive listening, because the person is not actively in-

volved in the listening act. The person does not have a purpose for listening. Have the students list circumstances under which they are engaged in passive listening. When is it acceptable, or even advantageous? When is passive listening inappropriate? When could passive listening even get you into trouble?

2. Explain to students that several other kinds of listening are important to them. Ask them if they can identify any other types of listening. Tell them they will experience several different types of listening, describe the listening experience, and suggest purposes for each type of listening.

Examples:

Attentive Listening—Lower Elementary

a. Give the students oral directions for drawing something without telling them the finished product. For example: Put a piece of paper and a pencil on your desk. Draw a circle the size of an orange in the middle of your paper. Draw a smaller circle above the first circle, with the bottom of the smaller circle touching the top of the larger circle. Draw a small triangle on the left-hand side of the top circle; make the narrow point going away from the circle. Draw a round eye on the top circle. Draw a rectangular-shaped tail on the right-hand side of the bottom circle.

Ask the children to tell you what they have drawn. How did they listen to the directions? Why did they need to listen carefully? What was the purpose for this kind of listening? When would they need to do this kind of listening? Why is this kind of listening important to them?

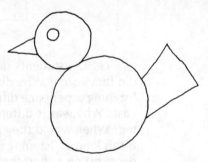

Attentive Listening—Upper Elementary

b. Tell the students to take out a piece of paper and a pencil. Say you are going to give them directions for drawing a picture, as follows: Draw each item as I tell you; I will not repeat any of the directions. Put the point of your pencil on the top center of your paper and draw a circle the size of a quarter. From the bottom of the circle, draw two straight lines about one-half inch apart and one-fourth of an inch long. Connect the bottom of the straight lines with a horizontal line. Extend the horizontal line about one-half inch on each end. Turn this connecting line into a rectangle by drawing two one-inch lines for the sides and drawing another bottom line. Put your pencil on the bottom left-hand side of the rectangle, draw a curved line about three inches long toward the bottom left-hand side of your paper. Put your pencil on the bottom right-hand side of the rectangle, and draw a curved line about three inches long toward the bottom right-hand side of the paper. Connect the lower ends of the two curved lines with a straight line. Put your pencil in the center of the bottom straight line; draw two small half-circles on either side of the center. Now place your pencil back up on the top left-hand corner of the rectangle; draw a two-inch straight line slanted toward the bottom left corner of your paper. Put your pencil back on the rectangle; draw a second line just below the first line. Put your pencil on the top right-hand corner of the rectangle. Draw a two-inch straight line slanted toward the bottom right corner of your paper. Draw a second two-inch slanted line under the first line. Draw small circles at the open ends of each of the slanted lines. Draw a face on the top quarter size circle.

Let the students describe their listening experience. How did they listen? Why did they have to listen carefully? Was the listening experience different than listening to the radio broadcast? Why was it different? What was their purpose for listening? When would they need to use this kind of listening? Why is this kind of listening important to the students? Have the students list on a chart the characteristics of this type of listening, and when they would use this type of listening. Have the students suggest ways they could improve attentive listening.

Directed Listening—Lower Elementary

a. Read a paragraph that requires students to listen for a specific purpose, such as important details, the main idea, a sequence of events, etc. For example:

"After you listen to this paragraph, I want you to tell me where Stephanie and Steve were after school and what they saw.

Stephanie and Steve, the Anderson twins, walked quietly into the kitchen. They knew they were two hours late getting home from school, and they expected their parents would be worried and angry with them. Mom and Dad both came to the kitchen as the twins tried to make their way across the room. After their parents hugged them, the first question was, 'Where have you been?' This is the answer Stephanie and Steve gave: 'We left school and started to walk home our usual way. As we walked by Dexter Park, we saw that the Haunted House was ready for Halloween. We thought we would take just a few minutes to peek inside. In the first room was a coffin with a vampire inside. As we walked down the hallway, a skeleton jumped out of a closet. We started to run, but were not sure how to get out. One door led to a room covered with cobwebs and large spiders. The next room had bats swooping down at us. Every other door we opened had white ghosts dancing toward us. One of the more friendly ghosts finally showed us the door to the outside. We hurried home as fast as we could.'"

Ask the students to draw a picture showing where the twins had been and what they saw. Discuss how the students listened and what they listened for. Were there any clues that helped them listen for their purpose? How could they improve this type of listening?

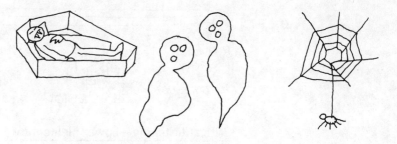

Directed Listening—Upper Elementary

b. Tell the students they will be listening to a paragraph in order to retell a sequence of events that happened in history. After they listen to the paragraph, tell them they will be expected to retell the order of events in the United States when the railroads were being built. For example:

"The United States had great distances that must be crossed to go from place to place. Heavy materials also needed to be moved from place to place. Many people felt that railroads could solve these problems. The first railroad built in the United States was a three-mile track in Massachusetts. Horses drew railroad cars containing the granite used to build the Bunker Hill Monument. In 1830, the Baltimore and Ohio company began to experiment with railroads. Horses drew the first cars, but a year later, the Baltimore and Ohio switched to steam locomotives. The first passenger-train service was started in South Carolina, and was pulled by a locomotive called 'Best Friend of Charleston.' One of the most important acts for railroad expansion was the signing of the Pacific Railroad Act in 1862. President Lincoln authorized the building of the transcontinental railroad that would connect the East and the West. The Central Pacific railroad company started laying tracks in Sacramento, California, and moved east. The Union Pacific built tracks from Omaha, Nebraska, westward. In 1869, the two railroads met at Promontory, Utah. A golden spike was driven into the track to celebrate this great event."

Have the students identify the sequence of events that took place in the paragraph. Next, have them describe their listening experience. How did they listen? What was their purpose for listening? Were there any clues in the paragraph that helped them listen for their purpose? When would they use this type of listening? Have the students list on a chart the characteristics of this type of listening, and when they would use this type of listening. Have them suggest ways they could improve directed listening.

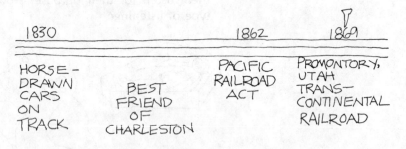

Critical Listening—Lower Elementary

a. For a critical listening experience for lower elementary, tape record a commercial used on a children's television show. Before you play the tape, ask the children to listen in order to identify the source of the tape and why the producer of the material wants them to listen to it. Have them listen to the tape and discuss: Who is trying to persuade us? What are they trying to persuade us to do? Should we believe everything we are told? Why or why not? How should we listen to this type of material? Why? How can we improve our listening when we listen to advertisements?

Critical Listening—Upper Elementary

b. Tape record a commercial or a political announcement. Prepare the students and discuss the listening experience in a similar way to that suggested for the lower-elementary activity.

Have the students list on a chart the characteristics of this type of listening and when they would use this type of listening. Have them suggest ways they could improve critical listening.

Appreciative Listening—Lower and Upper Elementary

a. Select a story to read to the students or a record to play for them. Before reading the story or playing the record, tell the students they will have an opportunity to share their favorite parts of the story or record with the group after they have listened to it. After the listening experience, have them tell what they enjoyed most and why they enjoyed it. Discuss this type of listening with the group; have them list the characteristics of appreciative listening, and tell when they would use this type of listening. Have students suggest ways they could improve appreciative listening.

3. Review the different types of listening, the purposes for listening, and the personal requirements and responsibilities for each type of listening. (This activity can be used as an introductory activity to instruction in listening improvement.)

ACTIVITY 3-3:
LISTENING TIMES

TYPE		TERM	
CLASS	☑	STA	☐
GROUP	☑	LTA	☑
IND	☐	LC	☐

Purpose:

1. To record the amount of time spent in listening during the day

2. To realize the importance of listening in both school and private lives

3. To identify when we listen and to what we listen

Materials:

A form showing daily time periods allowing students to identify both time spent in listening and sources of each listening experience.

Grade level:

Middle and upper elementary, middle school

Procedures:

1. Ask children if they have any idea about how much time during the day they spend listening. Write estimates on the board. Have them suggest some of the listening experiences they have at school and at home.

2. After students have provided estimates of both the amount of time they think they spend listening and what they listen to, do the following. Ask them if they think they spend more or less time listening than people did 50 years ago. Discuss answers and reasons for responses. Tell the students that research conducted over 50 years ago showed that adults spent more time in listening than in any other form of communication. In fact, the study showed that 11 percent of communication time was spent in writing, 15 percent spent in reading, 32 percent in speaking, and 42 percent in listening.[2] Ask the students for suggestions about how they could compare the time they or their parents spend listening with the time people spent in listening 50 years ago.

3. Using student suggestions, ditto a form to use for recording the time spent listening. This form might look like the following example:

```
┌─────────────────────────────────────────────────────────────┐
│          WHEN DO I LISTEN?   TO WHAT DO I LISTEN?             │
│                HOW LONG DO I LISTEN?                          │
│                                                               │
│   Time of Day    What I Listen To      How Long I Listened    │
│    7:00–7:30    _____     _____       │
│    7:30–8:00    _____     _____       │
│    8:00–8:30    _____     _____       │
│    8:30–9:00    _____     _____       │
│    9:00–9:30    _____     _____       │
│    9:30–10:00   _____     _____       │
│   10:00–10:30   _____     _____       │
│   10:30–11:00   _____     _____       │
│   11:00–11:30   _____     _____       │
│   11:30–12:00   _____     _____       │
│   12:00–12:30   _____     _____       │
│   12:30–1:00    _____     _____       │
│  (continue for remainder of day)                              │
│              Total time spent in listening = _____        │
└─────────────────────────────────────────────────────────────┘
```

4. Discuss with students how they can record their listening experiences and the amount of time spent in each listening activity.

5. Assign the listening survey for the following day. (If possible, ask parents who wish to take part in the survey to record their listening experiences and the time spent in listening.) Ask students to return their surveys to school so the class or group can tabulate the results.

6. Tabulate the results of the survey. Total the number of hours and minutes spent in listening for each student. Chart the range of hours and minutes found in the classroom. Tabulate the number of students who listened for those approximate time periods. For example:

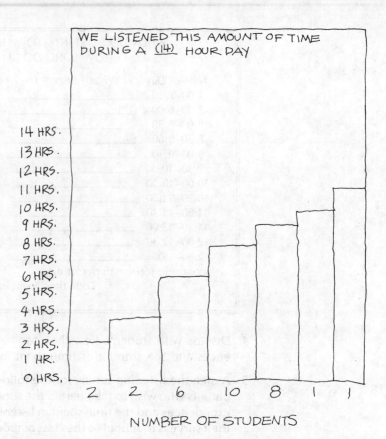

WE LISTENED THIS AMOUNT OF TIME DURING A (14) HOUR DAY

14 HRS.
13 HRS.
12 HRS.
11 HRS.
10 HRS.
9 HRS.
8 HRS.
7 HRS.
6 HRS.
5 HRS.
4 HRS.
3 HRS.
2 HRS.
1 HR.
0 HRS.

2   2   6   10   8   1   1

NUMBER OF STUDENTS

7. If parents or other adults take part in the survey, tabulate their listening times and compare the two charts.

8. Calculate an average of the amount of time students spend in listening. Change the amount of time into a percentage of the waking day. Now, compare this with the listening estimates found 50 years ago. Do the students listen more or less?

9. Finally, have students review their listening schedules to compile a list of their listening activities. What did they listen to? Have them list their listening activities and see if they can evaluate which type of listening activities were most important in their own lives. Older students can categorize their listening activities into types of listening and tabulate the amount of time they were involved in each type.

```
┌─────────────────────────────────────────────────────────────┐
│                    MY LISTENING ACTIVITIES                    │
│                                              How Often        │
│         Television programs            _____    │
│         Listening to directions        _____    │
│         Listening to a conversation    _____    │
│         Records                        _____    │
│         School subjects                _____    │
│         Announcements, etc.            _____    │
└─────────────────────────────────────────────────────────────┘
```

10. Comparisons can also be made between the time spent listening, speaking, reading, and writing. Percentages can be calculated for each type of activity in a day. These percentages can then be compared with the research results from 50 years ago.

	Percentage of Time Spent in Forms of Communication	
	50 Years Ago	**Today**
Listening	42%	
Speaking	32%	
Reading	15%	
Writing	11%	

THE LISTENING POST

TYPE		TERM	
CLASS	☐	STA	☐
GROUP	☐	LTA	☐
IND	☑	LC	☑

Purpose:
1. To develop and improve auditory awareness
2. To identify sounds in the environment
3. To identify environmental locations characterized by specific sounds

Materials:
Paragraphs describing a journey and the sounds heard on that journey; paragraphs can be taped with the sounds heard replacing the identifying words (this activity is similar to a rebus story that uses pictures; instead of pictures replacing words, sounds replace words; a numbered card showing correct answers for the sounds and the location of the sound journey

Grade level:
Lower and middle elementary (depending upon the sound discrimination necessary to identify the sounds and their locations)

Procedures:
1. Place sound journeys on tape. Read the experiences describing the journey into the recorder; wherever a sound is specified, use a sound effect rather than the words. Pause after the sound effect so students have an opportunity to identify the sound. Sounds may be obtained by taping actual sounds or using various sound effects records which contain appropriate sounds. Verbally number each sound journey on the tape. Prepare a numbered card showing the correct answers for the sound journey. (Use pictures when preparing cards for younger students.)

2. Examples of sound journeys and the corresponding self-correcting cards include:
   a. Sound journey number _____.
   "It is three o'clock in the afternoon and you are entering a small, yellow, foreign sports car for your journey through sound. You put your key in the ignition and hear the roar of the [car engine]. It is a beautiful sunny day, so you roll the window down to feel the warm air and hear the sounds around you.

You haven't gone far until you hear a [police whistle]. You have to stop your car and wait at the corner. As you wait you listen to the sounds. You hear people [talking] and [laughing]. You hear [trucks] going by and an [air hammer] is being used to do street repairs. You hear the [police whistle] again and you can continue on your journey. You have gone a few blocks and you must pull over to the side of the street. You hear a [fire truck siren] behind you. My, it's going fast. You continue down the street, and you know you must stop again when you hear the [railroad crossing bell]. You wait a few minutes and you can hear the [train engine] as it rushes by. You know you have been on your sound journey for 15 minutes because the [town clock] is chiming. You also know you are passing a school because you can hear children [yelling] on the playground. Whoops! You've been daydreaming. The light changed and you hear a [car horn]. The car passes you and you can hear the [car radio] playing music. As you pass the high school, you can hear the [band playing], and if you were close enough, you could hear the [marching feet]. Your journey is now over, but you've had a chance to listen to the sounds of the [city]."

Card number _____

Sounds, in order heard:
    car engine
    police whistle
    people talking
    people laughing
    trucks
    air hammer
    police whistle
    fire truck siren
    railroad crossing bell
    train engine
    town clock
    children yelling
    car horn
    car radio
    band playing
    marching feet
    Sounds of the City

---

b. Sound journey number _____.
   "Just before the sun came up, a [cock-a-doodle-do] sound filled

the air to wake me up and let me know it was time to get up and start this sound journey. I dressed quickly and ran out into the yard. As I ran across the yard, I almost stepped on a [quack]. The [quack, quack, quack] told me that I should watch where I am going. The next sound I heard was a loud [neigh], as I felt a wet nose nuzzle my arm for an apple. The [moo, moo] coming from the building told me that other animals wanted their breakfast. As I started to get the feed, a [squeak] ran from under the feed bin. The [meow] was on her feet and quickly followed the [squeak]. The [squeak] got to his hole before [meow] could get him. The [baas] were ready for their breakfast also, and said so. The [bow-wow] joined the group with his song to let everyone know he was up and ready for the day.

"The [moos] were given their breakfast and were preparing to be milked. The [honk], [cackle], [quack], and [gobble] were quick to get to [oinks] residence for any breakfast extras that might be left over. After all, [oink] is a messy eater.

"Everyone, the [cock-a-doodle-do], the [baa], the [neigh], the [meow], the [bow-wow], the [quack], the [cackle], the [gobble], the [oink], and the [moo] all settled down for a morning nap about 10:00. I was happy because I had an exciting sound journey on the [farm]."

Place identifying animal names or pictures on a card corresponding with the number of this story.

c. Other sound journeys can be prepared for locations such as the airport, the zoo, the waterfront, a haunted house, an amusement park, or a train trip.

3. Students can divide into groups to prepare their own sound journeys, place them on tapes, and have other students identify the sounds and locations of the sounds.

ACTIVITY 3-5:
LISTENING FOR DIRECTIONS

TYPE		TERM	
CLASS	☐	STA	☐
GROUP	☐	LTA	☐
IND	☑	LC	☑

Purpose:
1. To develop and improve attentive listening skills
2. To follow oral directions on a tape and place shapes in a described format
3. To reinforce identification of shapes (lower elementary)
4. To reinforce identification of colors (lower elementary)

Materials: Circular, square, half-circular, triangular, rectangular, and curved shapes cut from various colors of felt; feltboard; tape containing oral directions for each activity; color-coded drawing illustrating correct placement for each activity

Grade level: Lower, middle, and upper elementary (depending upon difficulty level of oral instructions and terms used on the tape)

Procedures:
1. Prepare a collection of different colored shapes cut from felt. This collection could include the following shapes cut from each of the basic colors: two circles; two smaller circles; two half-circles; two squares; two triangles; two rectangles; two curved shapes; two long, thin strips; and two short, thin strips.

2. Record on tapes the oral directions for turning the shapes into pictures. Number orally each activity on the tape. On separate cards, draw a picture of the resulting shape, color it correctly, number the card to correspond with the oral number on the tape, and place the completed cards in a box so students can use them for self-correcting their listening activity. Examples on the tape may range from simple to more complex directions, depending upon the students' attentive listening ability. When the dialogue is read onto the tape, pause long enough for the students to carry out the direction. The following examples include both the taped directions and the corresponding cards for self-correction.

Examples:
Sailboats—Lower-Middle Elementary

a. "Place two curved, blue shapes on the center of the feltboard. Place them so they both look like blue hills. Place a red, half-circle on top of the left, blue, curved shape. Place the red half-circle so the straight side is facing the top of the feltboard. Place a green, half-circle on top of the right, blue, curved shape. Place the green half-circle so the straight side is facing the top of the feltboard. Place a purple triangle above the red half-circle. Place the purple triangle so the tip of the straight line touches the red half-circle, and the point of the triangle faces the right side of the feltboard. Place an orange triangle above the green half-circle. Place the orange triangle so the tip of the straight line touches the green half-circle, and the point of the triangle faces the right side of the feltboard. Place a large, yellow circle in the right corner of the feltboard. Now look at your picture. What did you make? Check your listening skills by looking at card number _____ in the box."

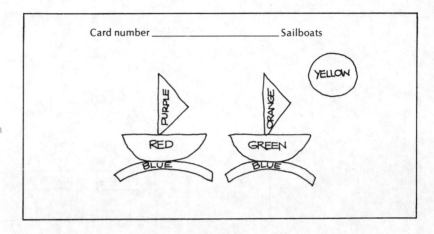

Card number _____ Sailboats

YELLOW

PURPLE

ORANGE

RED

GREEN

BLUE

BLUE

The Clown—Middle Elementary-Upper Elementary

b. "Place an orange half-circle on the middle of the feltboard. Place a half-circle so the curved part of the half circle is toward the top of the feltboard. Now, place a smaller, yellow circle directly below the half circle; the yellow circle should touch the bottom of the orange half-circle. Place an orange rectangle directly below the yellow circle; the rectangle should touch the circle. Place a long, thin, yellow strip next to the top, left-side of the orange rectangle; angle the strip toward the left corner of the feltboard. Place a long, thin black strip next to the top, right side of the orange rectangle, angle the strip toward the right corner of the feltboard. Place a red, half-circle under the orange rectangle so the curved side of the half-circle points to the left side of the feltboard and the tip of the straight side touches the center of the bottom of the rectangle. Place a brown, half-circle under the orange rectangle so the curved side of the half-circle points to the right side of the feltboard and the tip of the straight side touches the center of the bottom of the rectangle. Pull the bottom of the red and brown half circles about an inch apart. Place a short, yellow strip below the red half-circle; have the end of the strip pointing toward the left side of the feltboard. Place a short black strip below the brown half-circle; have the end of the strip pointing toward the right side of the feltboard. Look carefully at your design. What did you create? Check your listening skills by comparing your left picture with card number _____ in the box."

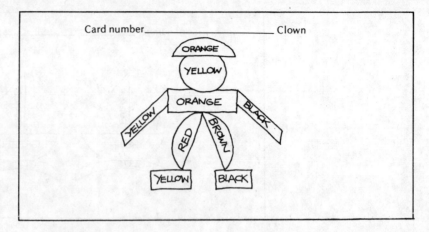

Card number_____ Clown

ORANGE
YELLOW
ORANGE
YELLOW   BLACK
RED   BROWN
YELLOW   BLACK

c. Many shape pictures may be described. Some other suggestions include:

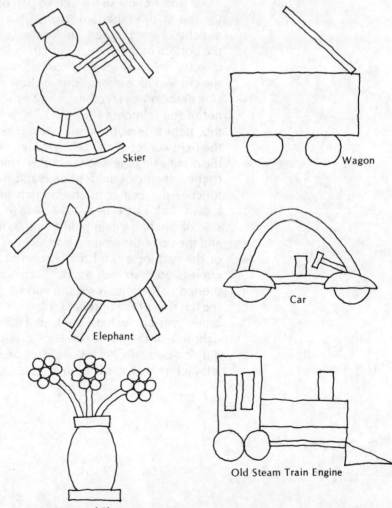

Skier

Wagon

Elephant

Car

Vase and Flowers

Old Steam Train Engine

3. This activity may also be used as a group attentive-listening activity by asking children to draw what they hear on the tape or what is read orally by the teacher.

4. Have children experiment with the shapes, then write their own directions for other children to listen to and follow. Have them evaluate both their ability to give directions and their ability to listen to directions.

ACTIVITY 3-6:
THE CLASS CRIER

TYPE		TERM	
CLASS	☑	STA	☑
GROUP	☑	LTA	☐
IND	☐	LC	☐

Purpose:

1. To develop and improve attentive listening ability

2. To repeat class announcements, assignments, and special news concerning the class

3. To perform tasks required by the class announcements, assignments, and special news

4. To learn how people got the news in Colonial times

Materials:

Sheet of paper with announcements or assignments for the day; a bell for special news, announcements, or assignments; pictures of a town crier

Grade level:

Lower and middle elementary

Procedures:

1. Background information: In Colonial times, there were very few newspapers; consequently, most towns had a town crier. The town crier walked through the streets calling out the news of the day. If the town crier had special news to tell, he rang a bell or banged on a drum. When the people heard the bell or the drum, they ran to the street to hear the news.

2. Show the class a picture of a town crier during Colonial times. Ask them if they know what the town crier is doing. If they do not know the job of the town crier, explain the town crier's duties and how he attracts attention.

3. Ask the students what the town crier might announce if he visited their class. Discuss suggestions with the class. Tell the students that you are going to use a "Class Crier" to inform the class about special announcements, news, and to tell them about class or group assignments.

4. Put the special announcements or assignments on a sheet of paper similar to one used by a town crier. Read the announcements or assignments to the class as if you were a Colonial town crier. You may also use a bell to announce very important assignments or announcements. Ask individual members of the class to repeat the special announcements or assignments.

5. Have the students evaluate their attentive listening ability. Can they repeat announcements and assignments presented by the town crier? Can they perform the assignments announced by the town crier? Do they accomplish whatever is asked of them in the announcements? Do they believe their attentive listening is improving?

6. Students can take turns as class crier, reading special announcements or news to the class. Develop a bulletin board of town crier announcements, assignments, and class news.

ACTIVITY 3-7:
LISTENING FOR MAIN IDEAS AND SUPPORTING DETAILS

TYPE		TERM	
CLASS	☐	STA	☑
GROUP	☑	LTA	☐
IND	☑	LC	☐

Purpose:

1. To identify the main idea in a paragraph after a listening experience

2. To identify the supporting details in a paragraph after a listening experience

Materials:

Examples of paragraphs in which the main idea is stated or inferred; paragraphs should also state several important details which support the main idea

Grade level:

All grades (vary difficulty of the paragraphs to conform with the students' ability level)

Procedures:

1. Read a paragraph and ask students to listen carefully for the main idea of the paragraph. For example:

"The ocean can be a very mean place at times. If you haven't heard yet, I didn't make it to Hawaii. I ran into a storm off the California coast. The storm tore a piece of rigging off the boat that was essential to keep my mast from blowing over the side. To top it off, the pounding caused a through hull valve seal to break. This caused me to take on too much water for comfort. Luckily, the Coast Guard arrived in time and towed me to the harbor. It was a hair-raising experience, but I saved myself and my boat."

2. Ask the students to identify the main idea of the paragraph and tell why they believe it is the main idea. Have them suggest a title for the paragraph and give their reasons for selecting the title.

3. Suggest to the students that the main idea of a paragraph or the title of a paragraph that states the main idea can be turned into a question. This question can then be asked in order to find the details that support the main idea. These supporting details should answer the question posed by turning the main idea into a question. Have the students try turning their main ideas into questions. Discuss which questions they believe are most accurate for the paragraph, such as:

> Why is the ocean a very mean place?
> What was my hair-raising experience?
> How did I save myself and my boat?

4. Now have them listen to the paragraph again. Ask them to identify the important supporting details. For example:

> I ran into a storm off the California coast.
> The rigging was torn from the boat.
> The hull valve seal broke and the boat took on water.
> I was towed in by the Coast Guard.

5. Discuss which question they believe is answered by the supporting details in the paragraph.

ACTIVITY 3-8:
WERE PILGRIMS DULL?

TYPE		TERM	
CLASS	☑	STA	☑
GROUP	☑	LTA	☐
IND	☑	LC	☐

Purpose:
1. To develop and improve listening comprehension
2. To identify important details in a selection which support or do not support a specific viewpoint

Materials: Paragraph describing some of the clothing found in the first Plymouth inventories

Grade level: Middle and upper elementary

Procedures:
1. Ask the students to think about the reading or studying they have done which describes the Pilgrims of Plymouth, Massachusetts. Ask the students to describe the clothes they believe the Pilgrims wore. Were the clothes mostly dull colors, or did the Pilgrims also wear brighter colors? Have the students write their answers to this question.

2. Tell the students they will have an opportunity to listen to a selection and discover whether their judgments are correct or incorrect. Tell them that inventories of clothing are available that describe the clothes worn by some of the Pilgrims. Ask the students to listen to a description of the Pilgrim's clothing; listen for verification of details suggesting dull-colored clothing; listen for verification of details suggesting brighter-colored clothing; and listen for details supporting or not supporting their own earlier evaluations of Pilgrim's clothing.

3. Read the following selection to the students (details for the clothing suggested by "A Record of Clothing From Early Plymouth"[3]):

"The inventories of people who died in the Plymouth settlement contain lists of their clothing. These inventories describe the colors of the clothing. The clothing of the Pilgrims has often been described as 'sad.' Sad does not, however, mean a dreary color; it refers to deep or dark colors such as dark green, blue, mulberry, and crimson, as well as black and gray. William Brewster, one of the original passengers on the Mayflower, had a blue suit, a green waistcoat (jacket), a violet coat, and several black suits. One of the women of Plymouth owned a black, a red, and a violet-colored skirt; two violet-colored jackets; white and blue stockings, one black, three blue, and two white aprons; and gray, red, black, and blue lengths of cloth to be used for clothing."

4. Ask the student to verify any details suggesting dull colors; verify details suggesting brighter colors; and finally, support or not support their own evaluations of Pilgrim's clothing.

PILGRIMS WORE DULL COLORS	PILGRIMS WORE BRIGHTER COLORS
1.	1.
2.	2.
3.	3.

ACTIVITY 3-9:
THE MYSTERY OF
THE KIDNAPPED CHEMIST

TYPE		TERM	
CLASS	☐	STA	☐
GROUP	☐	LTA	☐
IND	☑	LC	☑

Purpose:
1. To develop and improve the ability to listen for sequential order
2. To identify the sequential order in a listening selection

Materials:
Taped story of "The Mystery of the Kidnapped Chemist" (the selection can also be read orally to a group of students); The Sound Road Map

Grade level:
Middle and upper elementary

Procedures:
1. Place the following dialogue on tape for use in the listening center, or read the selection to a group of students. If the tape is used, number the activity, place complete directions on the tape, and describe the assigned follow-up activity to evaluate if listening occurred.

2. Solving the Mystery of the Kidnapped Chemist—Listening For Sequential Order; Name and number of tape (use sounds where stipulated in dialogue):

"You are going to have an opportunity to solve the case of the kidnapped chemist. The heroine in this story is a girl who invented a formula for turning people invisible. Two companies want the formula; one company is honest and the other one is not. When our heroine refuses to sell the formula to the dishonest company, they kidnap her, blindfold her, and put her in the back seat of a car. The kidnapper tells her she will be taken to a secret laboratory where she will be forced to make the formula. She cannot see where the car will be taking her. She wonders how she will be able to tell the police how to find the secret laboratory; she knows she will try to escape and she needs to know the location of that laboratory. The kidnappers have covered her eyes, but they have not covered her ears. She decides that if she listens carefully, she may be able to get enough clues to identify the route the car is traveling. She is afraid, however, that she will not be able to listen carefully enough to recognize all the sounds and to remember the order she hears them. The order is very important, since the sounds will form a sound road map, and provide the clues for locating the secret laboratory. When you finish listening to the clues, you will mark her trip on a sound road map. Ready? The car is starting!

The first sound she hears is a [church bell]. The sound is loud, so the car must be beside the sound. The car stops at the corner by the sound, and turns toward the right. She can hear a new sound off in the distance. The car is coming closer to [zoo animal sounds]. As she rides past these sounds, she knows it is 8:00, because she can hear the [clock striking]. Many sounds are now heard in the sky. She can hear an [airplane] overhead. The road is getting bumpy, and she can hear [road construction noises]. Something big just passed the car. A pleasant sound is heard as the car travels on. She can hear [children laughing and talking] in the distance. She must be driving in the country, because she can hear the sound

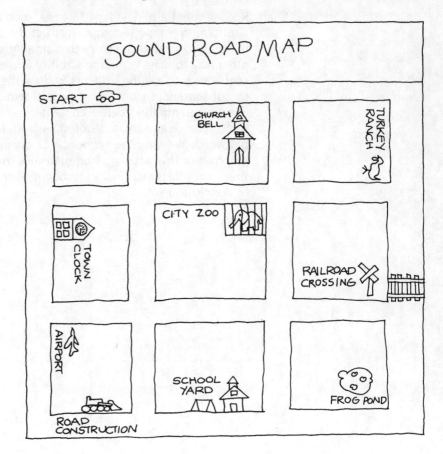

of [frogs]. She hears a [railroad crossing bell], and thinks the car is stopping at a railroad crossing. The car moves ahead, slows, and stops. Her kidnappers tell her to get out, because she has reached the secret laboratory. She strains her hearing, and thinks she hears the sound of [turkeys gobbling]. Can you help her remember her trip? Where did the car travel? Where is the secret laboratory? To show that you remember the car's movements, draw the direction the car took on the Sound Road Map in the listening center. After you have finished, listen to the tape a second time and check to see if you are correct. If you are not correct, draw in the right directions with a red pencil."

3. Other examples of sequential listening activities that may be placed on tapes, which are also very good for use with lower elementary grades, are as follows:

a. Select a number of interesting comic strips. Read the contents of the comic strips into a tape recorder. Cut the comic strips apart, number the correct sequential order on the back of each comic strip, and instruct the students to place each comic strip into correct sequential order after listening to the comic strip on the tape.

b. Read sequentially-developed stories, such as "Three Billy Goats Gruff," into a tape recorder. Instruct the students to use flannel-grams to retell the story to a small group of students. Another way to assess children's ability to place a story in correct sequence is to ask the students to draw the sequential order, or to put sentences from the story into sequential order.

c. Read sequentially-ordered content-area materials onto tapes (e.g., science and social studies). Ask students to listen for signal words showing the sequence or organization of the paragraphs. For this activity, find materials that use terms such as first, second, third, finally, to begin with, next, before, after, in conclusion, etc.

ACTIVITY 3-10:
POOR RICHARD

TYPE		TERM	
CLASS	☑	STA	☑
GROUP	☑	LTA	☐
IND	☐	LC	☐

Purpose:

1. To evaluate and interpret proverbs in Benjamin Franklin's *Poor Richard's Almanac*

2. To develop critical listening and thinking skills

3. To develop divergent thought processes and discussion skills

Materials:

Sayings from *Poor Richard's Almanac;* reference materials about Benjamin Franklin and the Revolutionary War

Grade level:

Middle and upper elementary, middle school

Procedures:

1. Background information: Benjamin Franklin published a yearly magazine called *Poor Richard's Almanac*. The almanac was first published in 1732. It contained weather reports, news about the tides, cooking lessons, poems, and other information for the common people. The almanac was entertaining as well as useful, and was very popular. The most famous part of the almanac became the proverbs or wise sayings that Franklin either wrote himself or took from the writings of other wise men. He often changed the words when he chose someone else's proverbs so that his readers would understand the proverbs. Many of the proverbs stress the desirability of hard work and frugality to help a person become virtuous, wealthy, and wise.

2. Explain the background of *Poor Richard's Almanac* to the students. Discuss the time in history when Benjamin Franklin lived and wrote the almanac.

3. Read some of the proverbs from *Poor Richard's Almanac* to the students. Ask them to listen to the proverb and explain what they believe the proverb means. Ask students to share the reasons for their interpretations. Ask them if they believe the proverb is still as worthwhile today as it was in the 1700s. Why or why not? Some of the proverbs are:

> Eat to live, not live to eat.
> Early to bed and early to rise makes a man healthy, wealthy, and wise.
> When you're good to others you're good to yourself.
> Content makes poor men rich; discontent makes rich men poor.
> The wise man draws more from his enemies than the fool from his friends.
> Keep conscience dear, then never fear.
> Pardoning the bad, is injuring the good.
> Wealth and content are not always bed fellows.
> Doing an injury puts you below your enemy; Revenging one makes you but even with him; Forgiving it sets you above him.
> Words may show a man's wit, but actions show his meaning.
> The sleeping fox catches no poultry. Up! Up!
> Beware of little expenses; a small leak will sink a great ship.
> There are lazy minds as well as lazy bodies.
> Who is strong? He that can conquer his bad habits.
> Lost time is never found again.
> The used key is always bright.

4. Develop a Class Almanac of proverbs.

5. Develop a bulletin board of Poor Richard's Proverbs and drawings illustrating the meaning of the proverbs:

ACTIVITY 3-11:
PLAYING DETECTIVE WITH FAIRY TALE HEROES

TYPE		TERM	
CLASS	☐	STA	☐
GROUP	☐	LTA	☐
IND	☑	LC	☑

Purpose:

1. To identify the fairy tale character represented by a descriptive paragraph

2. To identify details that support the character's identification

3. To identify details that do not support the character's identification

4. To reinforce stories heard or read

Materials:

Paragraphs describing fairy-tale characters (may be tape recorded, with answers placed on self-correcting cards, or they may be read orally by teacher while students analyze answers)

Grade level:

Lower and middle elementary (depending upon characters used; Activity #1 is easier than activities 2 or 3)

Procedures:

1. Prepare paragraphs describing characters from fairy tales. For example:

   a. "When I was a child, my mother told me to sell our old cow. I bought some beans from a man. He said the beans were magic. I brought them home and showed them to my mother. She scolded me and sent me to bed. She was angry and threw the beans out the window. In the night, the beans sprouted and began growing. When I woke up, I saw a large beanstalk which grew up into the sky. I climbed the stalk to the top. I walked along a long road until I came to a huge house. I asked a great big tall woman for some breakfast. She warned me that her husband was a giant who loved boiled boys on toast. Who am I?"

Answer: Jack and the Beanstalk

b. "One day I was going to take a cake and some other goodies to my grandmother, who wasn't feeling very well. My grandmother lives out in the woods, so I had quite a way to go. When I walked into the woods, I met a wolf. He asked me where I was going and what I was carrying in my basket. I stopped to pick some flowers, and finally reached my grandmother's house. I was surprised, because grandmother's door was open, and I could walk right in. When I told my grandmother that she had big ears she said, 'The better to hear you with.' Believe me, I had quite an adventure that day. Who am I?"

(*Answer:* Little Red Riding Hood)

Have the students identify the fairy-tale character and defend the reasons for making their identification.

2. For a critical listening activity, write paragraphs in which the majority of the sentences pertain to one character. Include one or

two sentences inconsistent with that character. Instruct the students to listen carefully to the paragraph, identify the character who is speaking, identify the details which support the identification of the character, and identify the details which are not correct for that character. For example:

"When I was a young girl, I was very happy until my mother, the queen, died, and my father married again. My stepmother was so jealous that she sent me out into the deep woods with a hunter, who was told to take my life. The hunter could not do this. *I roamed the woods until I found a huge castle with many rooms* (inconsistent). Inside this house, I found a table set with seven little plates, and seven little beds ready for the night. I was lucky, because the seven little men told me I could live with them. My stepmother was very angry when she found out I was living with the seven little men. *She mixed an evil spell and turned me into an apple* (inconsistent). The spell was finally broken and I lived happily ever after."

After the students listen to the paragraph, have them identify the character, list the supporting details, and tell why these details support their choice of character. Next, have them identify the two details that are incorrect for that fairy-tale character. Have them evaluate why the two statements are incorrect.

A COTTAGE IS NOT A CASTLE.

(*Answer:* Snow White) Incorrect details: I roamed the woods until I found a huge castle with many rooms (it was a small cottage). She mixed an evil spell and turned me into an apple (the spell was placed on an apple, Snow White was not turned into an apple).

3. Have students develop their own paragraphs describing a fairy-tale character. Ask them to place one or two incorrect statements in the paragraph. Have them share these paragraphs with other students, who will listen for supporting details and identify incorrect statements.

ACTIVITY 3-12:
PLAYING DETECTIVE
WITH FAMOUS AMERICANS

TYPE		TERM	
CLASS	☐	STA	☐
GROUP	☐	LTA	☐
IND	☑	LC	☑

Purpose:

1. To identify the persons in history who might have made particular statements or described themselves

2. To select details identifying a historical figure

3. To apply previous knowledge of a historical figure to evaluate whether a viewpoint is consistent with that person

4. To identify details that are inconsistent with a person or time period

5. To reinforce social studies and history

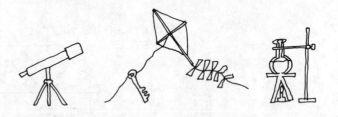

Materials: Paragraphs written to present specific people in history, their accomplishments, viewpoints, values, or backgrounds

Grade level: Middle and upper elementary, middle school (depending on the historical figures used and in which grade those people are studied; activities 2 and 3 are more difficult than #1, requiring critical evaluation of inconsistent statements)

Procedures:

1. Develop paragraphs or short stories about famous people in history; delete the name of the person in the description. You can write the dialogue in first person so students have to listen for supporting details to identify the person. Try to illustrate both male and female heroes, as well as heroes from various minority groups. Examples of paragraphs could include:

a. "I was very proud in 1905, when I was named to the Hall of Fame for Great Americans. You may be wondering how I happened to be given this great honor. When I was a child, I spent many hours with my father in his observatory. I later went to school and studied mathematics and read a great deal about navigation. One evening I was in my father's observatory looking through the telescope, and saw a faint and hazy object in the sky where no object had even been observed. This discovery made me famous. I was awarded Denmark's gold medal for the first person to discover a telescopic comet. I became a professor of astronomy at Vassar and made many more astronomical discoveries. I do not believe that women cannot succeed in the sciences. Who am I?"

(*Answer:* Maria Mitchell, the first American astronomer to discover a telescopic comet.)

b. "When I was growing up, I lived in Boston with thirteen brothers and sisters. My father wanted me to work for him. He made candles to sell to the people of Boston. I did not want to make candles; I wanted to write articles and print my own newspaper. I worked as an apprentice in my brother James's printing shop. We didn't get along very well, so after a few years, I moved to Philadelphia to look for a job in a printshop. I was fortunate, and by the time I was 22, I owned my own newspaper, *The Pennsylvania Gazette*. One of my most famous publications was an almanac which told people about the weather, important dates to remember, and included advice in the form of proverbs. I always had many ideas, and enjoyed inventing things. I invented a stove which fitted into a fireplace and sent heat out into a room rather than up the chimney. My most famous experiment proved that electricity and lightning are the same; in fact, I invented the lightning rod. I became involved with politics, and worked for the colonies during the American Revolution. I was proud of my work. I was the only person who signed all of these papers: The Declaration of Independence, the treaty with France, the peace treaty with England, and the Constitution of the United States. Who am I?"

(*Answer:* Benjamin Franklin)

c. "When I was a boy, I wanted to go to school more than anything else. This was not easy, however, because I had to leave home to go to school. The local schools would not let me attend. I even had to earn my own money while I was away from home. I washed and ironed clothes, cooked, and swept floors for people so I had enough money to sleep, eat, and buy books. This was not an easy life. In 1894, I finally earned a college degree in agriculture from Iowa State College. I chose agriculture because I felt that agriculture could open the door of freedom for my people. I took a job teaching at Tuskegee University in Alabama so I could help my people learn how to prepare land to grow better crops. One morning, as I was walking to the university, I saw a strange plant growing at the edge of a field. I asked a farmer what the plant was, and he told me it was useless goobers. I found out the plant was also called peanuts. Since the peanuts would grow in soil that would not raise cotton, I decided it could not be useless. I started to experiment with peanuts, and discovered over 300 products that could be made from this very useful plant. When I died in 1943, these words were written on my gravestone: 'He could have added fortune to fame, but caring for neither, he found happiness and honor in being helpful to the world.' Who am I?"

(*Answer:* George Washington Carver)

Have the students identify the famous person described in each paragraph. Have them identify important details, the point at which they could identify the person, and details that might be similar for more than one person in history.

2. For a more demanding critical listening activity, develop paragraphs as in the above activity, but include one or two sentences inconsistent with that person's values, accomplishments, or time in history. Instruct the students to listen carefully to the paragraph, identify the person who is speaking, identify the details which support the identification, and identify the details which are not consistent with that person or time in history. For example:

"When I was 17 years old, I joined a wagon train to help settlers moving west. I learned a great deal about the mountains and the western country. In 1842, I met Lieutenant John Fremont of the United States army. He was planning an expedition to California, to explore the land and report back to the government in Washington. He had heard that I was a well-known trail blazer, and asked me to be the guide for the journey. *Fremont offered to pay me five hundred dollars a month for my services* (inconsistent with time in history). When we finally crossed the mountains and reached California, we found that the United States had declared war on Mexico. We were told to capture Monterey, San Diego, and Los Angeles for the American government. We were successful. *A dispatch was sent back on the Transcontinental Railroad informing the President that California had been captured* (inconsistent with time in history). I returned to California again as a guide for General Kearny. We were ambushed by the Mexican army. I reached Fort Stockton, and help, by crawling through bushes, high grass, and thick brush. After that experience, I explored much of the western United States and became well known as an Indian fighter. Who am I?"

(*Answer:* Kit Carson) Inconsistencies: (1) Fremont offered to pay me five hundred dollars a month for my services. (The sum was $100 a month, $500 would have been unheard of in the 1840s.) (2) A dispatch was sent back on the Transcontinental Railroad informing the President that California had been captured. (The Transcontinental Railroad was not completed until 1869.)

After the students listen to the paragraph, have them identify the person in history, list the supporting details, and tell why these details support their choice. Next, have them identify the two details in the paragraph that are inconsistent with the time of history presented in the paragraph. Have them evaluate why the two statements are incorrect.

3. Ask students to develop their own paragraphs describing famous people in history. Ask them to place one or two incorrect statements in the paragraph and share these paragraphs with other students, who will listen for supporting details and identify incorrect statements.

4. Students can write conversations between two people in history, then read them for other students to identify.

5. This type of critical listening activity can also be developed around subjects other than famous Americans from history. Some other topics and suggestions for famous people might include:

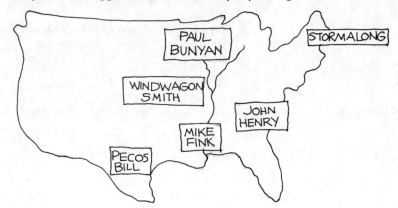

a. Which Tall-Tale Hero Am I?

Paul Bunyan	Davy Crockett
Pecos Bill	Mike Fink
Windwagon Smith	Captain Stormalong

b. Which World Hero Am I?

Winston Churchill	Golda Meir
Marie Curie	Mohandas Gandhi
Dag Hammarskjold	Sigmund Freud
Albert Schweitzer	Maria Montessori

c. Which Famous Black American Am I? [A source for identifications is *Profiles of Black Americans,* by Richard A. Boning (New York: Dexter & Westbrook, 1969).] Some possibilities are:

Patricia Roberts Harris (first black American woman to represent U.S. as an ambassador)

Shirley Chisholm (first black American woman elected to congress)

Ralph Bunche (worked for world peace as ambassador to the United Nations; winner of Nobel Peace Prize)

Bill Pickett (originated the art of steer wrestling)

Matthew Henson (co-discoverer of the North Pole)

Dr. Charles Drew (discovered blood plasma and organized Red Cross Blood Bank)

George Washington Carver (famous agricultural chemist who perfected many uses for the peanut)

Martin Luther King, Jr. (symbol for the Civil Rights movement)

Whitney M. Young (Civil Rights leader)

Sammy Davis, Jr. (entertainer)

Louis Armstrong (jazz musician)

Mahalia Jackson (gospel singer)

Wilt Chamberlin (professional basketball player)

d. Which Living American Am I? (Choices from current or past history)

e. Which Sports Hero Am I? (Choices from sports of interest to the students)

ACTIVITY 3-13:
FOOLS AND FOOLISHNESS IN FOLK TALES

TYPE		TERM	
CLASS	☑	STA	☑
GROUP	☑	LTA	☐
IND	☐	LC	☐

Purpose:

1. To discover that authors use literary techniques to influence the listener

2. To identify literary techniques that make the listener sympathize with, empathize with, or reject a character

3. To develop appreciation for literary techniques used in folktales

4. To respond to literary techniques used in folktales

Materials:

Examples of folktales depicting different kinds of fools; e.g., "The Golden Goose" (The Brothers Grimm); "The Man, the Boy, and the Donkey" (Aesop); "The Golden Touch" (Nathaniel Hawthorne); Simple Simon (Mother Goose); "Jabberwocky" (Lewis Carroll); "The Blind Men and the Elephant" (John G. Saxe); "The Akond of Swat" (Edward Lear)

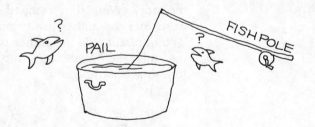

Grade level:

Middle and upper elementary

Procedures:

1. Background Information: Many folktales have been written about fools. These fools may be cowardly, absentminded, ignorant, gullible, extremely talkative, or greedy. Simpletons, like Jack in "Jack and the Beanstalk," often win in folktales. Other fools, such as the man in "The Man, the Boy, and the Donkey," lose everything be-

cause of their foolishness. According to Francelia Butler, "The literature about fools is appealing to children because fools are, above all, human—and therefore tales about fools bring them always a certain joy and delight in the human condition." [4]

2. Discuss these different kinds of foolish characters with the students. Ask the students if they can think of some folktales that use the theme of foolishness. How do they feel about the foolish character in the story or poem? Are they sympathetic toward the character, or do they dislike the character? Tell the students you will be reading to them some of the folktales and rhymes that tell about foolish characters. After they listen to the folktale or poem, they will have an opportunity to share how they feel about the character, what made them like or dislike the character, and what terms the author has used to make them feel that way. Some of the following selections may be used:

a. "The Golden Goose" (Brothers Grimm)—Although Dummling is considered a simpleton by his brothers, he performs a good deed for an old man and is given a golden goose. Anyone who touches the goose sticks fast. As Dummling progresses toward the city, he gains seven followers who cannot let go. Within the city is a princess who never laughs. The princess's father has proclaimed that whoever can make her laugh shall marry her. Dummling's procession is so funny that she laughs; Dummling marries her, and becomes heir to the kingdom.

   After the class listens to the story, have part of the class act out the story for the rest of the class. Then change roles, so all the children have an opportunity to observe this humorous scene.

   Discuss with the group their reactions to the simpleton in the story. Were they sympathetic? Why or why not? What words did the author use to make them feel this way? What kind of picture did the author paint with words? Was it funny, sad, silly, etc.? Have the group draw pictures to illustrate the foolishness in the story.

b. "The Man, the Boy, and the Donkey" (Aesop)—In this fable, the foolish person does not win. On the way to the market, the man takes advice from all of the people passing by. First, he puts the boy on the donkey, then he puts himself on the donkey; next, he and the boy ride the donkey, and, finally, the boy and the man tie the donkey's feet and carry the donkey on their shoulders. The final foolishness occurs when the donkey falls off the bridge and drowns because his feet are tied.

After reading the fable, have the students compare the fool in this story with Dummling. Did they react in the same way to this story? Why or why not? What technique did Aesop use to get his point across to the listener? What words were used to describe the man, the boy, and the donkey? Have the students select statements that influenced the man. Have them say the statements scornfully, as if they were the people passing on the road.

"See that lazy youngster."
"Shame on that lazy lout."
"Aren't you ashamed for overloading that poor donkey?"

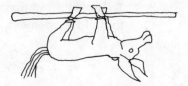

c. "The Golden Touch" (Nathaniel Hawthorne)—King Midas is an example of a man whose greed causes him to become a fool. King Midas values nothing but gold, until he is given the golden touch. When his food, water, and his child are all turned to gold, he discovers that gold is not the most important thing in the world.

This is a very good story for creative dramatics, puppetry, or story telling. Divide the students into smaller groups, and have each group plan a different creative way to present the story to the rest of the class.

Have them find other folktales which depict the theme of greed, and share the stories with the class.

d. Read several nonsense poems, rhymes, and limericks to the group. Let them listen for the enjoyment of the sounds in language. These poems may also be used for choral reading (see the oral language section of this book). Examples include: Simple Simon (Mother Goose);"Jabberwocky"(Lewis Carroll;) "The Blind Men and the Elephant" (John G. Saxe); and "The Akond of Swat" (Edward Lear).

ACTIVITY 3-14:
RADIO'S DAYS OF OLD

TYPE		TERM	
CLASS	☑	STA	☐
GROUP	☑	LTA	☑
IND	☐	LC	☐

Purpose:

1. To develop appreciative listening skills

2. To develop visual imagery

3. To illustrate characters and settings described in old radio broadcasts

4. To evaluate the use of sound effects and background music on a story

5. To define the climax of a story and describe the techniques used to build excitement

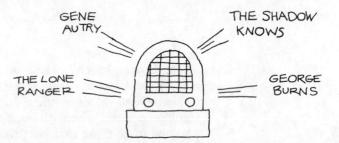

Materials:

Recordings or tapes of popular radio shows of the past; available shows include those of George Burns, Jack Benny, The Lone Ranger, Gene Autry, Hopalong Cassidy, Mr. Keen, Tracer of Lost Persons, The Shadow, Escape, Two Thousand Plus, My Friend Irma, Superman, The Green Hornet, and Sherlock Holmes's Adventures. (Sunburst Communications, Pleasantville, N.Y., publishes a *Tune-In* series of radio tapes and instructional materials for teaching listening and literature skills with radio broadcasts.)

Grade level:

Depends on broadcast selection and activities used with the selection; young children can react to theme songs on radio shows by painting to music or doing creative movement activities; activities requiring students to listen to longer segments, react to plot, or define climax are more appropriate for middle- and upper-elementary students. Records of old radio shows may be used with large groups, small groups, or individual students who wish to investigate a subject.

Procedures:

1. Ask students if they have ever heard some of the radio broadcasts from the 1940s and 1950s. (These broadcasts are often played over educational radio stations, or students may have recordings of them.) Ask the students why they believe radio was so popular forty years ago. Explain that they will have an opportunity to listen to some of these radio broadcasts. You may wish to suggest that they will also have an opportunity to produce their own radio show, complete with sound effects and background music, after they have listened to several radio broadcasts.

2. The listening activities you do with the students depends on the contents of the radio broadcast. Be sure you listen to the record or tape before you use it with the students. Introduce the broadcast, and prepare the students for the listening experience. These activities lend themselves to listening to radio broadcasts:

   a. Since students cannot see the characters in the story, ask them to listen to all the clues that suggest the physical appearance of the main characters, or one of the main characters. Have them draw a picture of the character and tell why they drew the character that way. Discuss with the students the clues they heard and how they interpreted these clues. (This activity does not have a right or wrong answer, unless obvious clues would call for the same interpretation by all listeners.)

   b. The setting for a radio show must also be imagined by each listener. Have students listen for clues about the location and time period of the story. If they do not have enough background experience with that time period, have them research the time period and illustrate the setting. They might depict the major setting of the story with dioramas or drawings. For a more extensive setting activity, divide the students into small groups and have them depict the setting on a roll of paper. They can place this roll setting in a box with a window opening and show it as the radio broadcast is replayed. "The Lone Ranger" stories may have several settings, such as a frontier town, an Indian village, a ranch, an old mine, an early railroad, etc. Students may also retell the story without using the radio broadcast.

After the students depict the setting, allow them to discuss whether or not they would like to live in such a setting.

c. After they have researched the time period, they can listen to the broadcast again and evaluate whether the broadcast is authentic for that time period. If the broadcast is a science fiction story set in the future or the far distant past, would the story be written in the same way? Has scientific knowledge changed during the 40 years since the broadcast was made? How would the story be written today? If the broadcast is a comedy, what do the jokes tell us about famous people or values of the time? Comparisons can be made with current comedians. What subjects do comedy writers use for jokes? Are there similarities between the subject matter of jokes told on television today and jokes told on radio broadcasts 40 years ago? Why may there be similarities?

d. Sound effects and music add to the radio listener's appreciation. Have the students listen to the sound effects, then discuss how the sound effects influence appreciation for the show. Compare the sound effects of a detective show with the sound effects of a western or comedy broadcast. Could the student identify the type of program by merely listening to the sound effects? Have the students list the sound effects they hear when they listen to different types of programs.

SOUND EFFECTS

Western Programs:

Mystery Programs:

Comedy Programs:

Science Fiction Programs:

Background music also influences the listener. Have the students listen to a program's theme song or background music, and discuss why that specific music was chosen. Ask them to listen to the background music, and allow them to do creative movement or painting while listening. Allow them to share how the music makes them feel.

e. Radio broadcasts allow students to listen to the development of a story's climax. Have them listen to a broadcast that develops a definite climax, identify the climax, and discuss the techniques used by the actors and sound effect technicians to increase the excitement building up to the climax. Have the students act out broadcasts, demonstrating the development of an exciting climax.

f. After students have listened to old radio shows and completed a number of listening activities, encourage them to develop their own radio broadcasts, complete with sound effects and background music.

4 Language Experience Activities

The language experience approach combines reading with the other communication skills of listening, oral expression, and writing. The approach uses a learner's own language patterns, vocabulary, and experiences to supply both meaningful and highly motivational reading materials. All the language wealth the child brings to school is called on to provide an orderly transition from speaking, to writing, to reading. Language experience activities do not separate reading from the other communication skills; this is especially helpful to the young child trying to understand the mysteries of learning to read.

The basic premise of the language experience approach is that each child's thoughts are valuable. They are to be expressed by the child, written down by the teacher (or by the child, when he attains adequate writing skills), and read by the teacher, the child, and anyone else who wishes.

Words that are meaningful to the child have been used to teach reading successfully under quite diverse circumstances. Sylvia Ashton Warner, using an approach she referred to as "organic language," taught Maori children of New Zealand to read under primitive conditions where both materials and student motivation were lacking. Her approach stressed the child's developing his own reading materials, using culturally important words such as "hut," "mother," and "food." The approach has also been used with remedial children at all levels of education, with non-English-speaking children, linguistically different children, children in special education classrooms, and children in regular education classrooms at all levels of instruction.

Language experience can be used in the classroom for several quite different purposes. At the kindergarten and first-grade levels, children dictate chart stories about their experiences. As they observe the teacher writing down exactly what they have said and then reading it, they are acquiring the readiness skills of grasping left-to-right and top-to-bottom progression; understanding the concept of words; visually discriminating among sentences, phrases, words, and letters; auditorily discriminating between words and sounds of letters; listening for comprehension; and following directions. Such experiences also result in vocabulary expansion, language expansion, and an appreciation for the value of reading. While some children at these early levels are using the language experience to develop meaningful readiness skills, other children in the same classes are actually reading the materials.

As children progress in reading and language arts instruction in first grade and beyond, the language experience is again used for more than one purpose. Language experience may be a total reading approach, as developed by Roach Van Allen [1] or as described by Russell Stauffer.[2] Or, the language experience approach may be used to expand and enrich the basal reader and other language arts instruction. Language experience is also useful when the skills taught in the basal reader must be retaught or reinforced. While many students find redoing the same basal sequence of activities boring or frustrating, they can often be motivated to learn by a meaningful language experience activity designed to help them develop a specific skill.

Another strength the language experience approach offers to the classroom teacher is its adaptability to large-group, small-group or individual activities. For example, a whole class might construct a chart story describing a field trip experience, or each student can compose a story after an entire class has had the same large-group experience. A small-group activity can be created for students who need to learn to follow a sequence of directions. After the small-group experiences, such as making a recipe, a group chart story can be written, or individual stories composed. The language experience can also be a completely individualized activity. A student can dictate or write a story about himself, his family, or a favorite pet. This flexibility provides many opportunities for individualizing instruction to meet different needs.

The language experience activities in this section may be used to teach, reinforce, and expand the specific skills taught in the language arts/reading curriculum. Each activity has a specific objective corresponding to the sequence of skills usually taught in the elementary grades. The activities include examples for facilitating readiness, sight word expansion, phonic analysis, structural analysis, descriptive vocabulary expansion, following a sequence of directions, use of antonyms, study skills, critical evaluation, comprehension, creative writing, and creative oral expression. The skills are not taught in isolation, but are developed through language activities that combine the communication skills.

Each activity lists an approximate grade level. These are the grade levels at which a scope and sequence chart usually lists those skills.[3] The grade levels are only approximations, since the children's ability levels must be considered; a child in a remedial reading, sixth-grade class, for example, may benefit from an activity that has a second or third grade designation.

Each language experience activity is developed in a specific sequence of experiences. "Experience" is a key term in this approach. Children are stimulated by *experiencing* a motivational activity. This activity provides something to think about, to talk about, to write about, and to read about. The resulting experience story is meaningful because the children have experienced the story before they are expected to either write, read, or answer questions about it. The following sequence is common for the language experience activities:

1. *Motivational activity.* Provide an experience to stimulate thinking, discussion, writing, and reading. Motivational ideas include field trips, pictures, experiments, holidays, poetry, music, tall tales, local issues, comparisons, families, pets, friends, myself, puppetry, make believe, birthday parties, content area units, art work, biographies, guest speakers, movies, literature, dreams, making a recipe, classroom animals, hobbies, or the weather.
2. *Discussion time.* Provide a discussion time so children can think, exchange, expand, and clarify ideas before they write.
3. *Dictation or individual writing.* If the story is dictated, either by a group or an individual child, record the words as presented by the group or child. Place the children in a position so they can watch you as you write on the chalkboard, chart, or large sheet of newsprint. If the language experience is being written individually by each child, provide as much assistance as necessary for them to write their own thoughts.
4. *Read the story.* Read the story back to the students immediately. Underline each word with your hand and allow the students to verify that this is exactly what they said. Allow them to read the story with you and by themselves, when they feel ready.
5. *Reinforcement.* Do appropriate reinforcement activities with the language experience story. For example, cut apart sentences in a sequentially-ordered story, mix them, and have students put them back into the correct order. Match sentences that are cut apart with sentences in a chart story. Match phrases or words with the same phrases and words in the chart story. Find words in the chart story that begin with a specific consonant or rhyme with a specific word. Do a role playing activity about a problem developed or resolved in an experience story.
6. *Word bank development.* Each child using the language experience approach develops a bank of words. The day after the experience story is written, individual children read the story, underline words they know, and are tested on the words in isolation. One way of testing words in isolation is to construct a word window.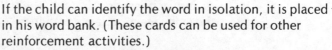

   This is made by cutting a window into a file card which allows the teacher to isolate words and test the child. Words that are known are placed on small word cards:

   If the child can identify the word in isolation, it is placed in his word bank. (These cards can be used for other reinforcement activities.)
7. *Reinforcement activities continue.*

ACTIVITY 4-1:
SAMMY CIRCLE'S ☺ DISCOVERY

TYPE		TERM	
CLASS	☑	STA	☑
GROUP	☑	LTA	☐
IND	☑	LC	☐

Purpose:

1. To involve students in a motivational activity resulting in oral discussion and a dictated story

2. To have students participate in a creative movement activity

3. To identify likenesses and differences in shapes by matching circles, squares, rectangles, and triangles

4. To interpret shapes through a creative art activity

Materials:

Sammy Circle, Stanley Square, Rita Rectangle and Tricia Triangle; chart story to illustrate "Sammy ☺ Discovery"; cardboard shapes of ○ , □ , ▭ , and △ ; chart paper for dictated story; art supplies for individual pictures

Grade level:

Kindergarten, first grade

Motivational Activity:

Begin the discussion by showing the students four characters in the shape of a circle, square, rectangle, and triangle. Introduce them by name:

| Sammy Circle | Stanley Square | Rita Rectangle | Tricia Triangle |

Encourage the children to describe each character, and to identify other items in the classroom or in their homes that have the same shape as each of the characters. Explain to the children that they are going to listen to a story about 4 children named Sammy Circle, Stanley Square, Rita Rectangle, and Tricia Triangle. After they listen to the story, they will become authors, and finish the story the way they want it to end. You can use the following chart story:

Sammy [circle face] Discovery

One beautiful morning Sammy [circle face] left his home to go out and play. Sammy [circle face] was thinking about his shape. Sammy didn't have any ———— or ⌐ , he was just one round circle. Sammy [circle face] didn't like ———— or ⌐ . He thought ———— and ⌐ were ugly.

As Sammy [circle face] rolled and bounced down the block toward the park, he saw that a new family had moved into the white house on the corner. Sammy [circle face] looked into the yard and saw three children playing. The first child was a [square face] . The [square face] had four sides that were all the same length [square] and the [square face] had 1 ⌐ , 2 ⌐ , 3 ⌐ , 4 ∟ . The second child was a [rectangle face] . The [rectangle face] had two sides that were one length ———— and two sides that were a different length | | . The [rectangle face] also had 1 ⌐ , 2 ⌐ , 3 ⌐ , and 4 ∟ . The third child was a [triangle face] . The [triangle face] had three sides that were the same length △ and 1 ∧ , 2 ⌐ , 3 ∠ .

Sammy [circle face] stopped to watch the [square face] , [rectangle face] , and [triangle face] play. Sammy [circle face] was surprised when he saw that the [square face] , [rectangle face] , and [triangle face] could do many things when they played. Sammy [circle face] was happy when Stanley [square face] , Rita [rectangle face] , and Tricia [triangle face] asked Sammy [circle face] to play with them. Sammy [circle face] , Stanley [square face] , Rita [rectangle face] , and Tricia [triangle face] played all morning. They ————————————————

Procedures:

1. Lead an oral discussion describing the circle, square, rectangle, and triangle. Introduce the shape characters from the story.

2. Introduce the story "Sammy [circle face] Discovery," which has been printed on large sheets of tagboard or newsprint. Have the children follow as you read the story, underlining each word with

your hand as you read it. Allow the children to "read" the rebus pictures when they appear in the story. Read the story a second time, allowing the class to read along with you.

3. Discuss some of the play activities a circle, square, rectangle, and triangle could do. Talk about movements, games, and acrobatics that would be fun to do if you were one of these shapes. Ask the students to tell you what they think the story title, "Sammy 😊 Discovery," means. "What do you think Sammy Circle discovered? Why?"

4. Have the students dictate a chart story finishing "Sammy Discovery."

Reinforcement:

1. Have students match the cardboard shapes of the ○ , □ , ▭ , and △ with the corresponding shapes on the chart story.

2. Ask students to pretend they are the shape characters in the story. Read the story to the class, allowing them to pantomime the actions of each character in the story. Have them pretend to be a circle, square, rectangle, and triangle at play. Have them experiment with the possible actions of each shape.

3. Allow children to choose one of the shape characters and draw a picture illustrating that character's possible actions. Compile a bulletin board of the shape pictures.

4. Play a guessing game in which children choose a shape, take the role of that shape, and pantomime its actions while members of the class guess what shape the student is.

5. Provide puzzles which allow children to manipulate the four shapes.

6. Using a flannel board and felt shapes, have students match identical shapes.

ACTIVITY 4-2:
SAMMY CIRCLE'S ☹ COLORS

Purpose:	1. To involve students in a motivational activity resulting in oral discussion and a dictated story
	2. To identify colors illustrated in a rebus chart story
	3. To match colors on cardboard circles with colors on a rebus chart story

Materials:	Sammy Circle drawn in each of the basic colors; chart story, "Sammy ☹ Colors"; chart paper for dictated story; art supplies for individual pictures

Grade level:	Kindergarten, first grade

Motivational Activity:	Begin the discussion by introducing "Sammy Circle." Draw Sammy on a card or sheet, but do not color in the circle. Explain that Sammy

Circle is unhappy because he wants to be colorful, but cannot decide which color he wants to be. He wants the children to "read" the chart story "Sammy ☹ Colors," which describes his problems. After they "read" the story along with their teacher, he wants them to draw a picture illustrating the solution to his problem, and dictate a short story telling about the picture. You may use the following chart story:

Sammy 🙁 **Colors**

A very unhappy Sammy 🙁 was sitting in his room. He wanted

to put on a bright new coat but he could not decide on the color.

Sammy 🙁 went to his closet and brought out his (red) coat.

The red coat reminded him of a (red) . He didn't get any

(r.) (r.) this year. He didn't feel like a (red) . Then

Sammy 🙁 brought out his (green) coat. The green coat made him

think of a (green) . He fell out of a (green) and didn't want

to think about (green) (green) . Next Sammy 🙁 brought out

his (blue) coat. The blue coat was the same color as his (blue)

He lost his (blue) yesterday. That made him cry. Sammy 🙁

brought out his (black) coat. The black coat reminded him of

(black) . He wanted to play outside and didn't want to think

about (black) (black) . Next Sammy 🙁 brought out his

(orange) coat. When he tried the orange coat on, he looked like

an (orange) . Sammy 🙁 was afraid someone would eat him.

Now there were only three coats left in the closet. Sammy 🙁

brought out his (brown) coat, his (purple) coat, and his

(yellow) coat. He didn't know what to do.

Will you help Sammy 🙁 decide which color coat to put on?

Tell Sammy 🙁 why you think he should wear that color. Also

tell Sammy 🙁 what you think he should do after he puts on

his coat.

Procedures:

1. Lead an oral discussion about Sammy Circle and his problems with colors.

2. Introduce the story, "Sammy 🙁 Colors," which has been printed on large sheets of tagboard or newsprint. Encourage children to follow along as you read. Allow children to "read" the rebus pictures. Read the story a second time, encouraging children to "read" with you.

3. Discuss the color choices Sammy Circle has for his coat. Encourage the children to discuss advantages and disadvantages for choosing each color. Which color did they choose? Why? What would they feel like if they were wearing a brown, purple, or yellow coat? What would they do after they chose their coat?

4. Have the students dictate a language experience chart story which solves Sammy's problem.

Reinforcement:

1. Have the students match the Sammy Circles drawn on colored paper with the appropriate rebus drawings on the chart story.

2. Randomly name colors depicted on the chart story. Have children point to the appropriate color on the chart.

3. Ask students to draw a picture illustrating "Sammy ☺ Colors,"

or their choice of the final color for Sammy's coat and the activities he would do after he dressed in his coat. Encourage them to dictate individual stories after they finish their pictures.

4. Match colored felt circles on the flannel board.

5. Have children who are ready match the printed word with the corresponding color circle.

ACTIVITY 4-3:
RHYMING REBUS GAMES

TYPE		TERM	
CLASS	☐	STA	☑
GROUP	☑	LTA	☐
IND	☑	LC	☐

Purpose:
1. To identify rhyming elements in a rhyming rebus chart and game cards
2. To dictate sentences and illustrate appropriate rhyming words to create rhyming game cards
3. To pantomime words on the rhyming rebus chart and game cards

Materials: Rhyming rebus chart; cards with pictures of rhyming elements; materials for rhyming game cards

Grade level: Kindergarten, first grade

Motivational Activity: Review meaning of rhyming words. Display charts showing sentences with rebus pictures illustrating the words for rhyming. Explain that each sentence on the chart contains a picture. The class or group will play a game in which they locate pictures that rhyme with the picture in each sentence. For example:

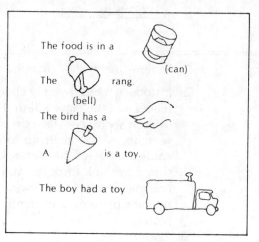

The food is in a (can)

The (bell) rang.

The bird has a

A ▽ is a toy.

The boy had a toy

Provide separate cards with pictures illustrating items that rhyme with each picture.

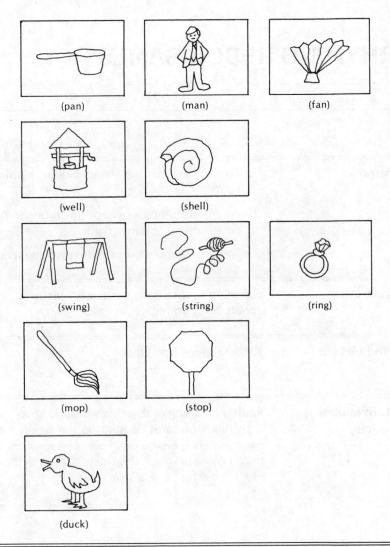

(pan)   (man)   (fan)

(well)   (shell)

(swing)   (string)   (ring)

(mop)   (stop)

(duck)

Procedures:

1. Review meaning of rhyming words.

2. Introduce rebus rhyming chart. Explain that you will read the sentences and the class will find pictures that rhyme with the picture in each sentence. Have the students follow as you read the first sentence. Allow them to look at the pictures on the individual cards and select the pictures that rhyme with "can." Ask them if they can think of other words that rhyme with "can." Continue reading the rest of the rhyming rebus chart, selecting appropriate rhyming pictures, and identifying other words that rhyme with the picture.

3. Tell the class or group they will have an opportunity to make their own rhyming picture game cards. Have them dictate sentences with a rebus picture suggestion. Print their sentences on cards, allowing the children to draw their own rhyming pictures. On separate, smaller cards, have them draw several pictures that rhyme with the illustration in the sentence.

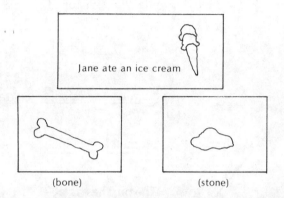

Jane ate an ice cream

(bone)   (stone)

You can also make another rebus rhyming chart as a group activity.

Reinforcement:

1. Have students match pictures on individual cards with the rebus pictures on the chart.

2. Play a pantomime game in which the students divide into teams to act out the rhyming words. For example, the child chosen to be "it" might draw the card [fan] . He could tell the group that the word he is thinking of rhymes with the first sentence on the chart, "The food is in a [can] ." An individual or a team then acts out the word they think it is.

3. Divide the rhyming game cards into groups of five. Place each group of 5 sentence cards and the individual pictures that accompany them into a large envelope folder. (Print the accompanying words on the back of the picture cards and place an answer key on the back of each card [Pan] .) Put the completed cards into a rhyming learning center where students can match the pictures individually.

4. Children who are reading can match word cards rather than picture cards with the rebus pictures.

The food is in a ⬭ .

| pan | man | fan | ran | tan | van |

The 🔔 rang.

| well | shell | tell | sell | fell | yell |

| smell | spell |

The bird has a 🪶 .

| swing | string | ring | sing | king |

| spring | bring |

The ▽ is a toy.

| mop | stop | hop | pop | crop |

| drop | shop |

The boy had a toy 🚚 .

| duck | buck | luck | tuck | stuck |

JILL, BILL, AND WILL
ON SAMPSON'S HILL

TYPE		TERM	
CLASS	☐	STA	☑
GROUP	☑	LTA	☐
IND	☑	LC	☐

Purpose:

1. To involve students in a motivational activity resulting in oral discussion and dictated sentences using rhyming words

2. To identify rhyming words in a story read by the teacher

Materials:

Rhyming triplet characters, Jill, Bill, and Will; chart story "Jill, Bill, and Will on Sampson's Hill"; paper for chart story

Grade level:

Kindergarten, first grade

Motivational Activity:

Begin discussion by introducing the rhyming triplets, Jill, Bill, and Will. These characters should be drawn on poster board or construction paper and properly labeled.

| Jill | Bill | Will |

Ask the children to listen to the names and tell you how they are alike (rhyming, ending sounds are alike, etc.). Tell the children that Jill, Bill, and Will want to find other words that rhyme with their names. Jill, Bill, and Will want the children to listen carefully to a story. Every time the children hear a word that rhymes with Jill, Bill, and Will, they should raise their hands.

Jill, Bill, and *Will* on Sampson's *Hill*

"Three triplets named *Jill, Bill,* and *Will* want to play on Sampson's *Hill. Jill* wants to *fill* a basket with berries. *Bill* wants to explore the funny old *mill. Will* wants to roll and roll down the green grassy *hill.* It is so *still* on Sampson's *hill.* No one *will* stop *Jill, Bill,* or *Will* on Sampson's *hill.* They can play all day on that *still,* green, grassy *hill.*" (Pretend you are Jill, Bill, or Will, what would you do on Sampson's Hill?)

Procedures:	1. Lead an oral discussion introducing the rhyming triplets. Review meaning of rhyming.
	2. Introduce story, "Jill, Bill, and Will on Sampson's Hill." Read the story while children listen carefully (eyes closed), and have them raise their hands each time they hear a word that rhymes with Jill, Bill, or Will.
	3. Have the children accompany you as you read "Jill, Bill, and Will on Sampson's Hill" from a chart story. Allow the children to fill in the rhyming words.
	4. Ask the children to pretend they are Jill, Bill, or Will, and have them dictate a sentence telling what they would do on Sampson's Hill. Ask them to use words that rhyme with Jill, Bill, and Will.

Reinforcement:	1. Have the students match Jill, Bill, and Will characters and other words that rhyme.
	2. Allow children to illustrate their stories about Sampson's Hill.

ACTIVITY 4-5:
RHYMING PICTURE STORIES

TYPE		TERM	
CLASS	☐	STA	☑
GROUP	☑	LTA	☐
IND	☑	LC	☐

Purpose:	1. To supply the missing word in a rhyming verse read by the teacher
	2. To dictate rhyming verse

Materials:	Rhyming picture story book, such as Dr. Seuss's *Cat in the Hat*

Grade level:	Kindergarten, first grade

Motivational Activity:	Read a rhyming picture story book, such as *Cat in the Hat,* rhyming poetry, or Mother Goose rhymes. Omit the rhyming word, allowing children to fill in the rhyming elements orally.

Procedures:	1. Discuss rhyming words, provide examples.
	2. Read the rhyming stories or poetry, omitting rhyming words. Allow children to fill in missing words.
	3. Allow children to dictate their own rhyming verses.

Reinforcement:	1. Provide rhyming sentences, such as: See the bug on my _____ (mug, rug, jug) Allow children to finish the sentences with any rhyming words.

INCREASING SIGHT WORD KNOWLEDGE

TYPE		TERM	
CLASS	☐	STA	☑
GROUP	☑	LTA	☐
IND	☑	LC	☐

Purpose:
1. To increase knowledge of preprimer (primer, first-grade, etc.) vocabulary by using preprimer words in model sentences

2. To increase the number of sight words known by finishing beginning model sentences with student's own words

3. To improve comprehension of preprimer (primer, first grade, etc.) vocabulary words by using them in context

Materials:
Model sentences which include desired preprimer, primer, first-grade, etc., vocabulary words; word banks for each child

Grade level:
First grade

Motivational Activity:
Discuss with children the enjoyment they get from writing their own sentences. Suggest they can use the same words the author of their reading book uses, but they can make the sentences their own by adding their ideas to the words the author uses. Compile a list of model sentences with the words you want to reinforce or teach. These model sentences use preprimer words from Dolch Basic Word List.

1. I help my _____.

2. I play in my big _____.

3. I can jump _____.

4. I make _____.

5. I can not find my _____.

6. I can go _____.

7. My _____ is funny.

Procedures:

1. Present the model sentences to the class, group, or an individual student.

2. Help the class, group or individual read the beginning of the sentence. Encourage the students to finish the sentence with their own words. Print the remainder of the sentence as the children dictate it. Reread the whole sentence, pointing to each word and stressing the preprimer vocabulary. If each child in a group adds his own ending to the sentence, write the child's name after the sentence.

    I help my Father rake the yard. (Jimmy)

    I help my brother wash the car. (Janet)

    I help my sister feed the dog. (Sandy)

3. Add words mastered to child's word banks (using technique described earlier).

Reinforcement:

1. Allow children to read their own dictated sentences and the sentences dictated by others in the group.

2. Illustrate the language experience preprimer model sentences. Have each child write his own sentence under the illustration.

3. If children still have difficulty remembering the preprimer vocabulary, use the Fernald VAKT approach with the words.

4. Place words learned from both model portion and language experience portion in child's word bank. Use word-bank words in new sentences.

5. Provide easy-to-read books and preprimers that give children an opportunity to use the vocabulary words.

ACTIVITY 4-7:
REINFORCING PHONIC INSTRUCTION

TYPE		TERM	
CLASS	☐	STA	☑
GROUP	☑	LTA	☐
IND	☑	LC	☐

Purpose:

1. To reinforce knowledge of beginning consonant sounds (blends, digraphs, etc.) with model sentences that use phonics and context clues

2. To increase the number of words known by finishing beginning model sentences with student's own words

3. To reinforce phonic skills in a contextual setting

Materials: Model sentences which reinforce desired beginning consonants, blends, digraphs, etc.; word banks for each child

Grade level: First grade

Motivational Activity: Introduce model sentences and suggest that children can use their knowledge of sounds to make the sentences into their own creations. Compile a list of model sentences that require completion using the desired sounds. These model sentences reinforce the phonemes /b/, /p/, /t/, and /d/ in initial positions. The remaining words reinforce the preprimer vocabulary.

---

1. I saw a b_____.
2. I want a p_____.
3. He came to the t_____.
4. I saw a big yellow d_____.
5. Will you eat the p_____?
6. We saw three t_____.
7. I like the funny b_____.
8. I can made a d_____.

Procedures:

1. Present the model sentences to the class, group, or individual student.

2. Review the phonic skills needed to finish the model sentences.

3. Help the class, group, or individual read the beginning of each sentence. Encourage students to finish sentences with their own words, using the appropriate beginning consonant sounds. Print the remainder of the sentence as dictated by the child. Reread the completed sentence, stressing the words with the appropriate beginning consonant. If each child in a group dictates his own sentence, write the child's name after the sentence.

   I saw a bright blue ball. (Tom)

   I saw a black bat. (Tim)

   I saw a big brass band. (Julie)

4. Add words mastered to child's word bank.

Reinforcement:

1. Have children read their sentences.

2. Illustrate sentences; write sentence under picture.

3. Have children bring concrete items to school as examples of items that begin with /b/, /p/, /t/, and /d/.

ACTIVITY 4-8:
THE DISAPPEARING PINEAPPLE

TYPE		TERM	
CLASS	☐	STA	☑
GROUP	☑	LTA	☐
IND	☑	LC	☐

Purpose:
1. To listen to a motivational story
2. To increase knowledge of descriptive terms and apply those terms in context
3. To participate in a creative drama activity

Materials:
Norman Stiles's *The Amazing Mumford and His Amazing Subtracting Trick* (Western Publishing Co., 1972); The Grover puppet, from "Sesame Street"; pineapple

Grade level:
First and second grades

Motivational Activity:
Introduce Grover puppet holding a fresh pineapple. Lead a discussion about the Muppet puppet. Ask children if they know who the puppet is. Ask the children what Grover is holding. Tell them they will be listening to a story about Grover and a magician who makes pineapples disappear. Suggest that, after they listen to the story, they will try to find a way to make this real pineapple disappear. Read *The Amazing Mumford* to the class or group.

Procedures:
1. Introduce Grover and the fresh pineapple. Lead an oral discussion about the puppet and the pineapple. Manipulate the puppet.
2. Prepare the children to listen to the story. Ask them to think about how a pineapple might disappear.
3. Read *The Amazing Mumford*.
4. Discuss the story, allowing children to tell how they think the magician made the pineapples disappear, and how they think Grover made the magician disappear.

5. Ask the children how they could make the real pineapple disappear. Do they know any magic? If not, is there a way they could do it without magic? (If children cannot think of any ways, place the pineapple on a cutting board and display a knife.)

6. Discuss possible adjectives for describing a pineapple's shape, feel, color, size, and taste. Allow children to examine the pineapple. List the descriptive adjectives next to a drawing of a pineapple. Cut the pineapple into slices and divide it among the children. List adjectives that describe taste.

7. Dictate a language experience story about the class's disappearing pineapple. Suggest that the class use some of the words that describe the pineapple.

Reinforcement:

1. Read the chart story developed by the class. (Match sentences, phrases, and words.)

2. Find the descriptive words used in the chart story.

3. Allow children to develop creative dramas about Grover or about "Our Disappearing Pineapple."

4. Plant the pineapple top. Write a chart story describing the steps in planting the pineapple and the care needed to keep the pineapple alive.

ACTIVITY 4-9:
MAKING BUTTER

TYPE		TERM	
CLASS	☐	STA	☑
GROUP	☑	LTA	☐
IND	☑	LC	☐

Purpose:

1. To involve students in a motivational activity resulting in oral discussion and a group or individual story

2. To apply structural analysis skills and identify root words with -ed and -ing suffixes

3. To read for details, follow printed directions, and state cause-and-effect relationships

4. To locate information from a table of contents or index

5. To reinforce sequencing skills through oral expression

6. To reinforce sequencing skills through a listening activity

Materials:

Recipe for butter; 1/2 pint whipping cream; 1/4 teaspoon salt; a pint jar; water; ice; bowl; recipe book; references on butter making

Grade level:

Second and third grades

Motivational Activity:

Show the students a quarter-pound of butter. Ask them where they can get butter. Ask them if people who lived a long time ago could buy butter at a store or creamery. Let them discuss what they think butter is made from and how it is made. Tell the students they are going to make their own butter. Show them a chart containing a recipe for homemade butter.

> ### HOMEMADE BUTTER RECIPE
> 1/2 pint whipping cream
> 1/4 teaspoon salt
> Pint jar with tight cover
>
> Pour the 1/2 pint whipping cream into the pint jar. Seal cover tightly onto jar. Shake the jar until the cream turns into butter. Open the lid on the jar and add salt. Stir the salt into the butter.

Procedures:

1. Lead oral discussion about butter.

2. Read recipe, review sequence orally.

3. Make the butter according to directions

4. Have students dictate a chart story or write an individual story about their experience making butter.

   Help students read recipe (if necessary). Discuss directions; have students list the steps for making butter; reread directions to verify sequential order. Following directions, make the butter. Sample the butter on crackers. Write a language experience story telling about butter making.

WE MADE BUTTER IN A JAR

We opened the pint jar top and poured the whipping cream into the jar. We closed the top very tight. Then we shook it up and down. It turned to butter at last. We opened the lid and added salt. Then we stirred it around. Next we put the butter on crackers. We ate the butter. It was so good that we wanted some more. We had fun shaking the butter and eating it.

Reinforcement:

1. Structural analysis
   Identify root words in the following: opened, poured, closed, turned, added, stirred, wanted, whipping, shaking. Discuss meaning of root words and how meaning changes by adding the prefixes -ed and -ing.

2. Comprehension
   a. Reading for details
      (1) What kind of cream should be used?
      (2) How should the lid be closed on the jar?
      (3) What should be added to the butter after shaking?
   b. Following printed directions
      (1) Circle the title of your story.
      (2) Underline all the action words, such as "stirred," in your story.
   c. State cause-and-effect relationships
      (1) What happened to the whipping cream because you shook it?

3. Study skills
   a. Using a table of contents or index
      (1) Use a cookbook index to locate a recipe using whipping cream or a dessert that uses whipping cream.

4. Oral expression (sequencing, giving directions)
   a. Choose a game; decide on the steps you would use to give the directions of the game to the class orally; tell the class what they should do first, second, etc., until you have given all the directions in the correct order. Allow the class to play the game. Are your directions clear and in order?

5. Listening (following directions)
   a. Listen to a tape at the learning center. Follow the directions and place the felt shapes on the flannel board in their described locations (or draw a picture, following the directions on a tape). (Activity 3–5 is an example of this activity.)

ACTIVITY 4-10:
OUR BOOK OF OPPOSITES

TYPE		TERM	
CLASS	☐	STA	☑
GROUP	☑	LTA	☐
IND	☑	LC	☐

Purpose:

1. To involve students in a motivational activity resulting in oral discussion and an individual story

2. To identify antonyms in pairs of words

3. To provide antonyms and their meanings when presented with a word

4. To find antonyms in a dictionary or thesaurus

5. To pantomime a term so that a group can identify the antonym

Materials:

Picture book of opposites, such as George Mendoza's *Book of Opposites;* paper for writing and drawing individual antonym picture books; story with terms underlined; dictionary and thesaurus

Grade level:

Second and third grades

Motivational Activity:

Show the students the *Book of Opposites.* Tell the students they are going to make their own picture book of opposites, and when the books are finished, each student will read his book to a kindergarten or first-grade child. (Make arrangements with a kindergarten or first-grade teacher so your students will have an audience for their books.) Review the meaning of the term "opposite" and introduce the term "antonym." Read the *Book of Opposites.*

Procedures:

1. Introduce the picture book, *Book of Opposites.* Describe the picture book the students will make after they have listened to you read the book. Talk about sharing their books with a kindergarten or first-grade class. Discuss the meaning of the terms "opposite" and "antonym."

2. Read the *Book of Opposites* aloud, allowing children to fill in the opposite terms. Some of the pictured antonyms are come–go,

nice–grouchy, on–off, big–little, light–heavy, short–tall, near–far, awake–asleep, same–different, start–finish, open–shut, and none–many.

3. Have the students give other words that are opposites, provide meanings for the terms, and use them in sentences. Write these antonyms on the board or on a chart.

4. Assign the students the task of writing and illustrating their own "Book of Opposites." Encourage them to use some of the terms suggested by the group and other words of their own choice. Share the book when finished.

Reinforcement:

1. Share individual "Book of Opposites" with the class, then have students read them to kindergarten or first-grade children.

2. Present a list of words and have students find the correct antonyms in a dictionary or thesaurus.

3. Provide a story with specific words underlined. Have the children rewrite the story, replacing the underlined words with antonyms. Have them finish the story, underlining the antonyms. Now have them give the story to a classmate to rewrite.

> Rewrite this story, changing the underlined words to an opposite or antonym word.
>
> A big man was walking through the green woods. He was going to visit a nice young witch. The nice young witch lived in a clean cabin in the hot woods. The witch could change boys into little elves or women into short elephants. The big man wanted the nice young witch to change him into a tiny _____
> _____
> _____
> _____
> _____

4. Place words that have antonyms on individual cards. Have students select a card and pantomine the word. The group will guess the antonym of the term being pantomimed.

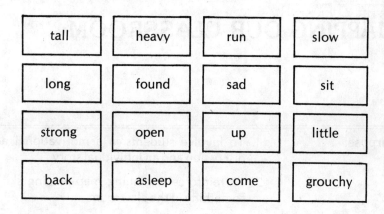

tall	heavy	run	slow
long	found	sad	sit
strong	open	up	little
back	asleep	come	grouchy

ACTIVITY 4-11:
MAPPING OUR CLASSROOM

TYPE		TERM	
CLASS	☐	STA	☑
GROUP	☑	LTA	☐
IND	☑	LC	☐

Purpose:

1. To involve students in a motivational activity resulting in oral discussion and an individual story

2. To reinforce beginning map-reading skills by making a map of something in the classroom

3. To create and interpret map legends

Materials:

Map of your desk or other location in the room; sheets of paper for map construction; map game for reinforcement activity; paper for individual language experience stories

Grade level:

Second and third grades

Procedures:

(This language experience activity would follow the early development of map-reading skills in kindergarten and first grade. Children of this age often depict land formations by creating mountains, rivers, etc., in boxes filled with sand or modeling clay. They may also have designed three-dimensional maps of their classroom or immediate neighborhoods by placing models of furniture or houses, buildings, streets, and plants on large tables. These activities can lead to many language experience chart stories for kindergarten and first-grade children.)

Review with the children their knowledge of the purpose for maps, and any map-reading experiences they may have had. Suggest that a map is an exact diagram of objects or places that really exist. Show the students a map drawn to depict some place in the classroom. Ask them to look closely at the map, then walk around the room to discover the location of the place drawn on the map. A map of the top of the teacher's desk, for example, might look like this:

After the majority of students have found the location illustrated on the map, discuss the meaning of each item on the map legend. Have students locate different items from the legend. Choose a child to describe the location of an item on the map, and have another child find that item on the teacher's desk. Discuss location, distances, and scale.

Next, ask students to choose a specific location in the room. Tell them they will draw a map of that location, creating their own map legends (e.g., library center, their desks, bulletin board, listening center, small-group instruction table, art center, etc.). After they have drawn their own maps, tell them they will write a story describing their map and activities they can do at their map's location. Ask them not to write the exact location on the map, so the rest of the group will have the opportunity to read their maps and discover the location they depict.

Procedures:

1. Lead a discussion reviewing purposes for maps.

2. Introduce map of teacher's desk or other location in the room. Allow children to discover location shown on the map, and discuss map legend, location of objects, distances, and scale.

3. Have each student choose a location in the room and draw a map of that location. Allow them to develop their own legends. Suggest that the map should consider scale, location of objects, and distances between objects. Ask them to include the legend on their maps, but tell them not to identify the locations they are mapping.

4. After their maps are completed, have the children write individual language experience stories describing their maps, and an activity that can be done at the location shown by each map.

Reinforcement:

1. Ask students to share their maps with the group. Allow students to read the maps and legends and guess the intended location. Have students try to find specific items drawn on the map. Does the map show the location correctly? After the group has identified the map's location, ask the map designer to share orally the accompanying language experience story. Place the stories and the maps on a bulletin board or in a map learning center.

2. Have the students draw maps of their own bedrooms at home, including a legend for each item depicted on the map.

3. Divide students into smaller groups, and have them make a map of the school and playground, including rooms, playground equipment, streets surrounding the school, sidewalks, and trees.

4. Provide an opportunity for students to develop their own games using identified map legends. The maps of areas of the classroom, the whole classroom, the school, and the playground could provide the references for these games. A game board for a playground map game might look like the following:

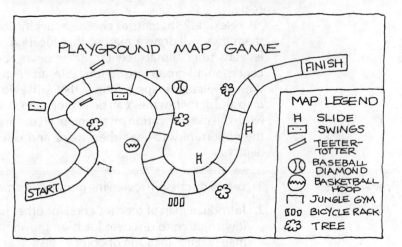

Have children make cards to shuffle and place upside down on the squares next to the various markers. These cards should provide directions for students landing on the square. For example,

Take a ride on the nearest swing.	When you reach the baseball diamond, go back 4 spaces.
Park your bike in the bike rack.	Move ahead to the next tree.

Move back to the nearest slide.	Try a trick on the first jungle gym.
You fell out of the swing, go back and rest by the nearest tree.	A friend is playing basketball, he wants you to join him.
Mary wants you to play with her on the first teeter-totter.	Push Jerry; he is on the last swing.

Have children shake a numbered cube to determine the number of spaces they may move. When they land on a square that has a card, they must read the card, identify the appropriate square using the legend, and comply with the card's directions. Place the students' map games in a map or game center.

ACTIVITY 4-12:
MAGIC WAVES

TYPE		TERM	
CLASS	☐	STA	☑
GROUP	☑	LTA	☐
IND	☑	LC	☐

Purpose:

1. To involve students in a motivating activity resulting in oral discussion and a group-dictated chart story

2. To improve comprehension of sequential order

3. To improve ability to follow directions

4. To participate in reinforcement activities by matching labels with stories, using sight words to complete sentences, or writing a creative story

Materials:

Empty glass bottle with cover; funnel; alcohol; blue food coloring; turpentine; rulers; marker or tape

Grade level:

Third and fourth grades

Motivational Activity:

Begin the discussion by showing students a wave model developed by the teacher (directions follow). Ask the children if they have seen similar models in stores. Ask them to tell you what they think might be in the bottle. Discuss the fact that the ingredients remain separated rather than mixed. Show an empty decorative bottle and tell the class they will make their own wave models, then write a story about their experience.

Procedures:

1. Lead an oral discussion on the mysterious wave machine, as described in the motivational activity.

2. Place the equipment and ingredients on a table. Clarify terms, such as alcohol, turpentine, blue food coloring, and glass bottle with lid. Label the items so students can visualize the printed term and see the proper association. (Use caution; materials are poisonous.)

3. Ask students to predict the sequence of events they think will occur. Have them place the items in the order they believe appropriate. Discuss the rationale for the order.

4. Read the directions for making the magic wave bottle. Have the children listen carefully to determine whether their utensils and ingredients are in the proper order.

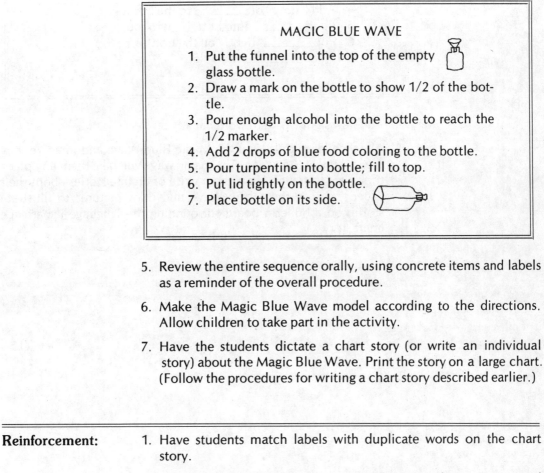

MAGIC BLUE WAVE

1. Put the funnel into the top of the empty glass bottle.
2. Draw a mark on the bottle to show 1/2 of the bottle.
3. Pour enough alcohol into the bottle to reach the 1/2 marker.
4. Add 2 drops of blue food coloring to the bottle.
5. Pour turpentine into bottle; fill to top.
6. Put lid tightly on the bottle.
7. Place bottle on its side.

5. Review the entire sequence orally, using concrete items and labels as a reminder of the overall procedure.

6. Make the Magic Blue Wave model according to the directions. Allow children to take part in the activity.

7. Have the students dictate a chart story (or write an individual story) about the Magic Blue Wave. Print the story on a large chart. (Follow the procedures for writing a chart story described earlier.)

Reinforcement:

1. Have students match labels with duplicate words on the chart story.

2. Cut a duplicate chart story into sentences. Mix the sentences and have students put them into correct sequential order.

3. Duplicate directions, leaving key words out of each sentence. Have students put label words in the proper places.

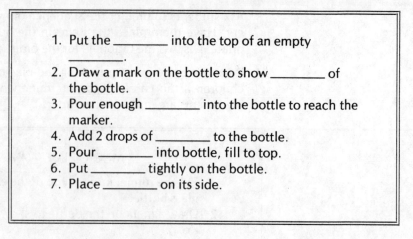

1. Put the _____ into the top of an empty
   _____ .
2. Draw a mark on the bottle to show _____ of
   the bottle.
3. Pour enough _____ into the bottle to reach the
   marker.
4. Add 2 drops of _____ to the bottle.
5. Pour _____ into bottle, fill to top.
6. Put _____ tightly on the bottle.
7. Place _____ on its side.

4. Add new sight words to word bank.

5. Allow children to look at the Magic Blue Wave and imagine they are looking at the ocean. The magic wave will take them any place they want to travel. Have them write or dictate stories about their experiences on the Magic Wave and draw pictures to illustrate stories on a bulletin board surrounding the language experience chart story.

ACTIVITY 4-13:
PLANNING MY VACATION

TYPE		TERM	
CLASS	☐	STA	☑
GROUP	☑	LTA	☐
IND	☑	LC	☐

Purpose:

1. To involve students in a motivational activity resulting in oral discussion and an individual language experience story

2. To use information from maps, including keys and legends, to answer questions about locations, distances, and directions

3. To select appropriate maps to determine populations, distances, land formations, points of interest, minerals, food production, etc., and answer questions about these subjects

4. To use information from various maps and reference books to write a language experience story about vacations they would like to take.

Materials:

Highway maps, economic atlas, world atlas, AAA materials (e.g., National Geographic Atlas of the World, Rand McNally Cosmopolitan World Atlas, These United States, tour books from the American Automobile Association)

Grade level:

Fourth through sixth grades

Motivational Activity:

Tell the students they are going to have an opportunity to plan a vacation. Before they plan their vacations, however, tell them you have been planning a vacation and would like them to help you. (This provides an opportunity to review map legends and introduce atlas reference skills.) The following example is developed around an imaginary vacation to Colorado, but, of course, you can use any location you wish.

Tell the class that you enjoy the mountains, and want to spend your summer vacation in Colorado. You need some assistance, however, because you want to see the most outstanding points of interest and still have time to hike in the mountains and see some ghost towns. Show students a map of Colorado (have several, so all the students can see) which shows highways, points of interest, cities, airports, railways, etc. Review the legends on the map, and discuss how they can help you plan a vacation. Have students find these legends on the map, then locate examples on the state map of interstate highways (I-75, I-70), other roads (U.S. 50, State 82), airports ✈ (Denver), scenic rivers 〜〜 (Gunnison), ghost towns ◯ (St. Elm), points of interest ◇ (Royal George), and national parks ☘ (Rocky Mountain National Park, Mesa Verde National Park, Dinosaur National Park). Ask the students if they think you will be able to travel from Colorado Springs to Fort Collins in one day. How can they find out how many miles apart these two cities are? Ask the students if there are any references to help you decide which points of interest you want to see. Some students will probably mention sources such as the American Automobile Association's Tour Books. Show them a tour book, and let the students read about some of the points of interest. Let students find "Places of Interest in Colorado" listed in the *Rand McNally World Atlas*. (This source also shows pictures of "Places of Interest in the United States.") Remind the students that you also want to go hiking in the mountains. Ask them if they have seen any sources that show mountain trails. For one source of mountain trails, show them the National Geographic *Atlas of the World* (pp. 48–50 show the 12 most-visited national parks, including Rocky Mountain National Park; elevations are also given). Find the elevation of Colorado on a topographical or relief map. Discuss the map legend that indicates elevation.

Let the students suggest places they would like to go on their own wishful vacations. (If you do not have maps from each section of the United States, Canada, Mexico, etc., you may restrict this activity to a specific part of the country or world.)

Procedures:	1. Ask students to help you plan your vacation; discuss information from maps and other references that can help you plan a trip. Ask students questions that require map-reading skills.
	2. Have students plan their vacations, using appropriate maps and references. If you have enough maps, ask students to mark their trips on the maps, then write experience stories describing where they are going, how they will get there, what they will see when they travel, what they will do for recreation, how many miles they will travel, etc.
Reinforcement:	1. Ask questions which require map-reading skills and atlas skills.
	2. Have students make a large relief map for the bulletin board, marking each proposed vacation on the map. Place language ex-

perience stories next to the bulletin board so they can be read by other students.

3. After students have studied their vacation maps, ask them to use this information to develop a treasure-hunt description. A treasure-hunt description for Colorado might be similar to the following:

A SEARCH FOR GOLD

Start your treasure hunt at the airport in the capital city of Colorado. The capital city is _____. Follow Interstate highway 25 south to the United States Air Force Academy; stop and see the academy museum. Continue south on Interstate 70 to Pueblo. How far did you travel from Colorado Springs to Pueblo? _____ Now turn west at Pueblo. Take U.S. 50 to Canon City. Stop at the point of interest west of Canon City. This point of interest is _____. Continue west on U.S. 50 to Gunnison. Stop and see the canyon west of Gunnison. This canyon is named _____. Now go west to Montrose. How far did you travel from Gunnison to Montrose? _____. Turn south on U.S. 550 and drive this highway paved in gold. Stop at the town named for a precious metal. What is the name of this town? _____. At this town, stop and take the narrow-gauge railroad, where the views are breathtaking. Stay on the railroad to Durango. How many miles did you ride on the railroad? _____ At Durango, turn west on U.S. 160. You have almost reached the treasure. Go west until you see the road to a national park. Turn south on the park road and drive until you see a real old palace in the cliffs. Get out of the car and climb the ladder to the palace. Congratulations, you have found the secret Indian gold! It has been buried here for hundreds and hundreds of years just waiting for you. Where was the buried gold? _____

Write the answers on separate cards and put the students' teasure hunts in a map learning center, or have students give treasure hunts to a classmate. Great hunting for everyone!

ACTIVITY 4-14:
GOLDEN FLEECE AWARDS

TYPE		TERM	
CLASS	☐	STA	☑
GROUP	☑	LTA	☐
IND	☐	LC	☐

Purpose:

1. To involve students in a motivational activity resulting in oral discussion and individual writing

2. To evaluate information critically using various sources to validate information

3. To use appropriate references to locate information

4. To present materials orally and role play two contrasting viewpoints

Materials:

List of Golden Fleece or other such awards presented by senators or other concerned groups; newspapers; reference materials

Grade level:

Fifth and sixth grades, middle school

Motivational Activity:

Ask the students if they know why awards are presented. Discuss awards mentioned by the students. Ask the students if they have ever heard of an award given for the worst, the most wasteful, or the ugliest. Tell them, if they do not provide the information, that several senators, congressmen, or newspaper writers give such awards. Senator Proxmire, for example, gives "The Golden Fleece Award" to the research grant that he and his staff consider the most wasteful expenditure of public funds. The following Golden Fleece Awards provide interesting topics for discussion and research:

EXAMPLES OF GOLDEN FLEECE AWARDS FOR
WASTEFUL EXPENDITURE OF PUBLIC FUNDS

1. $6,000 spent so an artist could photograph burning crepe paper being tossed out of an airplane.
2. $46,000 spent to study how long it takes to cook breakfast.
3. $27,000 spent to learn why inmates want to escape from prison.
4. $25,000 spent jetting around the country in a private plane to persuade people not to waste energy.
5. $102,000 spent to study the different effects of gin and tequila on sunfish.

Discuss these awards with students. Do they agree that each is an example of wasteful spending? What would they need to do before they could agree or disagree with the presentation of the award? What do they think the senator's staff needs to do before they give the award? Do they think the people to whom the awards are given like to receive them? Why? Is there a danger in presenting such an award? (The senator has been sued by the recipients of some of these awards.) Does this explain the research that goes into the study of each award before it is presented? Have students look at the various Golden Fleece Awards and suggest where they might find information about the topics of the awards.

Let the students choose a Golden Fleece Award and write a response to that award. (An alternative activity would be to have the group study each award and write a response to each one.) Encourage students to include reasons they think anyone wanted to do research on the subject; what benefits they think the research would have, if any, for man; why they think the senator's staff chose the topic for the Golden Fleece Award; whether the information obtained by the research has been gained for less money; and whether they would have chosen this subject for a Golden Fleece Award. Why or why not? Suggest they verify their response, if they can, by reading in appropriate references.

Procedures:

1. Ask students if they know why awards are presented. Discuss the purpose of awards.

2. Ask students if they have ever heard of an award presented for the worst, most wasteful, or ugliest. Explain, present, and discuss the Golden Fleece Awards.

3. Have students select a Golden Fleece Award and write their responses to the award.

Reinforcement:

1. Ask questions which require students to critically evaluate both the subjects of the Golden Fleece Awards and any references they use to find pertinent information.

2. Divide students into small groups according to which Golden Fleece Award they researched and wrote about. Have the rest of the students pretend they are members of the research organization that received the award for wasteful spending. Allow them to listen to the reasons for the award presented to them by the Golden Fleece Committee. After they have listened to the arguments for the Golden Fleece Award, have them ask questions of the committee.

3. Suggest that students select their own subjects for Golden Fleece Awards. (They may make up new names for their awards.) Unfair advertising, poorly-made consumer goods, excessive local spending, or other unfair practices make good subjects. Have them investigate the subject and offer reasons for presenting the awards.

4. Some committees present Onion Awards for ugly buildings, or other blights on the environment. Have students discuss why they think this category or award exists. Why would it be named onion? What would they consider an ugly building, or a blight on the environment? Suggest that students pick their own Onion Awards, draw a picture of the award location, and write their reasons for awarding the onion. In contrast, they could also give a Chrysanthemum Award (or other beauty symbol) for a beautiful building or an attractive addition to the environment. Discuss why a beautiful environment should be encouraged. Have students illustrate this beauty award and offer their reasons for presenting it. Develop a bulletin board illustrating the Onion and Chrysanthemum Awards and the accompanying language experience stories.

5 Writing Activities

Recent research in writing suggests that, for children to improve their writing, they need to develop self-critical powers and become involved in the evaluation and improvement of their own writing. Teachers must, then, provide children with many opportunities to write, and must interact with their students during the writing process, rather than evaluating only the final product. Donald Graves [1] finds that the teacher should interact with the children during stimulation activities prior to writing; during composing activities, in which the children dictate or individually write their own stories; and during writing conferences and follow-up activities. The activities in this section use an instructional sequence that allows the teacher to interact with groups and individual students during the writing process, as Graves advises. Another language arts authority, Beatrice Furner [2], suggests an oral exchange of ideas to help children expand and clarify their ideas before they compose. Oral exchange of ideas stimulates thinking, since students are motivated by other children's ideas and enthusiasm. Such discussion is an integral part of the activities included in this chapter.

The following instructional sequence should be used with every activity in this section:

1. A stimulation-motivational phase, to heighten interest, expand ideas, and establish the purpose for writing and the audience which is being addressed.
    a. The teacher may use an ongoing class activity to stimulate writing.
    b. The teacher may use everyday experiences to stimulate writing.
    c. The teacher may introduce a new experience to stimulate writing.

2. An oral exchange of ideas to encourage discussion during and after the stimulation activity.
    a. The teacher uses questioning strategies that extend and stimulate the discussion.
    b. The teacher uses brainstorming techniques that allow children to suggest rapidly ideas or vocabulary.
    c. Questions and answers are used to clarify ideas.

3. The composing period, in which children write or dictate their stories.
    a. Individual stories may be dictated to the teacher, teacher's aide, or an older student.
    b. Stories may be individually written by each child.
    c. Group chart stories may be dictated by the group and written by the teacher.
    d. The teacher interacts with children as they write, to help them clarify and develop their ideas.
    e. The teacher assists children, when asked, with spelling and other mechanics of writing.

4. The sharing period, in which students voluntarily share their writing with the intended audience.
   a. A creative story or other composition may be read to the group.
   b. Permanent collections of writings may be developed and shared.
   c. Bulletin boards or class newspapers may be used to share writing.
   d. Writings may be shared through creative dramatics, such as a puppetry presentation of a creative story.
   e. Invitations and letters may be sent to the intended audience.

5. The postcomposing activities, which allow the teacher to interact with the children, help them evaluate their writing, and work on demonstrated deficiencies.
   a. Children keep writing folders so they can evaluate their writing, see improvements in it, collect their best writings, and discuss their work with the teacher.
   b. Writing conferences occur in which individual needs are discussed, and the student receives individual guidance.
   c. The necessary conventions of writing are taught through the writing process.

The activities in this section are organized into five different types. The first group develops creative writing by suggesting everyday experiences, new teacher-introduced experiences, and ongoing class activities for stimulating creative writing. The second group of activities suggests methods for stimulating the writing of creative poetry. The third set of activities stimulates vocabulary development. The fourth set suggests writing activities that develop a sense of the importance of audience. The final group of activities provides suggestions for developing single paragraphs and multiparagraph compositions.

MYSELF AND MY FAMILY

TYPE		TERM	
CLASS	☑	STA	☐
GROUP	☑	LTA	☑
IND	☑	LC	☐

Purpose:

1. To stimulate creative writing through artistic interpretations of the child and his family

2. To stimulate oral expression by talking about something close to the child and his family

Materials:

An accordion-pleated book with a page for each member of the family and family pets (construct an accordion-pleated book by folding in half large sheets of heavy drawing paper; connect several sheets with tape to make a book large enough for pictures of the child's family and a story about each picture)

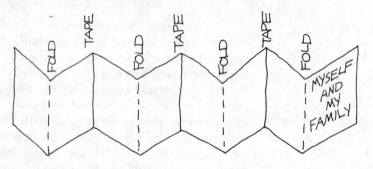

Grade level:

Kindergarten, lower elementary

Procedures:

1. Show children an accordion-pleated book with your picture on the front, and the title, "Myself and My Family." Read the title to the children or allow them to read it. Ask the children what they think would be inside this special book. Allow them to make suggestions, then show them your book. (Young children enjoy learning more about their teacher, so this activity stimulates oral discussion and questions.) Your book may use either photographs or illustrations, and should include a separate page for each member of your family and a short story describing each family member. After

you discuss your book, tell the children they will have an opportunity to make their own books about themselves and their families. Allow them to suggest subjects they would like to include in their own books.

2. Help children make their accordion-pleated books. Have them illustrate their covers and print the title of the book.

3. On subsequent days, have children illustrate a page for each member of their families, including pets. (Photographs may be used, if every child has access to pictures of their family members.) After they have drawn each picture, have them write or dictate a story about that person. Interact with each child as he is writing. Ask questions about the member of the family, to help children develop their stories. (The length of each story will depend on the level of each child. Kindergarten children may dictate short labels for their pictures, while second-grade children may write quite lengthy stories.)

4. Allow children opportunities to share their family books with the class and talk about their own families. Provide opportunities for other children to ask questions about each child's family.

MY LOVABLE DIRTY OLD BEAR

TYPE		TERM	
CLASS	☑	STA	☑
GROUP	☑	LTA	☐
IND	☑	LC	☐

Purpose:
1. To stimulate creative writing motivated by a topic close to children
2. To stimulate oral expression

Materials:
Literature selection, Edward Ormondroyd's *Theodore,* picture book of a dilapidated Teddy Bear (since many children have a favorite stuffed animal, suggest they bring their animals to school to share, and ask children who do not have an animal to draw a picture of one they would like to have)

Grade level:
Lower elementary

Procedures:
1. This creative writing activity is motivated by a book about a beloved Teddy Bear, and a picture of a much-handled Bear. Read *Theodore* to the class. Theodore is Lucy's stuffed bear. Although Lucy loves him very much, she is careless with Theodore. He is accidently placed under a pile of dirty clothes and taken to the laundromat. After he is washed, he is so clean he doesn't recognize himself. On the way home from the laundromat, Theodore falls out of the wagon. Lucy searches for him, but does not recognize the clean Theodore. He starts to feel more bearish when a dog drags him through the dirt, and he has several other adventures that help him recognize his old appearance. Lucy finally finds him, recognizes him, and joyfully brings him home. Theodore is happy when Lucy refuses to allow her mother to wash him. He feels that she loves him, and that she really understands bears.

2. After you read the story, show the children a drawing of a Teddy Bear that you once loved, or, if possible, show them a real Teddy Bear that has symptoms of handling and loving. Tell the children you had many happy adventures with your bear. Ask them if they can think of anything that might have happened to cause the bear to have a torn ear, etc. Was the bear taken on many adventures? How do they know this?

3. Allow the children to show and talk about their stuffed toys or pictures of their stuffed toys. Suggest that your Teddy Bear would like to share adventures with their toys. Have the children write or dictate an adventure they had with their stuffed animal. Young children may enjoy drawing a large picture of their toy, then writing or dictating a story inside the picture.

Have the students share their stories. These stories might then be put together to form "The Bearish Adventure Book."

ACTIVITY 5-3:
MY FAVORITE POSSESSION

TYPE		TERM	
CLASS	☑	STA	☑
GROUP	☑	LTA	☐
IND	☑	LC	☐

Purpose:

1. To stimulate creative writing motivated by a literature selection and discussion
2. To role play family-related experiences

Materials: Literature selection, Ezra Jack Keats's *Peter's Chair*

Grade level: Lower elementary

Procedures:

1. Read *Peter's Chair* to the class. Peter has a baby sister, so Peter must play quietly or he will wake her. Peter discovers that his mother fusses over the baby, and his father has painted Peter's crib and high chair pink. Peter is afraid his parents will paint his old, blue chair pink, and give that to the new baby also. Before they can do such a terrible deed, Peter takes the chair and decides to run away. He also takes his favorite toys with him. When he tries to sit in his chair, he discovers he is too big, and no longer fits the chair. He returns home, and decides to give his old chair to his baby sister. He even helps paint the chair pink.

2. Discuss Peter's reaction to this sister and his feelings when he finds his furniture has been painted pink. Ask the children if they have ever felt the way Peter does. Why do they think Peter wanted to run away with his chair and toys? Why do they think he decided to come back and give his chair to his sister?

3. Ask the children to think about their favorite toy, and pretend they are in a position like Peter's. How would they feel? What would they do? Then have them pretend they are Peter's baby sister. How would they feel about the same toy or possession? Finally, have them pretend to be Peter's mother and father. How would they solve this problem between Peter and his new baby sister?

4. Depending on the children's age and writing abilities, have them dictate or write a creative story about their favorite toy or possession.

5. Role play the situation described in number 3 above.

ACTIVITY 5-4:
HATS CHANGE MY IDENTITY

TYPE		TERM	
CLASS	☑	STA	☑
GROUP	☑	LTA	☐
IND	☑	LC	☐

Purpose:

1. To stimulate oral expression and creative writing through a teacher-introduced experience (a collection of hats)

2. To pantomime the actions of a character who might wear a specific kind of hat

3. To write a creative story about a character who wears a certain hat

Materials:

A collection of many different hats; ask children to bring a variety of hats, or begin a collection, such as a cowboy hat, fireman's hat, motorcycle helmet, nurse's cap, safari hat, policeman's hat, forest ranger's hat, baker's hat, football helmet, baseball cap, swimmer's cap, army helmet, trapper's hat, northeaster rain hat, straw hat, baby's bonnet, lady's hat, lady's large flowered hat, derby, top hat, yachtman's cap, hard hat

Grade level:

Lower and middle elementary

Procedures:

1. Provide a collection of different hats that suggest various occupations, characters, adventures, and actions.

2. Put on a hat. Ask the students to suggest who might wear a hat like the one you are wearing. What would the person look like? What would he or she do when wearing that hat? Suggest to the students that the hat caused the person to have a special adventure. Have them suggest adventures that might be appropriate.

3. Tell the students they will have an opportunity to put on a special hat, change their identities, and have an adventure. Discuss the various hats. Allow students to choose a hat, or mark hats with numbers and have students draw a number to determine their hat selection. Ask the students to put on their hats, think about their new identities, close their eyes, and imagine themselves as the person wearing the hat. Have them write a story about an adven-

ture they have while wearing the hat. Interact with the students as they write their stories individually.

4. Have students share their stories orally with the class or with a group of children.

5. Play a pantomime game in which students act out the occupations of people who might wear the various hats. Have other members of the group identify the occupation and the hat that would be worn by the pantomimed character.

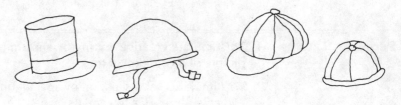

MY FIRST 100 YEARS

TYPE		TERM	
CLASS	☑	STA	☑
GROUP	☑	LTA	☐
IND	☑	LC	☐

Purpose:

1. To stimulate creative writing by showing an old doll, old toy, or picture of an old doll or toy

2. To stimulate oral discussion by speculating about the experiences and adventures of a toy and its owner

Materials:

An old or antique doll that has obviously been played with, an old toy soldier, etc., or a picture of an antique toy that looks as if it has been used by children

Grade level:

Lower and middle elementary

Procedures:

1. Show the toy to the students. Ask them if the toy looks like one they could buy in a toy store today. What is different about this toy? How do they know the toy is old? Who do they think might have owned this toy? Did the girl or boy love the toy?

   Continue a discussion about the historic time during which this toy was popular, and ask the students to speculate about adventures the doll or toy may have had with one or more owners. For example, did the toy go west on a covered wagon? Did the toy go down the Mississippi on a riverboat?

2. Ask the children to write a story about the adventures of the toy and its owner or owners. Interact with the children as they write their stories.

3. Allow students to share their adventure stories with the class or with a small group.

4. Another time, you might introduce an old toy by telling where you found or bought the toy, then let children speculate about the child who left, owned, or lost the toy. For example:

"I have been trying to solve a mystery about this old doll and the girl who owned and played with her. Maybe if you hear about how I got the doll, you can help me with this mystery.

There once was a big, old, deserted house on a farm in Iowa. A man who builds houses saw the farm and decided he wanted to tear down the old house and build a new house on the same spot. It was a beautiful site for a house. There were gnarled apple trees in the back yard, and a huge, green, grassy space covered with wild flowers in front.

This builder decided to check the house to make sure there was nothing in it before he sent for the wrecking crew to tear it down. As he was going through the old house, he came to a second-floor bedroom that looked as if it had belonged to a child. The walls were covered with faded wallpaper with pink roses, and a child's drawings could be seen on the walls. The room had a large closet that probably held the girl's clothes and other possessions. The builder opened the closet door to make sure nothing was inside. Something attracted his attention when he looked up at a high shelf. He put his hand up on the shelf, and found this old doll tucked away on that shelf.

Will you help me solve this mystery? Who do you think left this doll? Why do you think it was left? The doll looks as if it was played with a great deal. What adventures do you think the girl and her doll had? How do you think the girl felt when she discovered she didn't have her doll? How do you think the doll felt when it was left behind?"

ACTIVITY 5-6:
THE WONDERFUL MIRACLE

TYPE		TERM	
CLASS	☑	STA	☑
GROUP	☑	LTA	☐
IND	☑	LC	☐

Purpose:

1. To stimulate imaginative oral and written expression by having children encounter a new material for the first time

2. To investigate and answer sensory questions about a mysterious substance

3. To write a creative advertisement for a product using the substance

4. To write a creative story about the miracle substance

Materials:

Polyox Water-Soluble Resin—a safe, powder concentrate that mixes with warm water (and food coloring, if you want a colored substance) to form a substance with unusual properties—it forms long, sticky strings when a finger is stuck into and pulled out of it, and it reduces friction (Polyox water-soluble resin is used by firemen to deliver water at a faster rate and is also added to paints and toothpaste); [3] writing materials

Grade level:

All grades—young students can experiment with this substance and dictate a chart story; older children can try more detailed experiments and write individual stories or advertisements about products they would develop from the substance.

Procedures:

1. Tell the students they are famous magicians, inventors, or scientists. Tell them they have just created a new, magical substance, but are not sure what the substance will do or how they can use it. Show them the magic white powder. Ask them what they think it is. What does it look like? What does it feel like? What does it smell like? How do they think it could be used? Allow children to brainstorm ideas.

2. Suggest to the student magicians that they imagine something quite different might happen to the substance if water were added to the powder. Have them make suggestions about what they think might happen when water is added. Ask them to watch care-

fully as water is added to the magic powder. Allow them to experience and experiment with the magic substance. Give each magician a small amount of the substance on plastic wrap so they can experiment with it individually. Have them describe the experience and suggest its properties. How does it feel? How does it look? What will dissolve in it? How strong is it? How fast will it move? What can it do? What happens when I put my finger into it?

3. Allow the magicians to gather into small brainstorming groups. Have each group suggest as many magical uses as they can for this substance. Have them select their best idea and write an advertisement to introduce and sell their new substance. Have them present their advertisement to the rest of the class. Allow the other groups to ask questions about the new use or product.

4. Suggest that students write individual stories about what would happen if they were real magicians and created a miracle substance. What would their miracle look like? What special things could it do? How would they use their miracle?

5. Develop a bulletin board of miracle substance posters and creative stories.

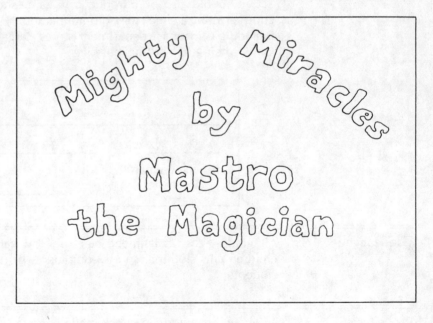

ACTIVITY 5-7:
WOW! I JUST WON $100

TYPE		TERM	
CLASS	☑	STA	☑
GROUP	☑	LTA	☐
IND	☑	LC	☐

Purpose:
1. To stimulate oral expression and creative writing through a teacher-introduced experience
2. To write a creative story stimulated by anticipated purchases in a catalogue

Materials:
A dittoed $100 check made out to each student (the amount is variable depending on age and expectations of the children — This activity could also be introduced in game-show format, with each child selecting a check for a different amount); variety of catalogues, including Christmas, department stores, large mail order, and specialty catalogues; writing materials.

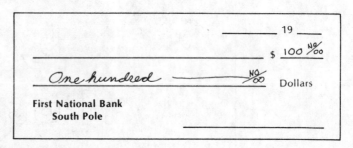

First National Bank
South Pole

Grade level:
All grades; the assignment can use toy catalogues for younger children and clothing, sports equipment, or hobby items for older students

Procedures:
1. Show the children a check made out to you. Ask them how they would feel if they received such a check. Ask them if they have ever seen television shows or read stories about people winning money or prizes. Ask the students how they would feel if they won money or prizes. Ask them what they would like to win. Give each student a dittoed check for the desired amount made out in the name of the student. Tell them they are going to pretend they

have just won a contest. The contest prize is a check, which they must turn in for merchandise of their choice.

2. Provide a variety of catalogues. (The type of catalogue depends on the children's age and interests.) Tell the children the rules of the contest state that they must select items from a catalogue that add up to the amount of their checks. Tell them they can select anything they choose. Discuss the type of items available in each catalogue.

3. Have the students make their selections, write a story about why they chose their merchandise, and include a description of themselves using their winnings.

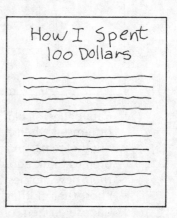

4. Catalogues can be used for many other writing activities; for example:
   a. Catalogues of camping equipment—Have students select materials they would need to go on a camping vacation with their families, and write a story about their trip. Tell them to include information about how they used the camping equipment they chose from the catalogue.
   b. Catalogues of household furniture, draperies, art objects, etc. —Ask students to think about a room in their house they would like to decorate. This room might be their bedroom, family room, etc. If they could decorate this room any way they desired, what would they include? Have them select items from the catalogues, place the cut-out items on a sheet of paper representing the room, and write a story describing the new room.

c. Catalogues of clothing—Have each child bring a photograph of himself, then have them select a complete new outfit, cut out the items, and place them on the photograph. Ask the children to think about what they would like to do while wearing their new clothes. Have them write a story telling why they chose their clothes, and what they would do while wearing them.

d. Choose an item out of a specialty catalogue and describe the person to whom you would give it.

e. Choose a famous person in history, or a well-known current celebrity. From a catalogue, have students choose one gift they think would be especially appropriate for that person. Have them write a story explaining why they chose the gift for that person.

AMERICAN INDIAN NAMES

TYPE		TERM	
CLASS	☑	STA	☑
GROUP	☑	LTA	☐
IND	☑	LC	☐

Students frequently study about American Indians in social studies, or read Indian folklore in literature or reading. The following activities use an ongoing classroom study to stimulate creative writing.

Purpose:
1. To stimulate creative writing through an ongoing classroom activity—the study of Indians
2. To interpret the nature relationships in Indian names
3. To write a creative story describing how an Indian child got his or her name
4. To write a story interpreting the students' selection of Indian names for themselves
5. To develop a symbolic language

Materials:
References about Indians; lists of typical Indian names; lists of Indian symbols used in writing

Grade level:
Third grade and above; the rebus writing activity, however, could be done by lower elementary children

Procedures:
1. Indian names were descriptive, and closely related to the animals or natural elements with which the Indians lived. Many of the names also carried a magical meaning. An Indian baby was named shortly after birth, either by a relative or the medicine man. The whole village participated in this happy occasion. The baby was often named for an animal, an occurrence in nature on the day the baby was born (thunder), or a brave deed performed by the name giver. A woman usually kept her name for life, but a man often replaced his name with a new name when he performed an act of valor or had a special dream. Discuss with students why Indian children might have names such as Eagle Claws, Running Ante-

lope, or Morning Star. Have students list Indian names they find in their stories. This list might include:

INDIAN NAMES

Girls' Names	Boys' Names
Flower	Eagle Hunter
Morning Star	Strong Deer
Blossoms	Black Fox
Dawn	White Eagle
Sun Woman	Running Wolf
Star	Peacemaker
Yellow Bird	He Who Is Feared
Soft Snow	Music Maker
Little Rabbit	Coyote
Good Leader Woman	White Buffalo
Growing Flower	Turtle
Graceful Walker	Gray Owl
Dancer	Dreamer
Small Speech	Story Teller
Rosebud	Shooter
She Is Alert	Trustworthy

2. Discuss children's interpretations of these names. "Even if you can't see the person, how would you describe a person with the name _____? Do you notice any differences between boys' names and girls' names? From your reading about Indians, why do you think there are these differences? Do the names tell you anything about the differences in jobs done by boys and girls in the Indian village?"

3. Have the children select an Indian name and write a story about how the Indian boy or girl got that name, or why the name is appropriate for the person.

ACTIVITY 5-9:
MY NATURE NAME

TYPE		TERM	
CLASS	☑	STA	☑
GROUP	☑	LTA	☐
IND	☑	LC	☐

Activity 5–9 is a continuation of Activity 5–8.

Procedures:

1. After discussing Indian names and writing a story about how an Indian got his name, ask the children to think about themselves. If they could select a descriptive Indian name or several Indian names to describe themselves, what name or names would they choose? Ask the students to write a story describing why they chose their "nature" names.

2. Since the "nature" names are based on something objective, they are easily drawn as pictographs, or sign language. The Indians frequently connected the visual representations of their names with a human head to signify ownership. For example an Indian signature for Eagle Horse might look like this:

Have the children draw pictographs illustrating the various Indian names. Finally, have them draw pictographs of their chosen "nature" names. Ask them to sign their stories with their pictograph signatures.

ACTIVITY 5-10:
INDIAN SYMBOLS—
WE CAN COMMUNICATE
WITH CONCRETE SYMBOLS

TYPE		TERM	
CLASS	☑	STA	☑
GROUP	☑	LTA	☐
IND	☑	LC	☐

Activity 5–10 is a continuation of Activities 5–8 and 5–9.

Procedures:

1. The Indians did not have the same alphabet we have today, but they wrote messages and told of their history. They used picture symbols to write their stories, and even drew pictures to illustrate their signatures. The Indian symbols, like their names, illustrated the natural environment of the Indian. Discuss some of the symbols the children believe Indians would have used. Allow them to draw some of the symbols they believe would be meaningful to Indians.

2. Make a chart of the Indian symbols, or show pictures from a book.

Indian Symbols

Indian Village

Meat Drying

Fish

Man

Feather

Bird

Snake

Sun

Tree

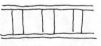

Lake Shore

Bear

Islands

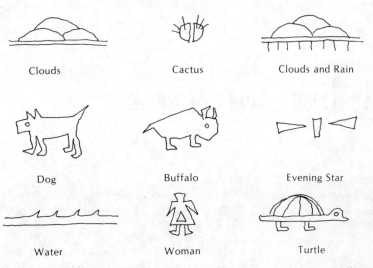

Clouds   Cactus   Clouds and Rain

Dog   Buffalo   Evening Star

Water   Woman   Turtle

3. Ask the children to pretend they are living in an Indian village a long time ago, and have them write a story using only Indian symbols. Group the children in pairs, so they can try to interpret one another's stories. Have them compare their pictures with the intended meaning.

4. Discuss the advantages and disadvantages of symbol writing. "What kinds of words are missing from the picture story? What do you add to make the story complete?" Show the children an example of rebus writing, which uses both words and pictures.

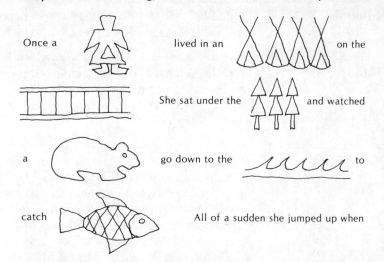

Once a [woman] lived in an [tepees] on the [fence/ladder] She sat under the [trees] and watched a [beaver] go down to the [water] to catch [fish] All of a sudden she jumped up when

Discuss the characteristics of words that can be shown by rebus pictures or symbols. Have the students finish the above rebus story by writing their own creative endings with words and pictures.

5. Suggest that students develop their own symbol language and rebus stories. Have them write their own creative stories, using both words and pictures. Display the class rebus stories next to the chart of the Indian symbols.

ACTIVITY 5-11:
MY OWN TOTEM POLE

TYPE		TERM	
CLASS	☑	STA	☑
GROUP	☑	LTA	☐
IND	☑	LC	☐

Purpose:

1. To stimulate creative writing through artistic interpretation and oral discussion

2. To develop reference skills, interpret a famous person through a totem pole representation, and write an accompanying story that interprets that person's life

3. To develop oral interviewing skills, interpret the child's family through a totem pole representation, and write an accompanying story

4. To interpret a student's legend through a totem pole representation and write a creative story describing the student's totem pole legend.

Materials:

Cardboard cylinder and construction paper for making totem symbols; writing materials; references and pictures of totem pole

Grade level:

Purposes 3 and 4 can be achieved at any level, since the story can be written or dictated. Purpose 2, however, requires the ability to read references or other sources to learn about the background of a famous person

Procedures:

1. Background: Totem poles are found along the North Pacific coast, from southern Canada to Alaska. The Northwest Indians carved and painted large tree trunks that sometimes rose to a height of 50 or 60 feet. The totem poles were erected in front of the house of the clan chief, and were symbols of the owner's prestige. The figures might tell the story of the clan legend, or of the great deeds of the totem-pole owner. Strange figures, faces, whales, fish, bears, ravens, and birds with outstretched wings told the story of the family ancestors, or other events that were significant for the family. The story began at the top of the totem and continued down from the distant and mystic past to the figure of the owner carved at the base of the totem. The Indian totems usually contained a representation of the owner's guardian totemic animal, which is why the poles are called totem poles.

2. Show pictures of totem poles, read references about totem poles, and discuss their symbolization.

3. Ask each child to select a famous person whom they would like to learn more about. Have them read a reference, biography, or other literature selection to increase their knowledge about the person. Ask them to think about how they could depict the person's life through figures similar to those used by the Indians. Have them draw a totem depicting the person's life, then write a story about it, explaining why they chose the specific incidents for the totem. This totem might be the story of a sports hero, a famous man or woman in history, or a character in literature. For example, totem poles could be developed for folk heroes such as Paul Bunyan, Mike Fink, Captain Stormalong, Daniel Boone, Davy Crockett, Johnny Appleseed, Windwagon Smith or Pecos Bill. A Pecos Bill Totem Pole might include the following incidents:

Birth of Pecos Bill

Bill Baffles Gallinippers

Bill Licks Pack of Coyotes

Bill Tames Widow Maker

Bill Invents Lariats

Bill Busts a Cyclone

4. For another totem-writing activity, suggest that students make totems telling their own family histories, or describing members of their families. Before they do this activity, ask them to interview their parents or other relatives to learn more about their own backgrounds. After they draw the totems, have them write a story explaining the characters on the totem and why they chose those symbols.

5. Another totem-writing activity allows children to fantasize about their own legends, or to develop a totem about their own experiences. Tell the students that Indian totems usually contained a representation of the owner's guardian totemic animal. Ask the children to think about the animal they would choose as their guardian; have them include the animal on the totem. Allow them to develop a fantasy totem or a real-life totem. Illustrate the totem, then write a story about the representations on the totem.

ACTIVITY 5-12:
SCHOOL IS . . .

TYPE		TERM	
CLASS	☑	STA	☑
GROUP	☑	ITA	☐
IND	☑	LC	☐

Purpose:

1. To write a creative poem after listening to a story about school and discussing school

2. To role play happy and sad school experiences

Materials:

Literature selection, Eleanor Schick's *The Little School at Cottonwood Corners*

Grade level:

Lower elementary

Procedures:

1. Read *The Little School at Cottonwood Corners* to the class. This book is about a preschool child who spends a day at the little school to find out what it will be like to attend school. After spending the day at school, she decides it will be wonderful when she is old enough to go to school.

2. Discuss the girl's reaction to school. Ask the children to pretend the girl is questioning them about school. How would they answer? Do they always feel the same about school? Why? What influences the way they feel about school?

3. Depending on the children's age and writing ability, have them dictate a group poem entitled "School Is . . ." or have them write an individual poem entitled "School Is . . ." This activity can be varied by presenting the children with some hypothetical situations. Would they write the poem the same way under each of these circumstances? For example:

Good Things That Happen at School	Unhappy Things That Happen at School
1. You just came home from a wonderful field trip.	1. You had to stay after school because you lost your math paper.

2. You met a new friend at school.

2. Your best friend at school is moving away and you don't think you have any other friends.

3. The teacher told you you are an excellent reader or storyteller.

3. You missed most of the words on the spelling test.

4. You learned how to write your name.

4. Someone took your last pencil and you were scolded for not finishing your work.

5. Your picture was chosen to represent the class in an art fair.

5. You lost the room's only softball during recess.

6. Your mom is room mother and she is bringing chocolate brownies today.

6. Your desk is messy and you have to stay in from recess to clean it.

3. Design a bulletin board containing the "School Is . . ." poems and pictures illustrating the poems. You can divide the bulletin board into "School Is Happy" and "School Is Unhappy" poems and pictures.

4. Role play the various happy and sad experiences children have at school. Allow children to suggest experiences. Pantomime the "School Is . . ." poems when they are read to the class.

ACTIVITY 5-13:
HAIKU

TYPE		TERM	
CLASS	☑	STA	☑
GROUP	☑	LTA	☐
IND	☑	LC	☐

Purpose:
1. To develop sensory images
2. To write a traditional Japanese form of poetry, the haiku

Materials:
Examples, definition, and diagram of haiku

Grade level:
Middle and upper elementary, middle school

Procedures:
1. Read several haiku poems to the students. Explain that "Japanese haiku are usually associated with one or another of the four seasons of the year; most of their images come either from nature or from the interaction of people with nature."[4]

2. Explain the format of haiku to the students: Haiku is made up of seventeen syllables, divided into three lines. The first line usually has five syllables, the second line seven syllables, and the third line five syllables.

3. Diagram the format for haiku.
   ___ ___ ___ ___ ___ syllables
   ___ ___ ___ ___ ___ ___ ___ syllables
   ___ ___ ___ ___ ___ syllables

4. Since Japanese haiku is usually descriptive of the seasons or nature, have the students go outdoors and listen to sounds, look at growing plants, clouds, and wildlife, and feel things in nature. Have the students jot down these sensory impressions, then ex-·periment with haiku. For example, a haiku poem might be written after a visit to the zoo:

   Cheetah in the zoo
   Pacing behind metal bars
   Longing for freedom

TYPOGRAPHICAL TRICKS
WITH POETRY

TYPE		TERM	
CLASS	☑	STA	☑
GROUP	☑	LTA	☐
IND	☑	LC	☐

Purpose:

1. To identify a form of poetry in which the poet arranges words to add to the effect of the words

2. To write a poem using a descriptive formation of words

Materials:

Examples of several poems written in shapes that add to the poem's meaning or imagery

Grade level:

All grades

Procedures:

1. Show the students examples of poems written in descriptive shapes—a poem about a snake suggesting the form of a snake, a poem about a city in the shape of a skyscraper, or a poem about a kite in the shape of a kite, for example:

A
KITE
IS FREE
TO FLY IN
THE SKY. IT CAN
GO UP, UP, UP INTO
THE CLOUDS WHERE
ONLY THE BIRDS
CAN FLY. IT CAN
SWOOP DOWN,
DOWN, DOWN
AND PLAY
TAG
WITH
THE BREEZE. I WISH I WERE FREE AS A KITE.

2. Discuss the reasons an author might use this format. Does it add to the imagery of the poem? Would you want all poetry to be written in this form? Why or why not? Have the students suggest subjects appropriate for this kind of poetry. Provide experiences where they can observe shapes and write about them.

3. Have students write their own descriptive shape poetry. Display the poems on a bulletin board.

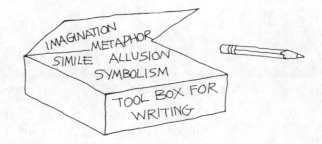

DEVELOPING IMAGERY WITH SIMILES

TYPE		TERM	
CLASS	☑	STA	☑
GROUP	☑	LTA	☐
IND	☑	LC	☐

Purpose:
1. To identify and define simile
2. To develop imagery through creation of similes using common terms and experiences in uncommon ways

Materials: Examples of common and uncommon similes; literature selections that contain similes

Grade level: Middle and upper elementary, middle school, depending upon degree of simplicity or sophistication of the similes

Procedures:
1. Explain to students that writers often paint a word picture for the reader by using an object or concept in a way that makes the reader "see" the words in a new way. Ask students to close their eyes and visualize the following examples:

   The surface of the lake was as smooth as a large pane of glass.
   When he opened his present, he was as happy as a kid eating a chocolate doughnut.
   The inside of the cave was as cool as a winter morning after a snowfall.

2. After you read each simile (expressed comparison), ask the students to describe what they "saw" in their minds. Ask them to explain what device was used in each sentence. Lead them to the realization that a simile is used to suggest that one thing resembles another. Similies use words such as "as" and "like" to express comparisons. Ask them why they think authors use similes.

3. Suggest to the students that some common similes are often overused. Ask them to suggest some of these common similes. Such a list might contain the following examples: as cool as a cucumber; as light as a feather; as blind as a bat; as pretty as a picture; as quick as a wink; as fresh as a daisy; as playful as a kitten; as happy

as a lark; as hard as a rock; as quiet as a mouse; as sharp as a tack; and as smooth as silk.

4. Tell students they are going to have an opportunity to paint their own word pictures, but they will do it with imaginative and original comparisons. Allow students to experience the environment, to look, see, feel, smell, hear, and talk about what they experience. Then have them write their own creative similes. This activity can be used in many learning situations. For example, students might go into a meadow in early spring, experience the wild flowers, the new leaves, ferns, and cloud formations, then write similes for:

As soft as _____; As pretty as _____; As light as _____; As green as_____; As loud as _____; As quiet as _____; As quick as_____; As slow as_____.

Another time, they might experience a harsher environment in a downtown city or factory area. If this cannot be done in person, they could experience the environment through a film, then write similes for:

As loud as _____; As harsh as _____; As strong as _____; As heavy as _____; As slow as _____; As hard as_____.

Personal feelings can be expanded by developing similes such as:
As nervous as _____; As excited as _____; As frightened as _____; As tired as _____; As lonely as _____; As relaxed as _____.

5. Have students make simile books, including their own similes and similes found in the literature.

ACTIVITY 5-16:
DEVELOPING IMAGERY WITH METAPHORS

TYPE		TERM	
CLASS	☑	STA	☑
GROUP	☑	LTA	☐
IND	☑	LC	☐

Purpose:

1. To identify and define metaphor

2. To develop imagery through the creation of metaphor

Materials:

Examples of metaphors; literature containing metaphors

Grade level:

Middle and upper elementary, middle school; depending upon degree of simplicity or sophistication of the metaphors

Procedures:

1. Explain to the students that writers also paint pictures by comparing two things without using the terms "as" or "like" (see *simile* in the previous activity). Read several examples of metaphors, have students describe what they hear, and compare the examples with the similes. Examples of metaphors (implied comparisons) you may use are:

   > Kindness is inviting ants to join your picnic.
   > Wisdom is knowing when to listen.
   > Fear is thinking you are lost.
   > Loneliness is a telephone that doesn't ring.

2. Allow students to experience different environments, as in the simile activity, then write their own metaphors. For example, on a cold winter day after a snowstorm, children can experience winter, snow, and cold on the school grounds, then write metaphors for:

   > Winter is _____; Cold is _____; Snow is _____;
   > Beauty is _____; Quiet is _____; Soft is _____.

   After experiencing an autumn day, students might respond to the following:

Autumn is _____; Color is _____; Windy is _____; Beauty is _____.

Personal feelings and values may be expressed through metaphors; for example:

Loneliness is _____; Happiness is _____;
Love is _____; Freedom is _____;
Anger is _____; Peace is _____;
Fear is _____; Hate is _____;
Sadness is _____; Kindness is _____.

3. Have students develop metaphor booklets containing their original metaphors and examples of metaphors from literature.

ACTIVITY 5-17:
SPACE WORDS

TYPE		TERM	
CLASS	☑	STA	☑
GROUP	☑	LTA	☐
IND	☑	LC	☐

Purpose:
1. To stimulate vocabulary development and understanding
2. To find space-related words in references
3. To use space-related words in creative stories and other compositions

Materials: Space stories and references about space; collections of space words and their meanings developed by the students

Grade level: Middle and upper elementary, middle school

Procedures:
1. Discuss with students the special vocabulary words that we now use as a result of space flights. During a brainstorming session, have students suggest space words and their meanings. Have them look up the meanings of any words they do not know. Put the word and its meaning on a space chart. Have the students add other words when they find them in space stories or science fiction. For example:

SPACE WORDS

Galaxy: A group of billions of stars like the Milky Way

Countdown: The time before blast-off when all systems are checked

NASA: National Aeronautics and Space Administration

Jettison: To throw away useless material

Lift-off; Launching the rocket from the pad

Light-year: The distance light travels in one year

Zero G: Lack of gravity, weightlessness

Satellite: A natural or artificial body which revolves around a larger body

Scrub: To cancel a flight

LEM: Lunar excursion module

Lunar rover: The machine used for travel on the moon's surface

2. Have students use space words to write their own space stories, both fiction and nonfiction. Students can divide into groups and write TV and radio scripts about space travel or science fiction.

KNOWING MY AUDIENCES
AND MY PURPOSE

TYPE		TERM	
CLASS	☑	STA	☑
GROUP	☑	LTA	☐
IND	☐	LC	☐

Purpose:

1. To understand that knowledge of audience and purpose for writing influences the writing

2. To understand that there are different purposes for writing

3. To understand that when a student communicates through writing, there is also a reader or audience for the writing

4. To understand that a writer needs to know his audience and purpose for writing before he can evaluate the writing's effectiveness

5. To help children understand audience and purpose during the writing process

Materials:

Examples of student-produced materials written for several different purposes and audiences

Grade level:

Any grades; depends on degree of difficulty of the written examples

Procedures:

1. Ask students if they always write for the same reason. Have them suggest the purpose they have for writing. A list such as the following might emerge:

```
┌─────────────────────────────────────────────────┐
│                                                   │
│              WHY DO WE WRITE?                     │
│                                                   │
│   1. We write true stories to tell about          │
│      experiences in class.                        │
│   2. We write letters to our friends and          │
│      relatives to tell them what we are doing     │
│      and to ask about what they are doing.        │
│   3. We write invitations to ask people to        │
│      come to our class.                           │
│   4. We write puppet shows to entertain our       │
│      class and ourselves.                         │
│   5. We write in our diaries to remind us abut    │
│      what we are doing and thinking.              │
│   6. We write stories for our class newspaper.    │
│   7. We write book reports to tell about books    │
│      we read.                                     │
│   8. We write charts to describe how we do        │
│      something.                                   │
│   9. We write about science experiments to        │
│      tell what happens.                           │
│  10. We write poetry and stories to entertain     │
│      ourselves, our class, and our parents.       │
│                                                   │
└─────────────────────────────────────────────────┘
```

2. Ask the students if the same audience reads each of these types of writing. Discuss the intended audience for each writing purpose listed. Discuss differences in the audiences, and how differences in the audiences might affect the content of the writing.

3. Read several examples of student writings to the group, or place the writings on transparencies. Ask the students to listen carefully to each example and to identify the purpose for writing and the intended audience. Selections can include comic strips, letters to parents, letters to friends, letters to companies asking for information, creative stories, creative poetry, book reports, daily schedules, science experiment charts, etc.

4. Read several examples of professional writing. Ask the students to listen carefully and identify the author's purpose for writing and the intended audience. Examples can include children's literature selections, magazine articles, news articles, comic strips, recipes, newspaper feature articles, editorials, etc.

5. Ask students if they think it is helpful to know the intended purpose and audience before they write. Draw conclusions about how understanding the purpose and audience for writing can make one's writing more effective.

ACTIVITY 5-19:
WRITING LETTERS

TYPE		TERM	
CLASS	☑	STA	☑
GROUP	☑	LTA	☐
IND	☐	LC	☐

Purpose:
1. To understand that personal letters have a different purpose and audience than do business letters
2. To identify the purpose and audience for a personal letter and contrast it with the purpose and audience for a business letter
3. To write a personal letter to a friend or relative
4. To write a business letter to someone unknown to the child

Materials:
Examples of personal and business letters; letter writing forms (see section 6)

Grade level:
All grades; a personal letter is an appropriate subject for all children, and older children may also write a business letter

Procedures:
1. This activity has the real purpose of writing a letter to a friend or relative. Begin this activity by showing the children an envelope with a personal letter enclosed. Ask them if they like to receive letters written just to them. If this letter was addressed to them, who would they wish the sender to be? What would they like to read in the letter? Who would be the audience for the letter? What would be the purpose of the letter?

2. Read examples of two letters; one should be an interesting personal letter to someone the writer knows, and the other should be a business letter requesting information from someone the writer does not know. Ask them to listen to each letter and identify the purpose and audience for each; for example:

July 23, 19____

Dear Sally,

   This is the most exciting time I have ever had at camp. Do you remember that I wanted to ride horseback every day? You just wouldn't believe the beautiful horse they gave me. His name is Cinnamon. He is brown and has a black mane and tail. He is real spicy, too. I feel just great when we run across the meadows. I'd like to ride on forever, or at least till I get hungry again.

   Speaking of food—do you remember what happened last year when we found a worm in the salad? You wouldn't believe what I found in my chili burger yesterday! A real grasshopper was sitting there staring at me! I screamed, and everyone stopped talking. Our table decided to protest this new food. The camp cooks say it will never happen again. They gave me an extra brownie. I think it was to keep me quiet so I wouldn't complain any more.

   Say hello to everyone for me. Don't have that slumber party you talked about until I get home. I'll tell you all about it when I see you next week.

                              Your best friend,

                              Jean

13 Rosewood Circle
Turnersville, N.J. 08012
Oct. 14, 19____

Alaska State Division of Tourism
Pouch E - 907
Juneau, Alaska 99811

Dear Sirs:

    The fourth-grade class at Jefferson Elementary School is studying about festivals in Alaska. Several free brochures for festivals are listed in the State of Alaska Visitor Guide. We would like to order the following brochures:

    L-001 Alaska Festival of Music
    L-002 Anchorage Fur Rendezvous
    L-003 Iceworm Festival
    L-004 Muskeg Stomp
    L-005 Equinox Marathon
    L-012 Cry of the Wild Ram
    L-024 Alaska State Championship Sled Dog

Thank you for sending us the brochures.

        Sincerely,

        Jerry Johnson
        4th-grade class
        Jefferson Elem. School

3. Contrast the differences between the purposes and audiences for a personal letter and a business letter. The children may come up with the following points:

Purposes and Audiences For Personal and Business Letters

	Purpose	Audience
Personal Letter	1. To exchange interesting personal information	1. Friend
		2. Relative

Business Letter	1. To request information	1. Business person who does not know me
	2. To give information about a business or product	2. Government official who does not know me
	3. To influence a policy maker.	

4. Discuss the contents of the personal and business letters. What is the subject matter of each? Are there any special requirements for each letter? (Such as: the personal letter is an informal, friendly exchange between two people who know each other well. It is like having a conversation. The business letter is more formally written. The letter usually requests or gives information to a busy company or business establishment that does not know the writer. The request or information needs to be clearly stated so the correct information or product will be received.)

5. Have the students write a personal letter to a friend or relative. Help the students during the writing process. Have the students mail the letters.

6. Provide a purpose for composing a business letter, such as the request for information from the Alaskan travel bureau. Write and mail the letters.

ACTIVITY 5-20:
WRITING INVITATIONS

TYPE		TERM	
CLASS	☑	STA	☑
GROUP	☑	LTA	☐
IND	☐	LC	☐

Purpose:

1. To understand that invitation writing has a specific purpose and audience

2. To identify the purpose and audience for an invitation

3. To write an invitation that includes information about what, who, why, when, and where

Materials:

Writing materials for invitations

Grade level:

All grades; the invitation can be dictated by young children and individually written by older children

Procedures:

1. This invitation-writing activity should accompany a classroom activity that stimulates the need to write a real invitation. For example, the following classroom projects might generate invitations or groups:

Project	Invited Audience
a. Puppet show	Parents or another class
b. Class art exhibit	Parents or another class
c. Choral reading program	Parents or another class
d. Guest speaker for a science unit, safety unit, health unit, etc.	Scientist, fireman, policeman, doctor, etc.
e. Band concert	Parents, community (could be a newspaper announcement)
f. Guest speakers during a study of occupations	Engineer, doctor, nurse, dentist, teacher, accountant, mechanic, etc.
g. Open house	Parents, community
h. Athletic events	Another school

2. Discuss the purposes for writing the invitation and the person or persons who will be invited. Suggest that the class pretend to be that person or group. What would they need to know? Contrast any differences between invitations written to schoolmates, parents, all members of the community, and guest speakers who are not known to the students. What characteristics of each audience might influence the way the invitation is written? Compile a list of student suggestions for invitations; for example:

OUR INVITATION SHOULD CONSIDER

1. What are we inviting our guest or guests to attend?
2. Who are we inviting to our class or school?
   Do we know each person we are inviting?
   How old are our invited guests? This will influence the words we use.
3. Why are we inviting our guest or guests?
   Do we want them to be entertained?
   Do we want them to tell us something? If so, what do we want to know?
   Do we want them to participate in an activity?
   If so, do they need to come prepared for something?
   Do we want them to see what we are doing and be proud of our school?
4. When do we want our guests to come?
   How long do we want our guests to stay?
5. Where do we want our guests to come?
   Did we give our guests all the information they will need to find our school, room, gymnasium, athletic field, etc.?
   If our guests do not know our school, did we include an address, directions, and a telephone number if they need more information?

---

3. Have each student write or dictate an invitation, or have the class dictate a group invitation. Interact with the students during the writing process. Help the students when necessary, so their invitation will be clear to the intended audience.

4. Have the students evaluate their invitations. If they were the intended audience, would they have all the important information after reading the invitations? Are their invitations clear to the audience at which they are aimed? Were the invitations attractive? Would they want to receive the invitations?

5. Have the students send or deliver the invitations to the appropriate audience.

ACTIVITY 5-21:
WRITING FOR MY OWN ENJOYMENT AND REMEMBRANCE

TYPE		TERM	
CLASS	☑	STA	☑
GROUP	☑	LTA	☐
IND	☐	LC	☐

Purpose:

1. To understand that diary writing has a specific purpose and audience

2. To write a daily diary entry recounting personal experiences and feelings for the child's benefit, expression, and enjoyment

3. To expand the diary into an autobiography

Materials:

Individual notebooks or diaries; examples of personal diary entries

Grade level:

All grades

Procedures:

1. Ask the students if they know of any kind of writing for which the only intended audience is the person who is doing the writing. Ask the students why they think a person would want to keep a diary. Discuss the kinds of experiences and feelings they would like to put into a diary. Discuss the value of keeping a written account of their experiences and feelings.

2. Discuss the writing style students would use in the diary. Who is the audience? Do they need to write long accounts explaining experiences or feelings, or would shorter notes be equally good? Why? Who should decide how the diary will be written? (Stress that a diary is a personal experience and is written only for the child; consequently, the child is the audience, and can write in a manner that is meaningful to him).

3. Provide an opportunity for each child to begin a diary. Allow a few minutes each day for them to write, or at least several times a week. Assure the children that the diary entries are personal and

will not be shared with you or anyone else unless the child wants to share them. Encourage the children to reread their earlier diary entries periodically. Can they learn about things that are meaningful to them? Is a diary useful and interesting? Why? (Many students find it particularly interesting to reread diary entries written when they were several years younger.)

4. Students can read autobiographies of famous people and discuss how the person writing the autobiography remembered details and experiences of his life. Would diaries written during all stages of the person's life be useful? How would the diary be helpful? Have the students imagine they have grown up and are now famous people. The world would like to know about them when they were younger. Where were they born, where did they live, what did they like to do, what experiences did they have, how did they feel about themselves and others? Have the students write their own autobiographies, using their diaries as references. Illustrate the autobiographies and design covers for the books.

THE LIFE OF
HELEN KELLER
HER EARLY YEARS

ACTIVITY 5-22:
WRITING A NEWS STORY

TYPE		TERM	
CLASS	☑	STA	☑
GROUP	☑	LTA	☐
IND	☐	LC	☐

Purpose:
1. To understand that news writing has a specific purpose and audience
2. To identify the purpose and audience for news writing
3. To write a clear, informative, and accurate news story

Materials:
Examples of news stories from school newspapers, city newspapers, and news magazines; writing materials

Grade level:
Middle and upper elementary, middle school

Procedures:
1. Ask students to bring examples of interesting news stories to school. Provide other examples of news stories from school or class newspapers, city newspapers, and news magazines. As students share their examples, ask them to listen carefully so they can define the purpose for each article, the kind of information included in each, and who they consider the intended audience for each article. Make a chart of the information discovered, similar to the following:

NEWS STORIES INFORM ABOUT EVENTS

Type of News Article	Purpose	Information	Audience
1. Sports report of the 6th-grade basketball game—school paper	To tell details of the game	Score, who played, where played, when played, how played	Elementary school children, parents, teachers

---

2. News report of tornado's destruction	To report details of tornado	Where did the tornado strike, when did it hit, who was hurt, what was the damage, how did people react	All people who read city paper

2. Discuss the purposes, types of information included, the requirements for that kind of writing, and the intended audience.

3. Brainstorm suggestions for news items that might make up the front page of a classroom newspaper; for example, baseball game at recess, an art exhibit in the gym, a guest speaker, the results of a science experiment, a report on a field trip to the zoo, a fire station, a television station, a museum, or a dairy, a class spelling contest, a puppet show presentation, a mock trial, a report of film seen in class.

4. Write news articles for the "Classroom Gazette." Interact with the students while they write to help them improve their ability to produce accurate and clear news stories. Discuss the need for editing and proofreading in newspaper stories. After editing and proofreading, duplicate the news stories for a classroom paper.

ACTIVITY 5-23:
THE CONTROLLING IDEA
IN A PARAGRAPH

TYPE		TERM	
CLASS	☑	STA	☑
GROUP	☑	LTA	☐
IND	☐	LC	☐

Purpose: 1. To identify the controlling idea in a paragraph

2. To write paragraphs with the controlling idea appearing in different positions in the paragraph

Materials: Examples of paragraphs written in the following formats:

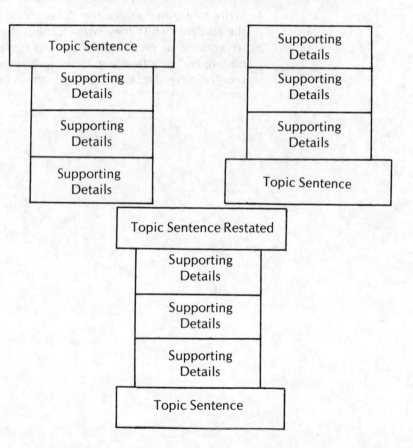

Grade level:	Middle elementary

Procedures:	1. Discuss the fact that topic sentences or the main idea of a paragraph may be found in different positions in the paragraph.
	2. Show examples and discuss these paragraph formations. (Use the same topic and supporting details, but write the information in the three different formations.) For example, the following paragraph formations all contain the main idea, "Spring is my favorite season of the year":

Spring is my favorite season of the year.

In spring, the wildflowers
make the meadows
bright with color.

The days in spring became
longer so I can play
outside.

Best of all, baseball season
starts in the spring, so
I can play my favorite
sport.

In spring, the wildflowers
make the meadows
bright with color.
The days in spring
become longer, so I can
play outside.
Best of all, baseball season
starts in the spring, so
I can play my favorite
sport.

Spring is my favorite season of the year.

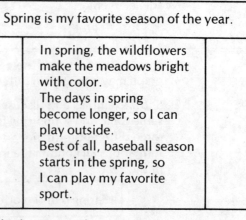

Spring is my favorite season of the year.

In spring, the wildflowers make the meadows bright with color.
The days in spring become longer, so I can play outside.
Best of all, baseball season starts in the spring, so I can play my favorite sport.

I think spring is the greatest time of the year.

3. Have the students turn the topic sentence into a question: Why is spring my favorite season of the year?—and discover if each of the supporting details answers the topic sentence question.

4. Next, have the students choose a topic sentence and write their own paragraphs illustrating each of the paragraph formations. This activity can be done by first dividing the students into groups and having them write group-suggested paragraphs, and later asking them to develop paragraphs individually.

ACTIVITY 5-24:
ORGANIZATION USING CHRONOLOGICAL ORDER

TYPE		TERM	
CLASS	☑	STA	☐
GROUP	☑	LTA	☑
IND	☐	LC	☐

Purpose:

1. To identify the chronological organization of a paragraph and a longer selection

2. To write a paragraph and a longer selection using chronological organization

Materials: Examples of paragraphs written in chronological order; examples of multiparagraph selections showing chronological organization (descriptions of historical events, class trips, experiments, and for making things frequently use chronological organization)

Grade level: Middle and upper elementary, middle school

Procedures:

1. Display and discuss several paragraphs written in chronological order. Read the paragraphs with the children, and let them figure out the organization of the paragraph; for example:

MAKING DECORATIVE CANDLES

You can make very pretty candles if you have paraffin wax, coloring, a can, and string. First, you melt the paraffin wax in the top of a double boiler. After the wax has melted, you may add wax coloring, if you wish. Now, tie a string or candlewick around a pencil. Place the pencil over the top of an empty orange juice can. Make sure the string hangs in the middle of the can. Pour the hot wax into the can. Let the wax cool and harden. Then, remove the candle from the can and cut the string to remove the pencil.

Lead the class into the discovery that the paragraph is organized according to the order of events. You could draw the order of this paragraph in the following manner:

Chronological Order   *Steps in Making Candles*
first	melt paraffin
to	add wax coloring
last	place string tied to pencil on can
	pour wax into can
	let wax harden
	remove candle from can

Ask the students to suggest other topics that could be written about in chronological order.

2. Provide a variety of one-paragraph and multiparagraph selections using chronological order. Ask children what types of subjects use this order.

3. Give children a variety of experiences, such as performing an experiment, going on a field trip, describing the steps in playing a game, making a recipe, or researching historical events. Have them write chronologically ordered one-paragraph and multiparagraph reports, depending on the subject matter.

ACTIVITY 5-25:
ORGANIZATION USING QUESTIONS AND ANSWERS

TYPE		TERM	
CLASS	☑	STA	☐
GROUP	☑	LTA	☑
IND	☐	LC	☐

Purpose:

1. To identify the organizational pattern of a paragraph or multi-paragraph selection that uses a question-and-answer format

2. To brainstorm ideas for questions to answer

3. To write a paragraph or multiparagraph selection that uses a question-and-answer format

Materials:

Examples of paragraphs written in a question-and-answer format (science and social studies materials frequently use this format, or literature selection may ask a question about a character, then describe the character)

Grade level:

All grades

Procedures:

1. Show and discuss several paragraphs written in question-and-answer form. Read the paragraphs with the children and help them discover the organization. For example, an early-elementary question-and-answer paragraph might be developed this way:

I PLAY WITH MY BEST FRIEND

What do I like to do with my best friend? Penny and I play every day after school. We like to take our skateboards over to the park. We race on the sidewalk and try to do tricks on the skateboard. When we get tired of the skateboards, we play on the swings. My friend and I like to fly high in the air.

Help the students discover the question-and-answer format of the paragraph. "Does each sentence in the paragraph answer the question at the beginning of the paragraph?" You could draw the order of this paragraph in the following way:

Question   What do I like to do with my best friend?
↓ Answer   Play after school
         Skateboard in the park
         ↓ Play on the swings

A longer, multiparagraph composition can follow the same format, with each paragraph asking and answering a question about the main topic; for example:

Santa Claus Around the World

Question   Who was the original Saint Nicholas?
↓ Answer   Discuss bishop of Myra, in Asia
         ↓ Minor, 4th century A.D.
Question   Who brings Christmas presents in the
         Netherlands and Belgium?
↓ Answer   Discuss Sinter Klaas and his assistant,
         ↓ Black Peter
Question   Who brings Christmas presents in Great
         Britain?
↓ Answer   ↓ Discuss Father Christmas
Question   Who brings Christmas presents in France?
↓ Answer   ↓ Discuss Père Noël
Question   Who brings Christmas presents in the
         United States?
↓ Answer   ↓ Discuss Santa Claus

2. Provide a variety of one-paragraph or multiparagraph selections using a question-and-answer format. Have students find different types of materials that use this format, including some of their textbooks.

3. Allow children to write their own questions and answer them in paragraph or multiparagraph format. Have students list, in a brainstorming activity, a number of questions they might like to investigate; for example:

QUESTIONS WE COULD INVESTIGATE

1. How do they celebrate Christmas in Mexico? (Russia, England, Norway, etc.)
2. What kind of training does an astronaut have?
3. What happens to a letter when it gets to our post office?
4. Why is a fir tree a symbol for Christmas?
5. Why does a plant need light to grow?
6. How does a cloud form into a rainstorm?
7. Why do your eyes blink?
8. How does a windmill pump water without using electricity?
9. Why does a microwave oven cook food more rapidly than a regular electric or gas oven?
10. What qualifications does the President of the United States need to have?
11. Why do I like Fridays?
12. What do we like to do on weekends?
13. What do we like to do at the zoo?

ORGANIZATION USING SPATIAL CONCEPTS OR PHYSICAL DETAILS

TYPE		TERM	
CLASS	☑	STA	☐
GROUP	☑	LTA	☑
IND	☐	LC	☐

Purpose:

1. To identify the organizational pattern of a paragraph or multi-paragraph selection that uses a spatial concept of direction or physical detail

2. To write a paragraph and a longer selection using a spatial concept of direction or physical detail

Materials:

Examples of paragraphs written in spatial ordering (materials that tell about happenings in one location, then in another location; stories or reports that proceed from inside to outside; paragraphs that take the reader on a visual trip from right to left or top to bottom)

Grade level:

Middle and upper elementary, middle school

Procedures:

1. Show and discuss several paragraphs written in spatial ordering. Read the paragraphs with the children and help them discover the organization; for example:

A VISIT TO A "MOTTE AND BAILEY" CASTLE[5]

Today, Sue and Brad Martin came to visit a very old, dilapidated castle that had once defended a village. They were very excited as they got out of the car and looked toward the castle. They saw the motte and the drawbridge that would take them into the castle compound. Their eyes followed the worn path up to the castle. The castle appeared to be built of thick stone walls, with slit windows that allowed the guards to watch the countryside. Sue and Brad had studied such castles. They knew if they could

---

look into the lower windows, they would see rooms used for storage. The middle windows would probably look into eating rooms, and the upper windows would look into sleeping rooms. When their eyes reached the top of the tower, they imagined they saw several guards pointing excitedly into the distance. Sue and Brad couldn't wait to start their exploration of the castle.

Lead the class into the discovery that the paragraph is organized according to direction. The paragraph illustrates a visual trip from the motte, the drawbridge, and up to the top of the castle tower. You could diagram the order of this paragraph in the following way.

```
Bottom        Looking at the castle
  ↑ Top         ↑ motte and drawbridge
                ↑ worn path to castle
                ↑ lower rooms
                ↑ middle rooms
                ↑ upper rooms
                ↑ tower
```

A longer story of this experience could use the same format as Sue and Brad explore the castle from the bottom to the top. Each paragraph could describe what they see in each level of the castle.

Authors of literature selections often use a directional format to describe a character. The following example of such a descriptive paragraph can be used with older elementary children.

THE OLD MAN IN THE PARK

While walking through the park, we saw an old man sitting on a bench. His shoes were new and shiny black. The shiny black of his shoes contrasted with his milky white ankles that were bare of stockings. His pants were cuffed, baggy, and torn. His shirt was made of faded flannel, a pocket was missing, and his sleeves were rolled over the elbows. The arms extending from the sleeves were gray, but his hands were calloused from hard work. On his wrinkled face was an expression of contentment and satisfaction, because today he had found a pair of new shiny black shoes.

---

2. Provide a variety of one-paragraph and multiparagraph stories or reports using directional organization. Ask children to suggest subjects that might use this organization.

3. Have children propose topics and write their own paragraphs, using directional organization.

ACTIVITY 5-27:
ORGANIZATION USING
A PROBLEM, CAUSE, AND
SOLUTION FORMAT

TYPE		TERM	
CLASS	☑	STA	☐
GROUP	☑	LTA	☑
IND	☐	LC	☐

Purpose:
1. To identify the organizational pattern of a paragraph or multi-paragraph selection using a problem, cause of problem, and solution of problem format

2. To brainstorm ideas for problem investigations

3. To write a paragraph or multiparagraph selection using a problem, cause of problem, and solution of problem format

Materials:
Examples of paragraphs or multiparagraph selections using this format (social studies, science writing)

Grade level:
Middle and upper elementary, middle school

Procedures:
1. Show and discuss several paragraphs written in a problem, cause of problem, and solution of problem format. Read the paragraphs with the children and help them discover the organization. For example, the problem of an argument on the playground might be written about in the following way:

> ### THE BASKETBALL AND MARBLE FEUD
>
> Every day this week, our third-grade class has had an argument at the beginning of recess. Some of the students want to use the blacktop on the school yard to play basketball. Other students want to play marbles on that same space. They get in each others' way and shout at each other. We are trying to solve

this problem. We could take turns. The basketball players could use the blacktop during morning recess. The marble players could use the blacktop during afternoon recess. We are also looking for other good places to play marbles. If we find a good spot, we will all be happy during both recesses.

Help students discover the organization of the paragraph. You could draw the order of this paragraph in the following way:

Problem
  ↓ Cause of Problem

  ↓ Possible Solutions
     to Problem

An argument at recess
  ↓ Some students want to play
     basketball and some want to
     play marbles in the same space.
  ↓ Taking turns on blacktop.
     Another place to play marbles.

2. Provide a variety of one-paragraph or multiparagraph selections using this form. Encourage students to think of materials that might use this format, including social studies texts and newspaper articles.

3. Provide opportunities for students to write their own paragraphs on longer articles. Brainstorm with the class, and list a number of problems they could investigate. Some problems might be closely related to the school and community, and would require investigation by observation and interviewing. Other problems may be related to content subjects or national concerns, and will require library research. (This will also depend on the students' grade level.)

PROBLEMS WE COULD INVESTIGATE

The taste and appearance of the spinach served in the school cafeteria

Discovering that your bicycle is missing

The pollution of the river near our school

A forest fire in our state park

The electricity was off for four hours this morning

A small percentage of voters voted in the last election

6 Activities for the Mechanics of Language

Without an understanding of sentence structure, it would be difficult for anyone to develop either written or oral sentences that make sense to a listener or reader. Modern grammarians advocate teaching grammar in such a way that children will understand their language.[1] Instruction should lead children into an exploration of their language and discoveries as to how it works. Sentence combining, sentence expansion, sentence transformations, and sentence pattern exploration are activities that allow children to explore and understand language.

Unlike grammar, usage deals with attitudes and language standards of a group, rather than with the way words are structured to convey meaning. Different levels of usage are appropriate for different audiences and purposes. Modern usage instruction stresses appropriateness to both audience and purpose; instruction is flexible, and increases the number of levels of usage available to the child. Many of the activities in the oral language section give opportunities for children to experiment with and expand their levels of usage.

Language standards have changed a great deal over the last few hundred years, and are still changing today. The first four activities in this section may be used to introduce children to the concept that language changes: spelling, graphic representations, and accepted usage change with time. Progressing from excerpts from Shakespeare's "Comedie of Errors" to examples of modern CB slang dramatically demonstrates this change in language. A study of the development of English and the major influences for change in the language is a logical extension of this activity.

Written communication has requirements beyond those of oral language. The ability to spell words correctly helps a child communicate with his intended audience. The spelling activities in this section emphasize reinforcement of spelling through motivational activities. A writer uses punctuation and capitalization as signals to help him convey meaning to the reader. This section concludes with ideas for a personal learning center to reinforce these aspects of writing mechanics.

ACTIVITY 6-1:
THE COMEDIE OF ERRORS

TYPE		TERM	
CLASS	☑	STA	☑
GROUP	☑	LTA	☐
IND	☐	LC	☐

Purpose:

1. To demonstrate the dynamic quality of language
2. To demonstrate that spelling, graphic representation, and accepted usage change with time

Materials:

Sentences written in Early English; one source is Charlton Hinman's *The First Folio of Shakespeare* (New York: W.W. Norton & Co., 1968)

Grade level:

Upper elementary, middle school

Procedures:

1. Ask students if they think our language has always been written and spoken as it is today. Discuss. Show them an example of early English copied from *The First Folio of Shakespeare*.

The Comedie of Errors

line 91, p. 103

> At length the ſonne gazing vpon the earth,
> Diſperſt thoſe vapours that offended vs,
> And by the benefit of his wiſhed light
> The ſeas waxt calme, and we diſcouered
> Two ſhippes from farre, making amaine to vs :
> Of *Corinth* that, of *Epidarm* this,
> But ere they came, oh let me ſay no more,
> Gather the ſequell by that went before.

From THE NORTON FACSIMILE, THE FIRST FOLIO OF SHAKESPEARE, prepared by Charlton Hinman, by permission of W. W. Norton & Co., Inc. Copyright © 1968 by W. W. Norton & Company, Inc.

2. Ask the students to look at the copy and try to read it. "Is it written in English?" Discuss. Read the sentences with the students. Ask

the students if they understood the language and if they could read the words. Encourage them to discuss the meaning of the words, the differences in acceptable usage, the differences in spelling, and letter formations.

3. Have students search for other spelling and usage differences. Compile a list of sentences written in Early English. Have the students suggest comparable current spellings and how they would say the sentences today. For example:

	Old English	Current English
p. 105 line 280	Good Sifter let vs dine, and neuer fret;	
p. 105 line 271	I greatly feare my monie is not fafe.	
p. 105 line 339	'Tis dinner time, quoth I: my gold, quoth he:	
p. 106 line 476	Why, but theres manie a man hath more haire then wit.	
p. 108 line 727	It would make a man mad as a Bucke to be fo bought and fold.	
p. 108 line 673	O villaine, thou haft ftolne both mine office and my name	

NOTE: Page references are from Hinman's *The First Folio of Shakespeare.*

4. Allow the students to suggest why they think language changes. Do they think the language they speak and write today is changing? (The following activity on "CB Slang" is a good comparative activity. Students can see some drastic changes in usage over a relatively short period in history.)

ACTIVITY 6-2:
CB SLANG

TYPE		TERM	
CLASS	☑	STA	☑
GROUP	☑	LTA	☐
IND	☐	LC	☐

Purpose:
1. To demonstrate the changing quality of language (might introduce a study of the history of language)
2. To demonstrate the need for an understandable vocabulary when speaking to or writing for an unknown audience which may not understand slang

Materials: Paragraph written in CB slang; references that define CB slang in terms of standard English

Grade level: Upper elementary, middle school

Procedures:
1. Instruct students to listen to the following paragraph. Ask them to listen carefully and pretend they are visiting the United States for the first time. They can all speak and understand "textbook English." After they listen to the paragraph, they will be asked to draw a picture illustrating their understanding of the paragraph.

CB SLANG

Breaker one nine. Let's modulate for a while. My twenty is hill town. A plain blue wrapper just blew by so brush your teeth and comb your hair, his picture taker's out. Better hang on the double nickel so you don't get any green stamps. There's a blinking winkin over my shoulder that's buying the orchard. Good trucking, stack them eights, and the good numbers to you.

---

2. Have the student draw a picture illustrating the meaning of the paragraph. Discuss the finished pictures and talk about the various interpretations. Ask the students if they think their pictures indicate what the writer of the paragraph really meant to communicate. Have students describe the intended audience for this communication. Discuss the importance of knowing your audience before you can communicate effectively through speaking or writing.

3. What does the paragraph actually mean? Direct the class to investigate CB slang, and to rewrite the paragraph with a vocabulary recognizable to a foreign visitor who speaks "textbook English."

STANDARD ENGLISH INTERPRETATION

I would like to break in on your conversation and talk to you for a few minutes. My location is San Francisco, California. A blue, unmarked police car just drove past me. He has his radar working, so I would advise you to slow down to 55 miles per hour in order to avoid any speeding tickets. There is a school bus behind me that has had an accident. I want you to drive safely, best regards to you, and goodbye.

---

4. Have students compare the clarity of the two paragraphs and the appropriate audience for each one.

5. Have students compile a chart showing CB slang expressions and their equivalent terminology in standard English.

CB Slang	Standard English Meaning
Advertising	Police car with warning lights flashing
Baby Bear	Rookie policeman
Baloneys	Tires
Bear bait	Speeder
Big ten-four	I approve of what I hear
Blinkin Winkin	School bus
Blowing your doors in	Passing a car or truck

CB Slang	Standard English Meaning
Brush your teeth and comb your hair	Reduce your speed
Buying an orchard	Vehicular accident
Ears	Citizen's band radio
How you be?	How are you?
Modulate	Talk
Motion lotion	Gasoline
Negative copy	I am unable to understand you
Peanut butter in ears	You are not listening to your CB set
Plain blue wrapper	Unmarked blue police car
Pumpkin	Flat tire
Singing waffles	Radial tires
Tar	Coffee
Wall to wall and treetop tall	I am getting very good audio reception

THE BEGINNING OF
THE ENGLISH LANGUAGE

TYPE		TERM	
CLASS	☑	STA	☐
GROUP	☑	LTA	☑
IND	☐	LC	☐

Purpose:

1. To investigate the development of the English language in England

2. To investigate major influences that have caused changes in the English language

Materials:

Map showing England and the countries of the continent which influenced English language; references on language development such as George H. McKnight's *The Evolution of the English Language, From Chaucer to the Twentieth Century* (New York: Dover Publications 1956); and Bruce Finnie's *The Stages of English* (Boston: Houghton Mifflin Co., 1972); Otto Jespersen's *Growth and Structure of English Language* (New York: Free Press, 1968); and Paul Roberts's *Understanding English* (New York: Harper & Bros., 1958).

Grade level:

Upper elementary, middle school

Procedures:

1. Discuss the fact that the English we speak today is the result of a long series of historical events and many different influences. The language of Shakespeare (see "The Comedie of Errors") is not the same language we speak today, although we can understand most of it. The English we speak had its origins in England, the same country in which Shakespeare wrote his plays. Many words were added to the English language, when people who spoke a different language either invaded or moved into the country. (Ask students to suggest some words they may know because people who speak a different language have moved into their community.)

2. Show a map of England and continental Europe. Have the students locate the areas that have influenced the English language. Compile a list of words that have been added to the English language because of influence from other countries. (Many upper-elementary and middle-school students begin studying European

history. A study of language development can stimulate the study of history.)

ROMAN INFLUENCE
Roman Traders Brought New Words:

wine	cheese	kettle	cup
Lancaster	Winchester	(names of cities)	

Roman Missionaries Brought New Words:

temple	synod	abbot
organ	hymn	candle

DANISH INFLUENCE

Late 700's, Denmark invaded England and added many new words:

house	mother	father

Words that have the /sk/ sound are Scandinavian:

skin	sky	skill	scrape	scrub
bask	whisk			

Plural forms of pronouns:

they	their	them

Adverb prepositions combining *take*:

take up	take in
take out	take down

Over 1400 English towns have Danish names; "by" added to the name is the Danish word for town and "thorp" means village:

Rugby	Grinsby
Althorp	Linthorpe

FRENCH INFLUENCE

Normans Ruled England

Foods:

biscuit	jelly	cream
veal	beef	bacon

Government Terms:

parliament	government	tax

Religious Words:

religion   parson   sermon
baptism   incense   crucifix

Household Words:

parlor   blanket   curtain
chair   lamp

Color Words:

vermilion   scarlet   blue

Recreational Words:

leisure   music   conversation
chess   dance

Educational Words:

logic   study   grammar
noun   surgeon   anatomy

3. Discuss the meanings of the various words and their uses in modern English. Create a bulletin board showing the origins of modern English words. Place appropriate words on charts next to the countries from which they came.

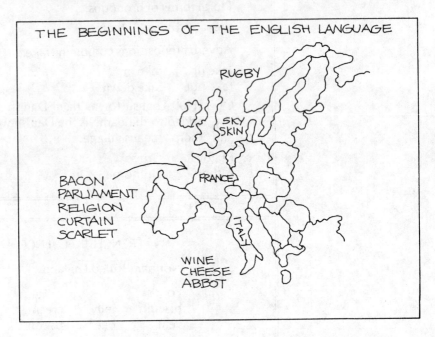

THE BEGINNINGS OF THE ENGLISH LANGUAGE

RUGBY

SKY
SKIN

BACON
PARLIAMENT
RELIGION
CURTAIN
SCARLET

FRANCE

ITALY

WINE
CHEESE
ABBOT

ACTIVITY 6-4:
THE ENGLISH LANGUAGE IN THE UNITED STATES

TYPE		TERM	
CLASS	☑	STA	☐
GROUP	☑	LTA	☑
IND	☐	LC	☐

Purpose:

1. To investigate the development of the English language in the United States

2. To investigate the major influences for change in the English language in the United States

3. To demonstrate the constantly changing quality of the English language

Materials:

Tapes of English speakers from England and the United States; references such as dictionaries that describe the history of American English, (e.g., Mitford Mathews's *Dictionary of Americanism on Historical Principles* (Chicago: University of Chicago Press, 1951); maps of the United States and Europe

Grade level:

Upper elementary, middle school

Procedures:

1. Ask the students if they believe that a person speaking English in England and a person speaking English in the United States would sound alike, or if all their words would mean the same thing. This would be a good opportunity to play a tape of a speaker from England, or to have a visitor from England talk to the students. Have the students listen for words that are used differently than in the United States, and listen for differences in dialect.

    The following story was written by Jacki Thomas, a graduate student from Bristol, England. She is illustrating some differences between English and American usage:

    Lavinia Predergast was awoken one day by a telephone call. It was her mother-in-law phoning to ask if she could come to stay with her and her husband for a fortnight. "Gosh!" she thought when she put the phone down, "this flat is a mess, I'd better start tidying up!"

But first she weighed herself on the scales—"Oh, that's good, still only 9 stone 3," she said with relief. Then she started rushing around to get the flat cleaned up.

She thought she would do the curtains while she was doing the washing, but she couldn't get the tap to the washing machine on, so she started washing up . . . no washing-up liquid left! So she had to get dressed to nip down to the corner shop and she threw her dressing gown on the bed. "It's gonna be one of those days!" she exclaimed. Even as she said it, she noticed the moths had got to the jumper her mother-in-law had knitted for her last Christmas, and she knew she'd lost the spare darning wool she had sent with it.

Lavinia put the baby in the pram and put her purse in her handbag, when the phone went again. It was her friend, asking if she could come round for a chat and a cup of tea, but Lavinia thought she'd be too busy to stop for elevenses today.

She wasn't long getting the washing-up liquid, and started washing the dishes as soon as she got back—she dried up the cutlery and crockery but left the frying pan and saucepans to drain. She washed out a few smalls and hung them out on the line with her new plastic pegs. She vacuumed the carpets, tidied up the living room, mopped the floors in the toilet and kitchen, then laid the table for lunch.

She just had time to get a couple of biscuits and get a glass of milk out of the fridge and was going to turn on the telly when she heard a car-door slam outside the flat; she looked out and recognized her mother-in-law's estate car—she was just getting her case out of the boot.

fortnight	two weeks
flat	apartment
curtains	drapes
do the washing	do laundry
washing-up liquid	detergent
nip	hurry
corner shop	small all-purpose store
dressing gown	house coat
jumper	sweater
darning wool	repair yarn
pram	baby buggy where baby lies down
purse	billfold, wallet
handbag	purse

come round	come over
elevenses	cup of tea, or coffee and cookies
cutlery	silverware
crockery	dishes
smalls	underwear
pegs	clothespins
9 stone 3	141 lbs.
tap	faucet
boot	trunk
estate car	station wagon
biscuits	cookies

2. Discuss—"We have learned that the English language was greatly influenced by people from other European countries when these people invaded England, came to live in England, or traded with the English." Since the English language spoken in England is somewhat different from the English language spoken in the United States, ask the students to suggest possible situations that might have influenced and changed the English language spoken in the United States.

3. Allow students to form groups to investigate a specific period and its influence on our language. Historically accurate fiction offers many examples of speech that is authentic for both time and place. Historical dictionaries are also useful. Some suggested study groupings include:

SKILLET

SPIDER

The Colonists Brought English to America
Pioneer America Added Colorful Language (e.g., to go on the warpath, to take to the woods)
European Immigrants Brought Their Language (e.g., a frying pan is called a skillet by some and a spider by others; a pail and faucet may be called a bucket and spigot)
Technology and New Inventions Add to Language (e.g., television is new to this century; acronyms, like *radar*, are created from the first letters of words: *radio detecting and ranging*)

Slang Expressions Add Color to Language and Change Meanings of Common Words (e.g., a term like "turkey" does not necessarily refer to the bird served for Thanksgiving dinner)

Have the research groups present their findings orally to the class, using the speech patterns of the period. Suggest creative methods for sharing the language of the periods, such as an original play, or a scene from authentic literature.

4. One way to study the influence of a nationality or a period in history on the United States is to investigate cities, towns, and areas that have names signifying foreign, Indian, or historical influence. Have students locate names in the area, state, or nation that demonstrate the influence of a group or period in history. Indian names show up on Menomonie and Winnebago, Wisconsin; Cheyenne and Ten Sleep, Wyoming; Ketchikan, Alaska; and Pontiac, Michigan. Spanish influence appears in El Cajon and Escondido, California, and La Junta, Colorado. German influence is felt in New Braunfels, Texas, and French influence in New Orleans and Lafayette, Louisiana, and in Ste. Anne de Beaupre, Quebec.

ACTIVITY 6-5:
BUILDING SENTENCE PATTERNS

TYPE		TERM	
CLASS	☑	STA	☑
GROUP	☑	LTA	☐
IND	☑	LC	☐

Purpose:
1. To develop an understanding of form class
2. To identify words and types of words that fit a specific pattern in a sentence

Materials: Examples of model sentences

Grade level: Lower elementary (sentences may be used orally with children who cannot read)

Procedures:
1. Show students sentences using a cloze technique. Have students suggest words that might fit the position. Talk about the types of words appropriate in each case. For example:

   Julie _____.

ran	jumped	laughed
hopped	sang	skipped

   The _____ jumped.

girl	boy	cat	cricket	dog
rabbit	lion	man	woman	

   The _____ clown laughed.

funny	clumsy	small	fat	skinny
tall	tiny	silly	red	

   Suzie walked down the street _____.

slowly	rapidly	hurriedly
clumsily	happily	quietly

2. These sentences can be finished with a pantomime activity; for example, a child chooses an action word to complete a sentence, pantomimes the action, and the rest of the group identifies the action and completes the sentence.

ACTIVITY 6-6:
SENTENCE EXPANSION

TYPE		TERM	
CLASS	☑	STA	☑
GROUP	☑	LTA	☐
IND	☑	LC	☐

Purpose:

1. To expand noun and verb phrases

2. To produce expanded sentences in the children's writing

3. To evaluate nonexpanded and expanded sentences

Materials: Examples of expanded and nonexpanded sentences to evaluate; examples of simple noun phrase plus verb phrase sentences to use for expansion activities

Grade level: Middle elementary

Procedures:

1. Have the students listen to two different sentences, one nonexpanded and one expanded. Ask them to draw a picture illustrating each sentence:

> The flower bloomed.
> The dainty alpine flower bloomed next to an icy mountain stream.

After they draw their pictures, ask them to describe the differences between the two sentences. Which sentence was more interesting? Which sentence gave more information? Show the students examples of other nonexpanded and expanded sentences. Discuss the differences in each pair. For example:

> The crowd cheered.
> The football crowd cheered wildly this afternoon.

> My brother skates.
> My younger brother skates on the champion hockey team.

> Everyone walked.
> Everyone at the picnic walked along the beach.

Sebastian laughed.
My uncle Sebastian laughed at all the clown's jokes.

2. Present some nonexpanded sentences to the students. Have them orally expand them as many ways as they can. Discuss the type of information given in each expansion; for example,

The boy ran.
The hunter started.
The bell rang.
Jacqueline returned.
Pepper smarts.

3. During children's writing experience, help them to use expanded sentences.

ACTIVITY 6-7:
HOLIDAY JUMBLE

TYPE		TERM	
CLASS	☑	STA	☑
GROUP	☑	LTA	☐
IND	☑	LC	☐

Purpose:

1. To unscramble sentences and place in logical syntactic order

2. To write logical sentences and scramble them for others to unscramble

Materials:

Scrambled sentences associated with specific holidays

Grade level:

Lower and middle elementary

Procedures:

1. Write a series of sentences describing specific holidays, or choose sentences the children have written about holidays. Do not use the name of the holiday in the sentence. For example:

---

night It dark was a and scary.
running goblins Ghosts past and house were the.
rang little One doorbell goblin the.
until frightened was I said trick he treat or.

---

beautiful was a It morning snowy.
early Kids up were very.
was excited Everyone.
bright were lights tree The.
tree under Presents the were.

---

258 **ACTIVITIES FOR THE MECHANICS OF LANGUAGE**

hard was very winter The first.
The for harvest Pilgrims were the thankful.
feast a Indians They to invited.
foods one the Turkey of was.

2. Have the students unscramble the sentences, decide what holiday is being described, and draw a shape around the sentence to illustrate the holiday. For example:

It was a dark and scary night.

Ghosts and goblins were running past the house. One little goblin rang the doorbell.

I was frightened until he said, "Trick or Treat."

It was a beautiful snowy morning.

Kids were up very early.

Everyone was excited.

The lights were bright.

Presents were under the tree.

3. Ask the students to write descriptions about animals or objects. Have them scramble their sentences and give them to other children to unscramble and identify the animal or object.

ACTIVITY 6-8:
PLAY SENTENCE DETECTIVE

TYPE		TERM	
CLASS	☐	STA	☑
GROUP	☑	LTA	☐
IND	☑	LC	☐

Purpose:
1. To study word forms (morphology) and identify words signifying plurality—plural noun forms, plural verb forms, and numbers
2. To become aware that a sentence contains several clues to plurality

Materials: Lists of sentences containing several clues to plurality

Grade level: Middle and upper elementary

Procedures:
1. Suggest to students that writers and speakers use several clues in sentences to inform a reader or listener that a sentence is plural. Ask the students to tell you any clues they use when they mean more than one.
2. Tell the students they will be playing sentence detectives, and will have an opportunity to find as many clues as they can that signify plurality of a sentence. (This activity may be played as a game, by dividing the students into smaller groups and having each group identify as many clues as possible.)
3. Present the students with sentences. After each sentence, have them identify the clues that led them to the subject's plurality or singularity. For example:
   a. The three squirrels were running from limb to limb.
   b. Glen saw a new red station wagon.
   c. The Siamese cats were Mrs. Hatfield's best friends.
   d. Some of the pencils were broken.
   e. The bird is sitting on a picket on the fence.

WHO, WHOSE, WHOM, AND WHICH

TYPE		TERM	
CLASS	☐	STA	☑
GROUP	☑	LTA	☐
IND	☑	LC	☐

Purpose:

1. To identify referents in sentences that use the relative pronouns who, whose, whom, which

2. To improve comprehension of sentences that use relative pronouns

Materials:

List of sentences with relative pronouns

Grade level:

Middle and upper elementary

Procedures:

1. Background—Research by Fagan[2] suggests that children in grades 4, 5, and 6 have difficulty comprehending sentences containing relative pronouns. Fagan recommends that students practice replacing referents in sentences containing relative pronouns.

2. Provide sentences containing relative pronouns; have students replace all referents with the words to which they refer; for example:
   a. Glen is the boy who delivers the newspaper on our block.
   b. The woman who called left her telephone number.
   c. The man, who lives down the street, is taking my sister to the airport.
   d. Here is the man whose camera I borrowed.
   e. Tony is the boy whom you met at my party.
   f. The shopping center, which is being built, will have my favorite ice cream shop.

3. Ask students to find sentences containing relative pronouns in their reading and share them with the group.

ACTIVITY 6-10:
PAST, PRESENT, FUTURE

TYPE		TERM	
CLASS	☐	STA	☑
GROUP	☑	LTA	☐
IND	☐	LC	☐

Purpose:

1. To reinforce past, present and future tenses of verbs

2. To write a paragraph in past tense, in present tense, and in future tense

3. To stimulate writing by using a personal subject—the child himself

Materials:

Three paragraphs about a person, object, or animal, with one in past tense, one in present tense, and one in future tense; paragraphs from literature or newspapers

Grade level:

Upper elementary

Procedures:

1. Discuss the fact that both authors and speakers use signals to let a reader or listener know when something takes place. Place paragraphs on transparencies, or duplicate them. Ask students to listen carefully while you read three paragraphs.

(*Present:*)   The large oak tree in our backyard is an apartment house for many animals. In the lowest apartments in the trunk live many different kinds of bugs. We can see a spider decorating her apartment with a beautiful web. Above the spider, a frisky gray squirrel is filling his cupboard with nuts. Two robins are hovering around their nest. As we look closer, we see they are the proud parents of five babies. This apartment must be a happy place to live.

(*Past:*)   The apartment in our back yard was not always so big and fully occupied as it is today. Many years ago, a squirrel buried an acorn on the open lawn. The warm rains came, and a sprout grew out of the acorn and up through the ground. Little by little, it grew bigger and bigger. We placed a stake next to the young tree so it wouldn't be cut by the mower. We watched the leaves turn red during many falls. Each spring, more branches and leaves grew on the tree. We hoped it would grow big enough for a bird to build a nest in the branches.

(*Future:*)   In three months, we will lose the apartment in our back yard. We are going to add a new room to our house. In order to build the room, we will need to cut down the tree, or cut a hole in the roof. We will use the lumber from the tree to make paneling for the new room. We will not forget this special oak tree.

2. Ask the students if all three paragraphs take place in the same time period. Ask them to identify the times. How do they know the first paragraph is right now, or in the present tense? Have them identify the verbs that signal the time as right now. How do they know the second paragraph happened in the past? Have them identify the verbs or other words that signal the past. How do they know the final paragraph will happen in the future? Have them identify the verbs and other words that signal future.

3. Suggest to the students that we can also write about ourselves in the past, present, and future tense. Have them suggest topics they can write about in each tense. Have them write paragraphs about themselves illustrating each tense. Interact with the students as they write their paragraphs, providing assistance as needed.

4. To reinforce the future tense, have students write predictions about the future.

ACTIVITY 6-11:
RIDE THE AMTRAK LINE

TYPE		TERM	
CLASS	☐	STA	☑
GROUP	☑	LTA	☐
IND	☐	LC	☐

Purpose: 1. To reinforce spelling

2. To write spelling words during a motivating activity

Materials: Game board showing a railroad track (may depict specific areas of the country, or be general in nature—if specific area is depicted, students can draw game board as social studies assignment after studying map of an area)

Grade level: All grades

Procedures: 1. Create a game board depicting an Amtrak or other railroad line.

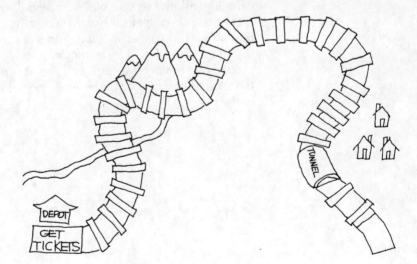

2. Write spelling word cards that give a word to be spelled, use the word in a sentence, and give directions for the speller if he spells the word correctly. For example:

> athlete
>
> An *athlete* is a person trained in physical strength and skill.
> Move ahead three spaces.

> thunder
>
> *Thunder* is a loud noise that follows a flash of lightning.
> Move ahead two spaces.

> You passed your spelling test.
> Move ahead three free spaces.

> You missed too many words on your spelling test.
> Move back two spaces.

3. Create railroad-related game-board markers for individual players. Markers might include an engine, caboose, passenger car, freight car, conductor's cap, engineer's cap, or train ticket.

4. This game can be played by two or more players. Shuffle the cards and place them face down in a pile. Have the first player select a card, and ask the second player to read the card to the first player. If the first player spells the word correctly, the player moves ahead the number of spaces indicated on the card. If the player misses the word, the player does not move ahead on the game board. The second player selects a card, and the next player reads the card to the second player. Continue until one passenger reaches the end of the line.

ACTIVITY 6-12:
TIC-TAC-TOE

TYPE		TERM	
CLASS	☐	STA	☑
GROUP	☑	LTA	☐
IND	☐	LC	☐

Purpose:
1. To reinforce spelling
2. To write spelling words during an enjoyable game activity

Materials: Lists of spelling words; tic-tac-toe game boards drawn on cardboard or on the chalkboard

Grade level: All grades

Procedures:
1. Several procedures may be used for spelling reinforcement with a tic-tac-toe format. Some possibilities:
   a. Divide the spelling group into two teams. Pronounce a spelling word for the first person on one team. Have the person write the word. If he writes the word correctly, the team member places an x or an o on the tic-tac-toe board. Next, pronounce a word for the first person on the opposing team. Continue pronouncing words to members of each team until a team has won horizontally, diagonally, or vertically.
   b. Divide the spelling group into two teams. Pronounce the spelling word for team one. Have each person on the team write the word. If all team members write the word correctly, the team places an x or o on the tic-tac-toe board. (This approach allows every team member to participate in the spelling activity. Team members, however, should be matched according to spelling ability.)
   c. Divide the spelling group into two teams, or divide the spelling groups into two individual players per game. Place spelling words on individual cards. Shuffle the spelling word cards and place them face down on a tic-tac-toe board. The first team chooses a square, the caller pronounces the word, and the first team member or the whole team writes the word. If the word is spelled correctly, the team places its x or o on the appropriate

square. If the team cannot spell the word correctly, the second team or individual can try to spell the word. Continue playing until a team or individual wins the game.

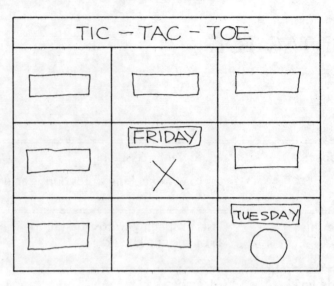

SYNONYM
CONCENTRATION GAME

TYPE		TERM	
CLASS	☐	STA	☑
GROUP	☑	LTA	☐
IND	☐	LC	☐

Purpose:
1. To expand vocabulary based on weekly spelling word list
2. To identify synonyms for words studied during weekly spelling lesson

---

Materials: Individual cards with one spelling word to a card, and cards with synonym for each word

---

Grade level: All grades

Procedures:
1. Cut individual cards from light-weight cardboard or construction paper. Write a spelling word and a synonym for each word on individual cards.

Spelling Words:

sway

fatal

contain

Synonyms:

wave

deadly

enclose

2. Shuffle cards and place them face down on a table:

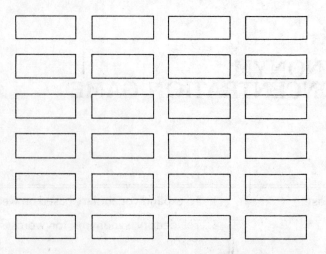

3. Divide the spelling group into two to five players. Students turn over two cards, trying to match a spelling word with its appropriate synonym. If the two cards match, and if the student identifies them as a match, the student keeps the pair. If the cards do not match, the cards are returned, face down, to the original position. The next player chooses a card and tries to find its match. As more cards are turned over, students must concentrate on the position of the cards so they will be able to find a pair. The winner of the game is the student with the greatest number of correctly matched cards.

4. This game may be changed to use antonyms or definitions. A group of students or an individual can prepare the game cards for others to play.

ACTIVITY 6-14:
RELATING
MEANING AND SPELLING

TYPE		TERM	
CLASS	☐	STA	☑
GROUP	☑	LTA	☐
IND	☐	LC	☐

Purpose:
1. To show the relationship between spelling and meaning
2. To identify the relationship between meaning and spelling

Materials:
Lists of word pairs demonstrating relationship between spelling and meaning

Grade level:
Middle and upper elementary, middle school

Procedures:
1. Background—Carol Chomsky's[3] work suggests that many spellings relate to semantic function in the language rather than to phonetic representation. Lexical spellings thus represent meaning, and lead speller and reader directly to a word's meaning. This research suggests that instruction should emphasize regularities in meaning between related words. This instructional approach may be used for spelling, vocabulary development, and reading.

2. Discuss with students the fact that many words give clues to spelling. If we understand the meaning of a word, meaning can help improve spelling. Ask students to pronounce and identify the relationship between *nature* and *natural*. Even though the two words are pronounced differently, there is a close relationship in meaning. Have students use the two words in sentences, compare the meanings, and identify the similarities in spelling. Study other words the same way, such as:

major	majority
culture	cultural
gymnasium	gymnastics
library	librarian
photograph	photography
microscope	microscopic

govern	governor	government
history	historical	historian

3. Ask students to become word detectives and look for their own examples of word families that share similar meanings and spellings.

4. Have students develop booklets of spelling word pairs or families that show a relationship between meaning and spelling. Have them use their words in sentences, and share their word detective books with other members of the class.

```
┌─────────────────────────────────┐
│      MY WORD DETECTIVE           │
│          BOOK                    │
│                                  │
│  SPELLING SHOWS MEANING          │
│                                  │
│    PHOTOGRAPH      (  )          │
│    PHOTOGRAPHER    (  )          │
│    PHOTOGRAPHY     (  )          │
│                                  │
└─────────────────────────────────┘
```

ACTIVITY 6-15:
ALPHABETICAL SENTENCES

TYPE		TERM	
CLASS	☑	STA	☑
GROUP	☑	LTA	☐
IND	☑	LC	☐

Purpose:
1. To reinforce alphabetical order
2. To write sentences using alphabetical order of the first letter of the word

Materials:
Example of a sentence written in alphabetical order; dictionaries

Grade level:
Lower and middle elementary

Procedures:
1. Show students examples of sentences written in alphabetical order. Ask them to read or listen to the sentences, and identify anything unusual about them. For example:

   Archie baboon can do everything faster: gather his island juice; kick little mangoes negligently; or pare quaint, round, seedy, tangerines under very wild xanthous, youthful, zinnias.

2. Have students write their own alphabetical order sentences. (Sentences do not need to extend through the whole alphabet.) Share sentences with the group.

ACTIVITY 6-16:
PERSONAL LEARNING CENTERS FOR WRITING

TYPE		TERM	
CLASS	☑	STA	☐
GROUP	☐	LTA	☐
IND	☐	LC	☑

Purpose:

1. To develop a useful personal learning center for spelling, handwriting, punctuation, capitalization, and letter writing

2. To reinforce spelling, handwriting, punctuation, capitalization, and letter writing skills

Materials:

Cardboard box (about the size of a desk top) for each child; lists of spelling words; manuscript or cursive writing forms; punctuation chart; capitalization chart; letter writing forms

Grade level:

All grades

Procedures:

1. Provide directions so each student can make his personal learning center. Cut the bottom, top, and front out of a cardboard box; this leaves the left side, back, and right side:

2. Tape large pockets onto the inside of the left, back, and right sides of the cardboard frame. (Construction paper or used file folders can be taped on three sides to form these pockets.)

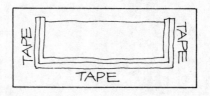

3. Next, discuss with the students the kinds of information that would be helpful to them when they write a story, a content area assignment, or a letter. (This information can change, and should be designed according to the needs of the individual children.) The following is suggestive of the types of information many students find valuable:
   a. Alphabetical lists of basic spelling words. Words from the spelling series used by the school, Dolch, or Thorndike lists of utilitarian words can be compiled and placed in a pocket marked "spelling." This basic list can be supplemented with words each child uses frequently in writing.
   b. Alphabetical lists of words the child frequently misspells. Older students may find it helpful to include a list of words often confused in writing; for example:

WORDS OFTEN CONFUSED IN WRITING

affect	-	to influence
effect	-	outcome
capital	-	city where government is located; a capital letter (A)
capitol	-	building in which legislature meets
desert	-	dry, barren region
dessert	-	a sweet served at the end of a meal
hear	-	to listen to
here	-	to this place
lose	-	to misplace
loose	-	not fastened
principal	-	something of importance; the administrator of a school
principle	-	a truth or belief
stationary	-	unmoving
stationery	-	paper used for writing letters
there	-	in that place
their	-	belonging to them
they're	-	contraction of "they are"
to	-	in the direction of
too	-	also
two	-	the number 2
weather	-	condition of the atmosphere
whether	-	choice or alternative

---

   c. A copy of the appropriate manuscript or cursive alphabet. Lower elementary students usually use manuscript, while middle and upper elementary students usually use cursive writing.

d. A punctuation chart. The items included will again depend upon the student's needs. Such a chart might include the following information:

PUNCTUATION CHART

Punctuation:	Example:
Period.	
1. Use periods at the end of a sentence.	This is Monday morning.
2. Use periods after abbreviations.	U.S.A., Fri., Aug., Mr.
3. Use periods after numbers in a list.	1. Seeds 2. Soil
Question Mark ?	
1. Use a question mark after a sentence that asks a question.	When are you going to the movie?
Exclamation Mark !	
1. Use an exclamation mark after a statement of excitement.	Great! We'll win!
Comma ,	
1. Use a comma to separate a series of three or more items.	We had hot dogs, corn, milk, and cake for lunch.
2. Use a comma between the name of a city and state.	We visited San Francisco, California.
3. Use a comma between the month and the year.	Our Independence Day was July 4, 1776.
4. Use a comma after the salutation of a letter.	Dear Mom,
5. Use a comma after the closing of a letter.	Sincerely,
6. Use a comma before a coordinating conjunction.	She wanted to buy a new coat, but she couldn't find one she liked.
Apostrophe '	
1. Use an apostrophe to show possession of a singular noun.	This is Toby's bicycle.
2. Use an apostrophe to show possession of a plural noun.	We saw the boys' basketball team play this afternoon.

3. Use an apostrophe to show that letters have been left out in a contraction.

You're, can't, isn't, I'll

e. A sample of the form and punctuation for a letter. For example:

Name of Street _____

City, State, Zip _____

Month, Date, Year _____

Greeting,

_____ Message _____

_____

_____

_____

Closing, _____

Signature _____

f. Guidelines for capitalization. For example:

USE CAPITAL LETTERS

1. Sentences begin with capital letters.

The dog was lost for one week.

2. Names begin with capital letters.

George Washington

3. Names of cities, states, countries, and rivers begin with capital letters.

Seattle, New Jersey, Canada, Mississippi

4. Names of days, months, and holidays begin with capital letters.

Monday, January, Memorial Day

5. Titles of books begin with capital letters.

Across Five Aprils

6. Titles such as Miss and Mr. begin with capital letters.

Miss, Mr., Mrs., Ms., Dr.

7. Greeting of a letter begins with a capital letter.

Dear Jackie,

8. The closing of a letter begins with a capital letter.

Your friend,
Sincerely,

4. Any other useful equipment can be included in the personal learning center, such as the child's personal writing folder, proofreading suggestions, or a dictionary and reference guide.

5. When the personal writing center is complete, the child can fold it flat for easy storage. He can use the center whenever he needs it.

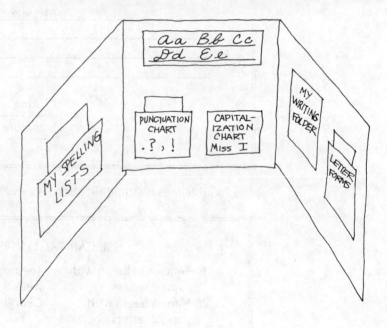

7 Activities for Literature

Literature activities encourage children to develop their imaginations and creativity, provide vicarious experiences, afford insights into human behavior, and stimulate literary awareness and growth.

Children should have opportunities to listen to the teacher read stories, or tell them, aloud. These enjoyable experiences should be a daily occurrence. Children should also have opportunities to share their own reading with others. It is advantageous, for both teacher and pupils, to identify specific interests. The teacher can thus select appropriate books to read to the children, as well as books they will most willingly read themselves. Since interest is one of the most important motivators for reading at all levels, the first activity in this section is an interest inventory for administering individually or to a group.

The other activities in this section demonstrate the variety of literature activities that can be developed with children. There are individual activities related to specific books or types of books, interest center activities, and units developed around literature. The activities allow oral discussion, reading for enjoyment, creative dramatization, art interpretation, creative writing, listening for appreciation, and reading or listening for specific purposes. The rationale behind the various activities and related research is available in language arts textbooks, a list of which appears at the end of Chapter 1.

ACTIVITY 7-1:
INVESTIGATING
CHILDREN'S INTERESTS

TYPE		TERM	
CLASS	☐	STA	☑
GROUP	☐	LTA	☐
IND	☑	LC	☐

Purpose: 1. To evaluate children's interests for the purpose of motivating the reading of literature

Materials: Interest inventory

Grade level: All grades; the inventory is read to young children, but older children may complete it independently

Procedures: a. Administer the following inventory:

(1) What do you like to do when you get home from school? __
_____

(2) What do you like to do on Saturday? _____

(3) Do you like to watch television? _____
If you do, what are the names of your favorite programs? __
_____
_____

(4) Do you have a hobby? _____
If you do, what is your hobby? _____

(5) Do you like to make or collect things? _____
If you do, what have you made or collected? _____
_____

(6) What is your favorite sport? _____

(7) What games do you like best? _____
_____

(8) Do you like to go to the movies? _____
If you do, what was your favorite movie? _____
_____

(9) Do you have a pet? _____

(10) Where have you spent your summer vacations? _____
_____
_____

(11) Have you ever made a special study? _____
rocks _____ space _____ plants _____ animals _____
travel _____ dinosaurs _____ other _____

(12) What are your favorite subjects in school? art _____ handwriting _____ social studies _____ reading _____ physical
education _____ science _____ spelling _____ arithmetic
_____ creative writing _____ English _____ other
_____

(13) What subject is hardest for you? _____

(14) What kinds of books do you like to have someone read to
you? animal stories _____ fairy tales _____ true stories
_____ science fiction _____ adventure _____ mystery
_____ sports _____ poems _____ humorous _____ other
kinds of stories _____

(15) What is your favorite book that someone has read to you?
_____

(16) What kinds of books do you like to read by yourself? animal
stories _____ picture books _____ fairy tales _____ true
stories _____ science fiction _____ adventures _____ mysteries _____ sport stories _____ poems _____ funny stories
_____ other kinds of stories _____
_____

(17) What is your favorite book that you read by yourself?

(18) Would you rather read a book by yourself or have someone
read to you?

(19) Name a book you read this week

(20) What books or magazines do you have at home?

(21) Do you ever go to the library?
How often?
Do you have a library card?

b. Tabulate your group's interests. Use the results to choose books
to read aloud to the group and to suggest books for students to
read individually.

ACTIVITY 7-2:
THE FANTASY OF MOTHER GOOSE

TYPE		TERM	
CLASS	☑	STA	☑
GROUP	☐	LTA	☐
IND	☐	LC	☐

Purpose:
1. To appreciate literature
2. To dramatize nursery rhymes creatively
3. To develop choral speaking with nursery rhymes
4. To write creatively a story stimulated by nursery rhymes
5. To interpret Mother Goose rhymes through art

Materials: Mother Goose books and pictures; large sheets of cardboard or large boxes for humanette puppets; language experience charts; materials for puppet construction

Grade level: Kindergarten, first grade

Procedures:
1. Young children love the happy rhymes and nonsense in Mother Goose rhymes. Give them many opportunities to listen to and recite Mother Goose rhymes.

2. Pantomime—As you recite a Mother Goose rhyme to the children, have them act out each part of the rhyme.

3. Pantomime—Allow children to take turns pantomiming their favorite Mother Goose rhymes while the class guesses their identity.

4. Choral Speaking—Because most rhymes are easily memorized, children need not be able to read to perform choral speaking activities with nursery rhymes. Practice different choral speaking arrangements, and try accompanying some of them with rhythm instruments or a bongo drum.

5. Creative Drama—Nursery phymes provide an excellent introduction to the concept that a drama has several parts—a beginning, middle, and ending. Have children listen to a nursery rhyme that has obvious parts, such as "Jack and Jill":

> Jack and Jill went up the hill to get a pail of water.
> Jack fell down and broke his crown,
> And Jill came tumbling after.

Ask the children to identify the first act in the rhyme; the second act; and the final act. Divide the class into groups, and have each group act out what they think would happen during the first part, the second part, or the final part. Encourage them to extend their parts by adding dialogue to each part, or pretending to be objects such as trees, flowers, or other creatures that might be on the hill. After each group has an opportunity to act out its part, put the parts of the nursery rhyme back together and have each group play its own part.

6. Role Playing—Put pictures of nursery rhyme characters into a pail (symbol for Jack and Jill). Provide a picture for each character in a nursery rhyme. Have the children select a character from the pail, form a group with the other characters in the rhyme, and role play their part in the jingle.

7. Humanette Puppets—A child can be transformed into a human-size puppet by making a cardboard figure large enough to cover the front of the child, or by using a box large enough to cover the body. Have students select nursery rhyme characters they would like to be and design humanette puppets. After they make the puppets, have them act out the rhymes.

8. Creative Writing (Language Experience Chart Stories)—After reading nursery rhymes, allow the children to select a nursery rhyme they would like to write a story about. This activity may be done many times, with different rhymes for stimulation. For example, after reading "Jack and Jill," ask students: "What do you think happened after Jack and Jill fell down the hill? What do you think their mother might have done? Would they go back and get more water?" After reading "The Old Woman and the Shoe," you might ask: "What would you do if you were the Old Woman in the Shoe? How would you take care of your children? What would it be like living in a shoe?" Or, after reading "Peter, Peter Pumpkin Eater," you might say: "Imagine that you lived in a pumpkin like Peter." (Provide a pumpkin for them to see and feel.) "How would you decorate your room? What could you do inside the shell? Would a pumpkin make a good home? Why or why not? What do you think your neighbors would think of your home?"

Draw a large object that symbolizes the nursery rhyme. Have the children dictate a story, which you will write inside the shape. Display the stories on the bulletin board. Encourage children to read their stories.

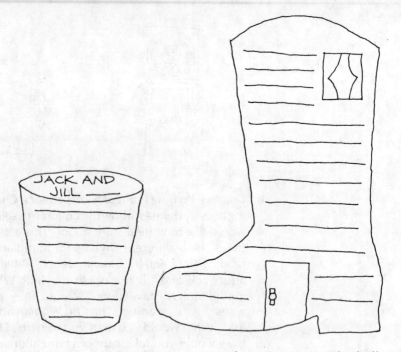

9. Art Interpretation—Create a "Mother Goose Land" bulletin board illustrating the homes and people who live in Mother Goose Land. The center of the board might contain a large figure of Mother Goose carrying a wand and riding on her goose. The children could paint a large mural depicting this land. Place the chart stories below the bulletin board.

10. Creative Drama (Puppetry)—After the children have listened to, pantomimed, and drawn pictures of many rhymes, allow them to select several rhymes to present as puppet shows. They might add to the puppet show by including their own language experience stories as part of the rhyme. Encourage them to make simple puppets showing their favorite rhymes. Invite another class to the festival to see the puppet plays, hear choral speaking, look at pictures, and read the children's chart stories. Write invitations to the Mother Goose festival on figures, drawn by the children, depicting nursery rhyme characters.

ACTIVITY 7-3:
MOTHER GOOSE IS ALIVE
IN UPPER ELEMENTARY

TYPE		TERM	
CLASS	☑	STA	☑
GROUP	☑	LTA	☐
IND	☐	LC	☐

Purpose:

1. To research and report historical references in Mother Goose rhymes

2. To research, report, and debate the origins of Mother Goose

3. To write a creative story motivated by current historical figures

4. To develop vocabulary stimulated by old English terms in nursery rhymes

5. To perform a creative drama extending a nursery-rhyme theme

6. To develop oral expression through choral speaking activities

7. To interpret through art the techniques used to illustrate nursery rhyme books

Materials:

Katherine Elives Thomas's *The Real Personage of Mother Goose* (Lothrop, Lee & Shepard Co., 1930); and several Mother Goose books: Marguerite de Angeli's *Book of Nursery and Mother Goose Rhymes* (Doubleday & Co., 1953) has both black-and-white drawings and pastel paintings; Feodor Rojankovsky's *The Tall Book of Mother Goose* (Harper & Row, 1942) has cartoon-like illustrations; Tasha Tudor's *Mother Goose* (Henry Z. Walck, 1944) has old-fashioned illustrations; and Blanche Fisher Wright's *The Real Mother Goose* (Rand McNally, 1944) contains an account of the origins of Mother Goose; also, encyclopedias; history references

Grade level:

Upper elementary, middle school

Procedures:

1. Research, Motivation—Discuss background with the students. The beloved children's character of Mother Goose is symbolized by a smiling old woman wearing a tall hat and a cloak. She often carries a wand and rides on the back of a goose. Many of the verses associated with Mother Goose are believed, however, to have been written for adults rather than for children. Many Mother

Goose rhymes were supposedly based on the lives of real people, during the times of Edward VI, Mary I, Elizabeth, Mary Queen of Scots, Queen Anne, William II, and George I. Many nursery rhymes, such as "Humpty Dumpty," appear to be only nonsensical rhymes, but in reality they may be satire (ridicule, sarcasm, irony, mockery) describing real events and real people. For example, "Ride a Cock Horse to Banbury Cross."[1] is believed to communicate a secret message to the people that Queen Elizabeth I of England was to leave the castle and travel to Spain for secret negotiations with the Spanish king. The rhyme was sung in pubs to let the people know subtly that they could see the queen and her entourage if they traveled to Banbury Cross. When they arrived, they would see the queen: "A fine lady rides on a fine horse, with rings on her fingers and bells on her toes." The line "She shall have music wherever she goes" refers to the fact that she was accompanied by her ladies-in-waiting and her musicians.

Assign a research project in which students identify several nursery rhymes written about a particular figure in history. Have the students discover the reason or incident behind the nursery rhyme, and tell what they think the nursery rhyme reveals about the person and how other people felt about that person. Examples of nursery rhymes for research are "Humpty Dumpty" (about Richard III), "Sing a Song of Sixpence" (about Henry VIII), "Little Boy Blue" (about Cardinal Wolsey), "Hey Diddle, Diddle" (about Elizabeth I), and "Three Blind Mice," "Little Bo Peep," "Mistress Mary," and "Little Miss Muffet" (about Mary, Queen of Scots).

2. Research, Oral Language—"Who was the real Mother Goose?" There are several versions of the identity of Mother Goose. The term was first used in a publication in 1697, when a French author, Charles Perrault, wrote a series of folktales and called them *Tales of Mother Goose*. Americans believe the original Mother Goose was Dame Goose of Boston; the French believe she was goose-footed Bertha, wife of Robert II, and there are other beliefs about the origin of Mother Goose. Have students research the origin of Mother Goose, choose the theory they favor, and present and defend their interpretation orally to the class. If several students select the same theory, a class debate could develop.

3. Creative Writing, Critical Thinking—After investigating nursery rhymes and the real people on whom they are based, allow students to choose a person from more current history, review that person's background, and write a satirical rhyme about the person. Ask the students to orally present their own nursery rhymes to the class, so the other students can guess the identity of the person in the nursery rhyme. The students can compile a book of current Mother Goose rhymes and call it "The Real Mother Goose Today."

4. Vocabulary Development—Many nursery rhymes use Old English terms no longer in common usage. Have students list such terms and supply the current meaning for the term. Finally, have them rewrite the nursery rhyme in current language.

Nursery Rhyme	Terms and Meaning	Today's Translation
Little Miss Muffet	tuffet -	
Sat on a tuffet	curds -	
Eating her curds	whey -	
and whey		

5. Creative Drama—Divide the class into small groups. Allow each group to select a Mother Goose rhyme and develop a longer creative drama about the theme of the rhyme. They may use puppets or costumes, if they wish. Have the groups present the dramas to a kindergarten or first-grade class.

6. Choral Speaking—Nursery rhymes provide excellent material for choral choirs. Allow students to select their favorite nursery rhymes, practice different choral arrangements, and present their choral nursery rhymes to a class of young children.

7. Evaluation of Illustrations (Art Interpretation)— The illustrations in Mother Goose editions range from humorous, cartoon-like illustrations, to quaint, old-fashioned characterizations. Have students compare the illustrations in several different Mother Goose editions. "What media does the artist use? What is the effect of each type of illustration? How does each one make you feel?" Have the students divide into small groups, select one type of illustration, research the artist's technique, and demonstrate the technique to the class. Create a bulletin board with examples of pictures using the various techniques.

ACTIVITY 7-4:
RABBIT HILL
(NEWBERY AWARD, 1945)

TYPE		TERM	
CLASS	☐	STA	☑
GROUP	☑	LTA	☐
IND	☐	LC	☐

Purpose:

1. To interpret and share literature selections through oral expression

Materials:

Robert Lawson's *Rabbit Hill*

Grade level:

Third and fourth grades

Summary:

Many animals live on Rabbit Hill, and they have frequently seen hard times. But change is in the air, and the animals speculate about what may happen in their lives because new people are moving onto the hill. Thankfully, the new people respect the animals. They do not use poisons or traps, they plant gardens without fences, and they believe animals have a right to live on the hill. The animals, in turn, guard the property for the new family.

Procedures:

1. Provide materials and allow students to make puppets of their favorite characters from *Rabbit Hill,* such as Father Rabbit, Little Georgie, Uncle Analdas, Willie Fieldmouse, or Porkey the Woodchuck. A simple rabbit can be made from a cardboard box, a paper plate, or a cylinder.

After they make the puppets, have a group of students put on a puppet play of their favorite part of the story for the rest of the class or for a lower-elementary class.

Rabbit Hill can also motivate children to create their own story about what might happen when humans are kind or unkind. After they listen to or read this story, allow children to divide into groups and choose to be either for or against the animals. Present a puppet show from each viewpoint. After the puppet presentations, discuss the consequences of each viewpoint with the class.

ACTIVITY 7-5:
SYLVESTER AND THE MAGIC PEBBLE (CALDECOTT AWARD, 1970)

TYPE		TERM	
CLASS	☐	STA	☑
GROUP	☑	LTA	☐
IND	☐	LC	☐

Purpose:
1. To interpret and share literature selections through oral expression
2. To interpret a picture book through oral expression

Materials: William Steig's *Sylvester and the Magic Pebble*

Grade level: Lower elementary

Summary: Sylvester, a young donkey, finds a red pebble that has the power to grant wishes. Sylvester makes the mistake of wishing to be a rock. Since the pebble must be held to grant a wish, Sylvester cannot turn himself back into a donkey. He remains a rock until one day his very worried parents are having a picnic on his back. Then, his mother picks up the magic pebble and places it on Sylvester's back. Sylvester wishes he were a donkey again and is miraculously restored.

Procedures:
1. After listening to or reading this book, the children may do a number of oral creative drama activities. First, the teacher can give each student a pretty "magic" pebble. They can think about and discuss what they would wish for if they found a real magic pebble. Next, the can create a play to demonstrate their wishes.

2. Several wishes can be combined into a new creative story by a group of children and presented to the rest of the class.

3. Lead a discussion with the children about how they think Sylvester's parents felt when Sylvester did not come home. "What did Mr. and Mrs. Duncan think happened to him? How did they try to find him? How would your parents feel if you did not come home? What would your parents do? Which wish do you think was the best one of all? Why?"

ACTIVITY 7-6:
SAM, BANGS, AND MOONSHINE
(CALDECOTT AWARD, 1967)

TYPE		TERM	
CLASS	☑	STA	☑
GROUP	☑	LTA	☐
IND	☑	LC	☐

Purpose:
1. To interpret and share literature selections through written expression
2. To interpret humorous fiction through writing

Materials: Evaline Ness's *Sam, Bangs, and Moonshine*

Grade level: Lower elementary

Summary: Samantha (Sam for short) has a habit of daydreaming and telling fanciful stories about herself. She says her mother is a mermaid, her cat Bangs can talk, and that she owns a fierce lion and a baby kangaroo. Her father calls her stories moonshine, and tells her she must understand the difference between real and moonshine. Problems develop because Sam's friend Thomas believes all of Sam's moonshine. Sam finally realizes that moonshine is not good when Thomas goes out to find her mermaid mother on Blue Rock. A storm develops and Thomas almost drowns; he is rescued just in time by Sam's father.

Procedures:
1. After the children read or listen to the story, have them write two poems, one titled "Moonshine is," and the other, "Real is."

2. Make a chart titled "Moonshine and Real." Write on the chart which things are moonshine and which are real from *Sam, Bangs, and Moonshine*. Add other items to the chart that you know are real or moonshine. Draw pictures on your chart to illustrate real or moonshine.

MOONSHINE
A FIERCE LION

REAL
BANGS THE CAT

3. Have the students pretend they are Sam, and like to tell "Moonshine Stories." Tell them to write a story about moonshine and what happened when they told their stories.

ACTIVITY 7-7:
SHADOW OF A BULL
(NEWBERY AWARD, 1965)

TYPE		TERM	
CLASS	☐	STA	☑
GROUP	☐	LTA	☐
IND	☑	LC	☐

Purpose:

1. To interpret and share literature selections through written expression

Materials:

Maia Wojciechowska's *Shadow of a Bull*

Grade level:

Fourth and fifth grades

Summary:

Manolo is a young Spanish boy whose father was a great bullfighter. Everyone in the town believes Manolo is destined to be a bullfighter, but Manolo is fearful of bulls (his father was killed during a bullfight). He tries to overcome his fears, and is afraid to tell anyone about them. During his first fight, he finally gains the courage to tell everyone that he does not want to fight bulls. He finally is able to feel proud of himself.

Procedures:

1. Tell the children to pretend they are Manolo, and the men are trying to prepare them for their first bullfight. Have them write a diary for the week before the bullfight. Extend the diary to the day of the bullfight, then the day after the bullfight. Ask them how they feel after they tell everyone about their wishes. How do the people treat them?

2. The bullfight is an important activity in Spain. Have the students write a letter to a travel agency or tourist bureau, asking for more information about bullfights. Try to get a travel poster illustrating a bullfight.

THE BRONZE BOW
(NEWBERY AWARD, 1962)

TYPE		TERM	
CLASS	☐	STA	☑
GROUP	☑	LTA	☐
IND	☑	LC	☐

Purpose:	1. To interpret and share literature selections through writing
	2. To interpret historical fiction through writing

Materials:	George Speare's *The Bronze Bow*

Grade level:	Sixth grade and above

Summary:	Daniel bar Jamin is an eighteen-year-old living in Israel. He hates the Romans, and feels his purpose in life is to free Israel. The Bronze Bow is a symbol of a group dedicated to driving the Romans from their country. Daniel finally meets Jesus, who teaches him to love. He realizes what real love means when he is able to invite a Roman soldier into his home.

Procedures:	1. Have the students pretend they are presenting recommendations to the Newbery Award Committee. Have them write a letter to the committee stating why *The Bronze Bow* does or does not deserve to win the Newbery Award.
	2. Have the students pretend they are with Daniel when he visits Jesus at the home of Simon the fisherman. Have them write a letter to one of the guerilla band describing what they see as Jesus speaks to the people and explaining their personal feelings during this experience.
	3. Tell the students the bronze bow was selected as a symbol because it was very strong, and it would be impossible for a man to bend a bow made of bronze. Have them investigate the use of symbolism in literature. Make a chart showing symbols of strength that are used in literature.

```
                    SYMBOLS OF STRENGTH

    Example:          Found in:          Why it was a good
                                                   symbol:

    A bronze bow    The Bronze Bow      The group of
                    by Elizabeth Speare  Israelites needed
                                         great strength
                                         to fight mighty
                                         Rome. (Love is
                                         the strongest
                                         of all)
```

ACTIVITY 7-9:
THE LITTLE HOUSE
(CALDECOTT AWARD, 1943)

TYPE		TERM	
CLASS	☐	STA	☑
GROUP	☑	LTA	☐
IND	☑	LC	☐

Purpose: 1. To interpret and share literature selections through art activities

Materials: Virginia Lee Burton's *The Little House;* flannel board

Grade level: Kindergarten through second grade

Summary: The Little House is built on a hill in the country. It leads a contented life, watching the four seasons pass and the children playing. After a number of years, the house notices that the lights of the city are coming closer. Finally, the house is all alone in the middle of the city, and becomes rundown and very unhappy. A lady goes by and recognizes the home as belonging to her grandparents. She has it moved to the country and restored to its original beauty. The house is happy again, as it watches the seasons, the sun, the moon, and the children.

Procedures: 1. After reading this story, have the children illustrate the book with flannel board pictures. Have them draw the major pictures from the book. Place pieces of flannel, pellon, felt, or other substances that will stick to the felt board on the back of the pictures, and retell the story with the flannel board pictures.

FINDERS KEEPERS
(CALDECOTT AWARD, 1952)

TYPE		TERM	
CLASS	☑	STA	☑
GROUP	☑	LTA	☐
IND	☑	LC	☐

Purpose: 1. To interpret and share literature selections through art activities

Materials: William Lipking and Nicolas Mordvinoff's *Finders Keepers*

Grade level: Kindergarten through second grade

Summary: Two dogs, Nap and Winkle, find a bone. They each want the bone, and look for someone else to help them decide who the bone belongs to. They ask a farmer, a goat, and a barber for help; they get ridiculous answers that do not solve their problem. They meet a big dog who helps them solve their problem by taking the bone. After Nap and Winkle fight the dog to get their bone, they realize the only way to solve the problem is to share the bone.

Procedures:

1. After they listen to or read the book, allow children to draw a large mural depicting the sequence of scenes from the book:
   a. Nap sees the bone, Winkle touches the bone
   b. Nap, Winkle and the farmer
   c. Nap, Winkle and the goat
   d. Nap, Winkle and the barber
   e. Nap, Winkle and the large dog
   f. Nap and Winkle share the bone

2. Tell the children each to pretend: "You and a very close friend both want the same toy. You do not want to share the toy. How could you try to solve your problem in a funny way? Draw your own picture book to show your story." Allow the children to write

the accompanying dialogue by dictating their stories, if they are not yet able to write their own. Have them share the picture books with the class.

3. Design a bulletin board called "Sharing Makes Us Happy." Have the children search magazines and picture files to find pictures of children, people, and animals sharing.

ACTIVITY 7-11:
THE EGG TREE
(CALDECOTT AWARD, 1951)

TYPE		TERM	
CLASS	☑	STA	☑
GROUP	☑	LTA	☐
IND	☑	LC	☐

Purpose: 1. To interpret and share literature selections through art activities

Materials: Katherine Milhous's *The Egg Tree*

Grade level: Lower and middle elementary

Summary: Two children spend their Easter vacation with their grandmother on a Pennsylvania Dutch farm. This award-winning picture book has pages of authentic Pennsylvania Dutch designs. The family decorates an egg tree every year, then invites friends to come and see the tree. Directions are given for making the egg tree.

Procedures: 1. After they read or listen to this book, allow children to make their own Easter egg tree as described in the book. Eggs can be decorated with wax crayons, then dipped in egg dye, or they can be painted with water colors.

2. People came to see the Pennsylvania Dutch tree in this story. Plan a time to invite another class, or parents, to view the tree. Design egg-shaped invitations and decorate them with Pennsylvania Dutch designs.

3. *The Egg Tree* shows numerous Pennsylvania Dutch designs. Practice drawing the designs on construction paper eggs. Hang the egg shapes from a mobile.

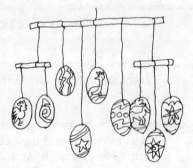

THE 21 BALLOONS
(NEWBERY AWARD, 1948)

TYPE		TERM	
CLASS	☐	STA	☐
GROUP	☐	LTA	☐
IND	☑	LC	☑

Purpose: 1. To interpret and share literature selections through art activities

Materials: William du Bois's *The 21 Balloons;* reference books on ballooning

Grade level: Upper elementary, middle school

Summary: Professor Sherman is fascinated with balloon flight. He flies a balloon over the Pacific Ocean and lands on the island of Krakatoa. Here, he finds that the inhabitants are inventors of super-gadgets. Since the island is volcanic, the people plan together an invention that they hope will allow them to escape if necessary. (The volcano does erupt.)

Procedures:

1. The people of Krakatoa were very inventive. One invention raised the bed up through the roof so the inventor could sleep on top of the roof when the nights were very hot. Tell the children to make a model of their own super-gadgets and explain the purpose of the invention to the class.

2. Have the students read other references about balloons, then design models of a balloon craft. Have them explain the balloon principle to the class.

3. Have them make a time line of the history of balloon travel and draw in illustrations for each time period.

BALLOONING TIME LINE

1783	1785	1793
World's first recorded balloon flight with passengers.	Blanchard and Jeffries cross the English channel.	First balloon flight in U.S.

1794	Civil War	1931
French win battle because of balloon signals	Union Army had an Aeronautics Corps using 7 balloons	Piccard reaches 51,000 feet in aluminum gondola

1957		1978
Davis Simons reaches 102,00 feet		First successful transatlantic balloon flight — Double Eagle II

ACTIVITY 7-13:
MAURICE SENDAK AND HIS LITERATURE— AN INTEREST CENTER

TYPE		TERM	
CLASS	☐	STA	☐
GROUP	☐	LTA	☐
IND	☑	LC	☑

Purpose:

1. To be able to explain why Sendak became interested in books and in writing his own stories, how he developed his artistic talents, and how he gathered ideas for writing and drawing

2. To write a creative story motivated by sketches of children

3. To write a creative story motivated by cartoons

4. To write a creative story motivated by music

5. To write a creative story motivated by *Where the Wild Things Are*

6. To react to music that motivates Maurice Sendak

7. To design a bulletin board with ideas for Sendak's books

8. To compare, in an oral presentation, the illustrations and writings of Lewis Carroll, Edward Lear, and Maurice Sendak

9. To experiment with the art medium Sendak uses and discuss the effectiveness of his illustrations

10. To interpret a character through the use of papier-mâché

11. To develop and perform a creative drama activity motivated by *Where the Wild Things Are*

12. To develop literature appreciation and interpret poetry through choral speaking.

Materials:

Books illustrated by Maurice Sendak:
Marcel Ayme's *The Wonderful Farm* (1951)
Ruth Krauss's *A Hole is to Dig* (1951)
Ruth Krauss's *A Very Special House* (1953)
Sesyle Joslin's *What Do You Say, Dear?* (1958)
Janice May Udry's *The Moon Jumpers* (1959)
Else Holmelund Minarik's *Little Bear's Visit* (1961)

Charlotte Zolotow's *Mr Rabbit and the Lovely Present* (1962)
Isaac Bashevis Singer's *Zlateh the Goat and Other Stories* (1966)

Books illustrated and written by Maurice Sendak:

Kenny's Window (1956)
Pierre: A Cautionary Tale (1962)
Where the Wild Things Are (1963)
Higglety Pigglety Pop (1967)
Seven Little Monsters (1977)

Books by Lewis Carroll and Edward Lear

Grade level:	Lower elementary; middle elementary; many of the activities are also appropriate for older students
Procedures:	1. Place information about Sendak's professional background on a tape, or type the information on cards or paper. Sendak's background is interesting, and provides insights into the motivational processes of a successful author and illustrator. The dialogue for this tape might read as follows:

As you listen to this tape [or read this paper], I want you to think about three questions: How did Mr. Sendak become interested in books and in writing his own stories? How did Mr. Sendak develop his artistic talents? How does Mr. Sendak gather ideas for writing and drawing?

Maurice Sendak, a favorite children's author, was born in Brooklyn, New York, on June 10, 1928. He is so popular with children that he has been called the "Picasso of children's books." He was given this title because he has drawn the illustrations for over 60 books. One of his books, *Where the Wild Things Are*, won the Caldecott Medal in 1964 for the best picture book.

Maurice Sendak's father interested him in stories when Mr. Sendak was a young child. His father told him bedtime stories from Eastern European Jewish folktales. He loved books, and even wrote his own books and drew the pictures for them. By the time he became a teenager, he was so interested in stories and writing that he decided he would be a writer and illustrator.

When Mr. Sendak was growing up, he drew pictures of kids playing, and later, used many of these ideas in his books. When he was in high school, he took many art courses. One of his favorite pastimes was drawing comic strip adventures about the other kids in school. He even had a part-time job working on the Mutt and Jeff characters for comic books. After he graduated from high school, he worked for a window display company, and made papier-mâché models of story book characters. He designed window displays for both books and toys.

Mr. Sendak became an illustrator for children's books when he was asked to draw the pictures for Marcel Ayme's book, *The*

Wonderful Farm, in 1951. The next year, he illustrated Ruth Krauss's book, *A Hole is to Dig.* These books started his rapidly growing career as an illustrator and author of his own books. Mr. Sendak uses the sketches he made of children to give him ideas for his many books. He also listens to music while he works.

2. Creative Writing—When Maurice Sendak was a boy, he drew pictures of kids playing. Later, he used these pictures to get ideas for his books. Have the children draw pictures of kids on their own sketch pads, then have them use their drawings to motivate their own illustrated story.

3. Creative Writing—Maurice Sendak drew cartoons about the adventures of children who got into trouble at school. Have students pick a comical situation and draw cartoon characters to illustrate the story. Write the dialogue in comic strip form.

4. Creative Writing, Appreciative Listening—Maurice Sendak listens to music while he works. Some of his favorite composers are Mozart, Beethoven, and Wagner. Have students listen to a recording by one of these composers. Have them describe what they visualize while they listen. Then, have them draw a series of pictures motivated by the music. Listen to the music again, and write a story to accompany the pictures.

5. Art Interpretation of Literature—Maurice Sendak designed window displays for new books. Have a group of children select one of Sendak's books and design a bulletin board as if it were a window display in a department or bookstore.

6. Oral Language: Comparisons of Writing, Styles, and Illustrations—Maurice Sendak's books have been compared with the writings of Lewis Carroll and Edward Lear. These writers also use both fantasy and reality. Have older students read a selection by each of these authors. Have them give an oral presentation comparing the author's use of pictures, content of stories, and writing styles.

7. Comparisons of Illustrations and Art Media—Maurice Sendak's illustrations vary from black-and-white pen-and-ink drawings to full-color illustrations. Have children look carefully at the illus-

trations in each book. Have them tell why they feel each type of drawing is effective. (*The Moon Jumpers* uses both black-and-white ink drawings and full-page illustrations that develop the greens and blues of a moolit summer's evening.) After they have examined the author's use of color or black-and-white drawings, have the students experiment with Sendak's art techniques.

8. Art Interpretation—Maurice Sendak constructed papier-mâché models of storybook characters. Ask the students to select their favorite Sendak character and make a papier-mâché model of that character.

9. Creative Drama—After reading *Where the Wild Things Are,* discuss how we often daydream and make ourselves the hero of the story. What kinds of activities do you dream about when you are the hero? Talk about how you would feel if you were sent to your room, what makes you fantasize, and what you would fantasize about. Have the childen act out their dreams in a creative play session.

10. Creative Drama—Have the students make masks depicting the wild things in *Where The Wild Things Are.* Let them be the wild things by wearing the masks. Perform a creative drama of this story and other adventures Max might have during another visit to the wild things.

11. Creative Writing—Have the children pick one of their favorite monsters in *Where the Wild Things Are.* Ask what the monster's name is, what it likes to do, whether it is a good or bad monster, what it thinks about Max, what the child and the monster would do if they met. Have them write stories about their special monsters.

12. Choral Speaking—Read "Pierre: A Cautionary Tale" to the class. Develop a choral arrangement by having the class join in, whenever the repeated line is stated.

HANS CHRISTIAN ANDERSEN—A FAIRY TALE INTEREST CENTER

TYPE		TERM	
CLASS	☐	STA	☐
GROUP	☑	LTA	☐
IND	☑	LC	☑

Purpose:

1. To develop listening comprehension

2. To role play experiences from Hans Christian Andersen's life

3. To develop and perform a creative drama activity

4. To compare the story "The Ugly Duckling" to Hans Christian Andersen's life

5. To write a creative story motivated by fairy tales

6. To interpret a fairy tale through art interpretation

7. To tell a story orally

Materials: Eva Moore's *The Fairy Tale Life of Hans Christian Andersen* (New York: Scholastic Book Services, 1969); Hans Christian Andersen fairy tales; materials for puppets and puppet theater

Grade level: Middle elementary, upper elementary

Procedures:

1. Hans Christian Andersen wrote 156 of the best-loved fairy tales. His life experiences also suggest many language arts related activities. The following background information may be put on a tape or related by the teacher to motivate interest in Hans Christian Andersen:

   Hans Christian Andersen, author of "The Ugly Duckling" and many other fairy tales, was born on April 2, 1805, in Denmark. He was the son of a poor shoemaker. Hans's father didn't have money to buy Hans toys, but he gave him handmade puppets and a puppet theater. He also told Hans marvelous stories. Hans enjoyed dancing and singing, and hoped someday to become an actor. He was very thin, however, and had big feet. He was clumsy, and was frequently told he would never be either an actor or a dancer. He had many unhappy experiences when the other boys, and his teachers, made fun of him at school. He stopped going to school because he was so unhappy. He had friends, though, who felt he had a talent for writing. But they told him that, before he could really become a writer, he would need to go back to school to improve his spelling and grammar. Hans finally finished school, and was happy now because he could do what he had dreamed of. His first book was a success. He also enjoyed telling stories to children, and even put on puppet plays for them. He wrote his own plays for the puppet theater. His first book of fairy tales was called *Fairy Tales Told for Children,* and included "The Princess and the Pea" and "The Tinder Box," Next, he wrote "The Emperor's New Clothes" and "The Little Mermaid." He started publishing a new fairy tale book every year so that both children and adults would have new stories for Christmas. Andersen wrote plays and other books, but it is his fairy tales about the Ugly Duckling, the Steadfast Tin Soldier, Thumbelina, and over 150 other characters that make Hans Christian Andersen loved by grown-ups and children. When Hans was 62 years old, the people of Odense, the town where he was born, gave him a celebration that lasted a whole week. The boy who had been a poor ugly duckling was now cheered by all.

2. Reading for Information, Role Playing—Directions for the students: Read *The Fairy Tale Life of Hans Christian Andersen or* another reference on Hans Christian Andersen's life. Choose one of the following periods of his life:

Five-year-old Hans enjoys his father's puppets
Hans starts school and doesn't enjoy it
Hans's father makes red dancing shoes
Hans meets the Danish Prince
Hans tries to become a dancer, an actor, and a singer in the city of Copenhagen
Hans goes back to school so he can learn to write, and has problems with Master Meisling
Hans becomes a writer
Hans goes to his celebration in Odense

With a partner, decide which of you will play the role of Hans Christian Andersen and which of you will play the role of a newspaper reporter. Role play an experience in which a reporter is interviewing Hans about a period in his life. Change roles and become the other person in your role playing.

3. Creative Drama—Directions for the students: Choose a period in Hans Christian Andersen's life. With a group of four other stu-

dents, pretend you are filming a "You Are There" episode for a television program. With your group, present your interpretation of that period in Andersen's life to the rest of the class. (You want your presentation to be authentic, so be sure to do research on life in Denmark in the 1800s. What did the people wear? How did the people travel? What did the cities look like? What did a school look like? What did the people do for entertainment?)

4. Critical Thinking—Directions for the students: Read Hans Christian Andersen's "The Ugly Duckling." You already know a great deal about Andersen's life and the unhappiness he suffered, as well as his moments of happiness. Can you compare Andersen and the ugly duckling? Was Andersen ever considered an ugly duckling? Why? What happened in Andersen's later life that is similar to what happened to the Ugly Duckling? Write a short paper on your comparison between "The Ugly Duckling" and Andersen's life.

5. Critical Thinking, Oral Discussion—Directions for the students: "The Ugly Duckling" and "Cinderella" are similar in many ways. Read "Cinderella" and compare it to the "Ugly Duckling." How is the ugly duckling like Cinderella? How were the ugly duckling and Cinderella treated? How did they feel about their treatment? What happens to the Ugly Duckling and to Cinderella at the end of their stories? Is there anything about Hans Christian Andersen's life that resembles Cinderella? Why would he write from the viewpoint of the poor person in Cinderella? After you have thought about the answers to these questions, share your reactions, in an oral discussion, with the rest of the class.

6. Creative Writing—Directions for the students: After reading "Thumbelina," imagine what your life would be like if you were only as big as your thumb. Write a creative story describing the experiences you might have during one day in your life.

THE EMPEROR'S BOUTIQUE

7. Art Interpretation—Directions for the students: The emperor in "The Emperor's New Clothes" thought he had the most beautiful clothes in the kingdom. Read this story, and draw a picture

showing what you think the emperor's clothes would look like if they were really the most beautiful clothes in the kingdom. Place your drawings on a bulletin board showing the "Emperor's Boutique."

8. Creative Drama—Hans Christian Andersen thoroughly enjoyed writing and presenting puppet productions to children. Provide an opportunity for your students to divide into groups, choose an Andersen fairy tale, and develop the story as a puppet production. Present the story to the rest of the class.

9. Oral Language, Story Telling—Hans Christian Andersen enjoyed listening to stories as a small child, and he also spent hours telling stories to children. Prepare an Andersen fairy tale to tell to the class. After your presentation, allow the class members to choose a fairy tale and tell the story to a group of classmates.

10. Creative Writing—Directions to the students: Andersen often gave inanimate objects lifelike qualities so these characters would seem more real to children. An example of an inanimate object that has life is "The Steadfast Tin Soldier." Read the story, then choose an object or toy you could write a story about. When you are finished, share your story with the class, then place it on the creative writing bulletin board.

CAROL RYRIE BRINK'S *CADDIE WOODLAWN*—AN INTEREST CENTER FOR HISTORICAL FICTION

TYPE		TERM	
CLASS	☐	STA	☐
GROUP	☑	LTA	☐
IND	☑	LC	☑

Purpose:
1. To listen to a tape about the author, Carol Ryrie Brink, and answer questions about the author
2. To develop the oral language skill of interviewing
3. To interpret a literature character
4. To develop reference skills
5. To interpret a scene through creative writing
6. To write a creative story motivated by literature
7. To read for comprehension of detail
8. To read for the purpose of evaluation
9. To interpret literature through an art medium
10. To develop discussion skills through value clarification activities
11. To develop math skills

Materials: Carol Ryrie Brink's *Caddie Woodlawn* (New York: Scholastic Book Services, 1975); reference books describing samplers, candle making, early transportation, and Indian villages; tape and tape recorder; writing materials, construction paper, and art materials for modeling an Indian camp; several catalogues showing prices of candy, tops, combs, and handkerchiefs

Grade level: Third through fifth grades

Procedures:
1. Record information about the author, Carol Ryrie Brink, on a tape, or type the information on cards or paper. Tell the students

that, after listening to this tape, they should be able to answer the following questions: (1) How is Carol Ryrie Brink related to Caddie Woodlawn? (2) How did Mrs. Brink gain her knowledge about Caddie's adventures? (3) Why did Mrs. Brink write *Caddie Woodlawn*? (4) is *Caddie Woodlawn* a true story?

Suggested information for tape:

Carol Ryrie Brink had a very special reason for writing *Caddie Woodlawn*. The heroine of the book was Mrs. Brink's grandmother. When Mrs. Brink was eight years old, she went to live with her grandmother. Her grandmother, Caddie, told her many stories about growing up in Wisconsin in the 1800s. During Mrs. Brink's childhood, she amused herself by drawing, writing, reading, and telling herself long stories.

When Mrs. Brink was an adult, she remembered the stories of Caddie's childhood, and thought other children would also like to read them. She wrote *Caddie Woodlawn* while her grandmother was still alive. She wrote letters to her grandmother to ask questions about details she could not remember.

Carol Ryrie Brink says the facts in *Caddie Woodlawn* are mostly true. Some of the facts are changed slightly to fit the story. *Caddie Woodlawn* won the Newbery Medal for the best children's book in 1936.

2. Oral Language, Interviewing, Writing—Carol Brink wrote *Caddie Woodlawn* because she enjoyed her grandmother's stories. Ask the children to interview older relatives or other older people in the community. In their interviews, they should ask people to retell experiences they remember from childhood, or stories they heard from their grandparents. During the interviews, the students can also gather information about what these people did for entertainment, how they traveled, where they got their food, how they dressed, and what toys they played with. Have the children share their information orally with the rest of the class, or write stories using the information. Develop a bulletin board to display the stories.

3. Oral Characterization—Ask the students to choose a character from *Caddie Woodlawn* and tell about that character as if they were that person. Allow other children to guess the identity of the character. Some of the characters in the book are Caddie, Mr. Woodlawn, Minnie, Indian John, Hetty, Tom, Mr. Tanner, Mrs. Woodlawn, Warren, and Uncle Edmund.

4. Reference Skills, Oral Language—Caddie played in the woods with her brothers, Tom and Warren, rather than making samplers or dipping candles like the other girls did. Have the children investigate how a sampler is made, or the processs for dipping candles. Ask a research group to explain the process to the rest of the class.

5. Creative Drama—Allow a group of students to choose a scene from *Caddie Woodlawn* to dramatize for the rest of the class. Allow students to work in groups so they will experience the roles of both player and audience. Some scenes for this activity might be: Caddie dropping the nuts on the floor in front of the Circuit Rider; Caddie riding to the Indian camp to warn the Indians of an intended attack; the prairie fire that almost destroys the school house; or Uncle Edmund talking the family into taking Nero to St. Louis.

6. Creative Writing—Caddie was frightened when she rode through the night to warn Indian John about the men who were going to attack the Indians. Ask the children to think about a time when they were frightened. How did they feel? What were their thoughts? How did they overcome their fear? Have the children write a story about a frightening experience they have had.

7. Creative Writing—Have the students choose a favorite chapter from *Caddie Woodlawn*. Ask them to pretend they are Caddie, and write a diary entry for that chapter.

8. Reading for Details—After reading *Caddie Woodlawn*, have students complete the following chart with drawings that show details for each category.

LIFE IN WISCONSIN IN 1864		
Clothing	Transportation	Home Furnishings
Entertainment	Education	Food

9. Evaluative Reading—Place in the learning center several reference and history books that give factual descriptions of the 1860s. Ask students to compare their readings about the historical period with the picture of daily life presented in the book. Are the historical facts accurate in *Caddie Woodlawn?* Make a list of accurate facts and a list of any inaccurate information.

10. Reference and Art—Caddie has a special friend named Indian Joe. Caddie even visits the Indian camp. Provide several reference books describing the Indians who lived in that part of Wisconsin. Students can read reference material about these Indians, then design and build a model of an authentic Indian camp.

11. Map Skills—Nero, the Woodlawn's dog, goes on a long trip with Uncle Edmund. They travel in a steamship all the way from Downsville to St. Louis. Nero runs away after he reaches St. Louis, and finally reaches his home in Wisconsin.
    a. Look at a map of the United States. Draw in the route Nero and Uncle Edmund followed to reach St. Louis.
    b. On page 53 of the Scholastic Book Services edition, there is a river named that is not near Downsville. What is the current name of the river on which Nero and Uncle Edmund started their journey?

NERO'S JOURNEY

c. Now look at the map again. Imagine the route that Nero traveled on his lonely trip back to Wisconsin. What states did he go through? What was the country like? Draw in the route you think he followed.

12. Several types of transportation characteristic of the 1860s are mentioned in *Caddie Woodlawn:* Indian canoes, horses, steamships, horse-drawn wagons, rafts. Provide reference pictures and books describing these forms of transportation. Ask children to construct a mobile illustrating these early means of travel.

13. Discussion, Values Clarification—Caddie makes some major decisions in the process of growing up. The following experiences can be used for discussion. The children should also relate personal experiences they have had in similar circumstances.

    a. Do you believe it would have been all right for the settlers to attack the Indians because the settlers thought the Indians were going to attack them? Why or why not? Did Caddie do the right thing when she warned Indian Joe? Who do you believe showed the most courage, Caddie or the settlers? Why? What would you have done if you had been Caddie? Have you ever had an experience in which someone thought you were going to do something harmful? What would happen if we always acted out of fear, or believed everything we heard?

    b. Caddie spent her valued dollar on gifts for three Indian children because she wanted to "drive that awful lonesome look out of their eyes." Do you believe Caddie acted correctly when she bought the gifts for the Indian boys? Why or why not? What would you have done if you were Caddie?

14. Math, Comparison of Values—Caddie spent her dollar for candy and other gifts for the Indian boys. List the gifts on a card, and ask the children to investigate the cost of buying similar items today.

CADDIE'S GIFTS	1864	198__
Hoarhound sticks (enough for 3 children)	?	
Striped peppermint sticks (enough for 3)	?	
Pink wintergreens (enough for 3)	?	
Three tops	?	
Three combs (good quality)	30¢	
Three large turkey-red handkerchiefs	30¢	
Total	$1.00	

THE SALEM WITCH-HUNTS—
A HISTORICAL FICTION UNIT

TYPE		TERM	
CLASS	☑	STA	☐
GROUP	☑	LTA	☑
IND	☐	LC	☐

Purpose:

1. To compare and discuss two pieces of historical fiction on the New England witch-hunts

2. To write a diary from the viewpoint of an accused witch

3. To write a comparison of the facts in a fictional story and a factual account

4. To write a creative article for a classroom newspaper

5. To orally interpret and present a character from the witch-hunts

6. To investigate, create, and act out a Salem witch trial

7. To create a puppet show that demonstrates fear of an unusual person

8. To investigate superstition versus scientific facts

9. To interpret folk literature through an art medium

10. To debate the position that physical characteristics do or do not determine character

11. To write a business letter

12. To critically evaluate and compare two periods in history characterized by a mania for persecution

Materials:

Historical Fiction:

Minshell, Evelyn White. *Dune Witch*. Westminister Press, 1972. (A girl's appearance and lilting voice cause villagers to believe she is a witch.)

Petry, Ann. *Tituba of Salem Village*. Cromwell, 1964. (Tituba, a slave from Barbados, lives through the terrifying days of the Salem witch trials.)

Speare, Elizabeth George. *The Witch of Blackbird Pond*. Houghton Mifflin, 1958. (This Newbery award-winner describes the experiences of Kit Tyler as she befriends a suspected witch and later is the subject of a terrifying witch-hunt and trial.)

Other useful references:

Alderman, Clifford Lindsey. *The Devil's Shadow: The Story of Witchcraft in Massachusetts*. Messner, 1967. (Presents the details of the witch-hunts, which began with accusations of several hysterical girls and led to the death or imprisonment of several hundred accused witches. There is a chapter on possible explanations for the witch hysteria.)

Alderman, Clifford Lindsey. *Witchcraft in America*. Messner, 1974.

Black, William George. *Folk Medicine*. Burt Franklin, 1970.

Jackson, Shirley. *The Witchcraft of Salem Village*. Random House, 1956.

Grade level:	Upper elementary, middle school

Motivation for the unit:	Elizabeth George Speare's fictional *The Witch of Blackbird Pond* could provide motivation for a unit on the Salem witch-hunts. This book describes Kit Tyler's experiences when she comes to live with her Puritan cousins in Connecticut. Kit befriends an old woman who is suspected of being the witch of Blackbird Pond. Kit is finally arrested and tried for witchcraft; she is saved, following an exciting climax.

In addition to this historical fiction, the teacher can provide related facts to provoke interest in the subject, among them:

a. During the late 1600s, many people were accused of witchcraft in Massachusetts and Connecticut.
b. The famous witch-hunt which took place in Salem in 1692 started when a doctor stated that several hysterical teenage-girls' behavior was due to the "evil eye." Within 6 months of this accusation, 20 persons were sentenced to death and 150 were sent to prison.
c. The Boston minister Cotton Mather spread interest in trials when he wrote *Wonders of the Invisible World* (1963).
d. Judge Samuel Sewall finally became conscience-stricken and asked forgiveness for his mistakes.
e. Belief in witchcraft faded in the 1700s, when people gained more scientific understanding of previously frightening phenomena.

Introduction of unit:	A "time tunnel" can be made from a large box and placed at the door of the classroom. As the children enter the room, they are told they are entering Salem Village during the year 1693. There should be several props in the room to remind students of Puritan days (more props

can be added during the unit). Numerous pictures and reference books should be on display.

Procedures:	Language Arts:

1. Creative Writing—Tell the students to: "Read several accounts of witch-hunts in both fictional books and factual references. Write a diary, pretending you are being accused of witchcraft. Include descriptions of the people and the surroundings, events leading to the accusation, the trial proceedings, your personal feelings, and the conclusion of your experience."

2. Written Composition—Tell the students to: "Read a fictional story about the witch trials. Now, read about the witch trials in a history book and an encyclopedia. Write a two-page paper comparing the facts presented in the fictional story to those in the encyclopedia and history book."

3. Creative Writing—Develop a class newspaper titled *The Salem Post* or *The Salem Times*. Some of the students may play the reporters' role, and interview classmates who are accused persons, jury members, eyewitnesses to strange happenings, or judges. Students may write editorials concerning the witch-hunts, and factual stories based on reference materials. Other sections of the paper might include a foods section, with recipes from Puritan times; a home section, describing the interiors of Puritan homes; or a fashion section, illustrating the dress of the Puritan period.

4. Oral Language—Tell the students to: "Choose a character from research in the Salem witch-hunts. Dress as that character, and tell his or her story to the class from that character's point of view." Possible characters for this activity are Kit Tyler, from *The Witch of Blackbird Pond;* Hannah Typper, the suspected witch from the same book; Cotton Mather, the Boston minister; or Judge Samuel Sewall, the Massachusetts judge who eventually begs forgiveness for his mistakes.

5. Creative Drama—After reading about the Salem witch trials, have the students perform a mock trial, with the accused, the judge, the witch jury and the witnesses.

6. Creative Drama—The Salem witch-hunts emphasized people's fear of those who are different or unusual. Develop a puppet show about what might happen when people do not understand someone who is different, and show how fear of an unusual person is overcome.

7. Critical Thinking and Discussion—The subject of *The Witch of Blackbird Pond* is similar to *Tituba of Salem Village*. The two stories, however, have a very different tone. Kit is a high-spirited cousin who comes to live with relatives, while Tituba is a black slave who belongs to a pious minister and lives under constant

suspicion. Have students read these two stories dealing with the persecution of people who do not follow Puritan beliefs, then lead a discussion comparing the two books. Topics for discussion include the causes and effects of persecution in each story, a comparison of the authors' styles, a comparison of each story's effect on the reader, and a discussion of the results of persecution in more modern times.

Science-related Language Arts:

Many of the medical "cures" or charms used in Puritan days were based on superstition. Some of the people accused of witchcraft engaged in this type of medical practice, or developed charms for various reasons. A study of these cures provides opportunities for verifying scientific facts versus superstition, developing oral language skills, and developing written composition skills.

1. Reference Skills—An early cure for a cough required shaving the patient's head and placing the hair in a bush where birds would carry the hair away. When the birds took the hair, they were also believed to take the cough away from the patient. Have students investigate how a cough is cured today. Which method is more realistic? Why?

2. Interpreting Folk Literature, Oral Expression—Folk medicine used the numbers three and nine. A child with whooping cough was passed under a three-year-old donkey three times, and passed over the donkey three times for nine successive mornings. Have students investigate the significance of the numbers three and nine in folklore and present their findings to the class.

3. Interpreting Folk Literature—The phases of the moon were believed to influence health. A cure of asthma required the patient to walk three times around the house at midnight during a full moon. To cure rickets, a lock of a child's hair was buried at a crossroad when the full moon was shining. Read several stories from folk literature that have themes about superstitions related to the moon. Develop a bulletin board about superstitions and health cures related to the moon.

4. Using References, Developing a Journal—Have the students develop a medical journal, listing the folk cure for the ailment on one page and describing the recommended modern cure on the facing page. For example:

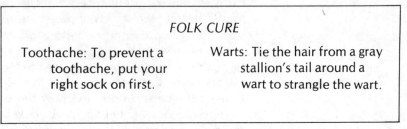

FOLK CURE

Toothache: To prevent a toothache, put your right sock on first.

Warts: Tie the hair from a gray stallion's tail around a wart to strangle the wart.

```
┌─────────────────────────────────────────────────────────┐
│                  MODERN MEDICINE CURE                     │
│                                                           │
│   Toothache:                    Wart:                     │
│                                                           │
│                                                           │
└─────────────────────────────────────────────────────────┘
```

5. Written Composition—Girls went to witches to seek love charms, or to learn the identity of their future husbands. Have students investigate folklore to discover love charms. Make a class love charm booklet. These examples may be used for a beginning:
   a. When a girl ate salt herring, walked backwards, and went to bed immediately, she would dream about her future husband.
   b. When a snail is placed on the cold ashes in a fireplace, the snail will write the initials of the future husband.
   c. If a girl eats an apple on Halloween while looking in a mirror, she will see her future husband over her shoulder.

6. Oral Language, Debate—Superstitions often related to physical characteristics. For example, teeth were considered an index to a person's character. Large teeth were believed to be a sign of strength, and small, regular teeth showed a perfectionist. If teeth were set apart, the person was prosperous. Eyebrows were also thought to relate to character. If a person had eyebrows that met across the nose, the person was considered unlucky and deceitful. Have the students find examples of other physical characteristics that have been used to describe personality. Ask if they believe they are justified. Why or why not? Have them present their findings during a class debate. One team of debaters will take the position that physical characteristics show a person's character; the other team will argue that physical characteristics do not determine character.

Social Studies-related Language Arts Activities:

1. Letter Writing, Oral Language—Have students write a letter to the Salem Chamber of Commerce asking for information about restoration of the historic section of this city and points of interest. Have a small group of students prepare an oral report illustrating the points of interest the class should see if it were to visit historic Salem.

2. Critical Thinking, Reference, Oral Discussion—The Salem witchhunts illustrate the effects of persecution, fear, and lack of understanding. Choose another period in history, such as the persecution of Jews In Nazi Germany, and read a book of historical fiction from that period, verifying the facts in an encyclopedia or history book. Compare causes of the persecution, personal reactions to the persecution, and how the persecution or conditions were resolved. (Marilyn Sach's A Pocket Full of Seeds and Esther Jautzig's The Endless Steppe are useful for this activity.)

STORYTELLING

TYPE		TERM	
CLASS	☑	STA	☑
GROUP	☑	LTA	☐
IND	☐	LC	☐

Purpose:
1. To select an appropriate story for storytelling
2. To prepare a story for telling
3. To tell a story to an appreciative audience

Materials: Stories suitable for storytelling

Grade level: Upper elementary, middle school

Procedures:
1. After you have told several stories to the class, discuss possible advantages of telling a story rather than reading a story.

2. Discuss the selection of a story for telling with the children. List several characteristics of good stories for oral telling. For example:
   a. Folk tales are good because they were originally told orally.
   b. Choose a story with a strong beginning that will quickly interest your listeners.
   c. The story should contain action.
   d. The story should contain only a few characters.
   e. The story should have a definite climax.
   f. The story should have a satisfactory ending.

3. Discuss with the students the procedures storytellers use to prepare a story. They do not memorize their story, but they do go through the following steps:
   a. Read the story completely about three times.
   b. List mentally the sequence of events in the story.
   c. Re-read the story, taking note of forgotten events.
   d. Go over the main events again, and add the details; then think about the meaning of the events.
   e. Tell the story before a mirror.
   f. Practice two or three more times, then try using vocal pitch changes to show changes in characters.

g. Use changes in posture or hand gestures to represent different characters.
h. Use pauses to separate scenes.

4. Discuss with the students the ways they can introduce their stories; for example:
a. Ask a question.
b. Tell why you choose that story.
c. Tell something interesting about the author.
d. Provide background information about a country or a period in history.
e. Display objects related to the book or story.

5. Have the students practice telling their stories to each other in small groups. When they feel confident, ask them to tell their stories to a group of younger children. (Teachers of lower elementary children are usually cooperative, and the older students enjoy such an attentive and appreciative audience.)

8 Media Activities

It has been estimated that by the time most students graduate from high school, they will have spent 11,000 hours in class and 15,000 hours watching television.[1] There is growing criticism of television programs for children, and much concern over declining achievement scores, the model presented by television, and the passive nature of the television viewer.

We need not consider the existence of television, however, as entirely negative. A responsible teacher can present children with activities that utilize their television viewing habits to motivate reading, creative drama, and creative writing. Media activities can help a child develop selective viewing habits and critically evaluate what he sees. Analysis of television commercials, in particular, provides instruction in critical listening and identification of the persuasive techniques that bombard the viewing public. Television programs and commercials can be powerful tools for instruction.

The television-related activities in this chapter investigate children's television interests; survey actual time spent watching television; instruct in selective viewing; motivate reading; evaluate fantasy and factual presentations; identify commercials seen during children's programming; and evaluate persuasive techniques used in public interest commercials.

Films are another medium that can stimulate language arts, through creative drama, creative writing, discussion, and reading. Experimentation with film and film production allows students to communicate in this medium as well as in writing and oral expression. The film-related activities in this chapter utilize cartoons and other films to develop appreciative listening; listening comprehension; art interpretation; oral discussion; creative writing; creative movement; media interpretation through filmmaking; group investigations and oral reporting; critical evaluation of cartoon versions and original book versions of stories; creative dramatizations; and character analysis.

A third extremely influential medium that can be used as an educational aid is the newspaper. Newspapers provide dynamic, up-to-date instructional materials. A newspaper covers a wide variety of interests—news, editorials, business, society, sports, fashions, and entertainment. Newspapers provide factual material, as well as material classified as opinion or even propaganda. A newspaper thus provides material not only for functional reading activities but also for critical evaluation activities. The activities in the newspaper section of this chapter develop categorizing skills; introduce students to the newspaper; develop vocabulary and thinking skills through a study of the significance of newspaper and magazine names; interpret a book through newspaper format; study headlines as main ideas and relate them to fairy tales; develop critical evaluation through comparative shopping; study advertising techniques designed to appeal to a specific population; critically evaluate fact versus fiction and fact versus opinion; and study and survey the newspaper- and magazine-reading habits of adults and students.

INVESTIGATING VIEWING INTERESTS AND HABITS

TYPE		TERM	
CLASS	☑	STA	☑
GROUP	☐	LTA	☐
IND	☐	LC	☐

Purpose: 1. To identify children's television viewing interests and habits

Materials: Television Interest Inventory

Grade level: All grades; should be read individually to young children, whose answers are written down by the teacher; students who can read and write their own answers may complete their own inventories.

Procedures: 1. Administer the following interest inventory to the class:
   a. Do you watch television? Yes _____ No _____
   b. If you do, what kinds of programs do you like to watch?

   cartoons _____   detective shows _____
   news _____   police shows _____
   game shows _____   westerns _____
   mysteries _____   science shows _____
   comedy _____   stories about families _____
   science fiction _____   animal programs _____
   music _____   educational TV _____
   sports _____   other _____
   specials _____   _____

   c. What are your favorite television shows? _____

   _____

   _____

   d. Who are your favorite characters on television? _____

   _____

   _____

   e. Do you watch any educational television programs? Yes _____
   No _____
   f. If you watch educational television how often do you watch it?

   _____

g. What are your favorite educational television programs?
_____
_____

h. How many hours do you watch television after school? _____
i. How many hours do you watch television on Saturday? _____
j. When you watch television, do you watch the programs with your parents? _____
k. Have you ever read a book about a television show? Yes _____
   No _____
   Which ones? _____
   _____

l. Have you seen any television programs about subjects you would like to learn more about? Yes _____ No _____
m. If your answer is yes, which subjects would you like to know more about? _____
   _____

n. How do you choose the programs you are going to watch?
   _____

o. Are there any kinds of programs you do not like? _____
   Which kind? _____

2. Compile the information to obtain an overview of the television interests of your class. This information can be used to motivate individual children's reading and writing, to stimulate creative activities with the group, and to develop critical evaluation activities.

SURVEY OF TIME SPENT WATCHING TELEVISION AND PROGRAMS WATCHED

TYPE		TERM	
CLASS	☑	STA	☐
GROUP	☐	LTA	☑
IND	☐	LC	☐

Purpose:

1. To compute time spent watching television during one week

2. To compute time spent watching different kinds of television programs

3. To compare time actually spent watching television with previously stated interests

Materials:

Mimeographed sheets for listing television programs watched and time spent on each program

Grade level:

All grades

Procedures:

1. Discuss with the class how they could discover exactly what programs they watch during the week and how much time they spend watching television.

2. Develop a mimeographed sheet the children can fill in easily with the programs they watch and the time they spend watching each program. The log might look like this:

Television Programs Watched on (*Weekday After School*)

Time	Name of Program	Minutes Spent Watching	Kind of Show
4:00	_____	_____	_____
4:30	_____	_____	_____
5:00	_____	_____	_____
5:30	_____	_____	_____
6:00	_____	_____	_____
6:30	_____	_____	_____
7:00	_____	_____	_____
7:30	_____	_____	_____

8:00 _____ _____ _____

8:30 _____ _____ _____

Total Time Spent Watching Television: _____

Another worksheet should be developed for the weekends, since possible viewing times cover a more extensive period.

3. As a group activity, compose a letter to the children's parents explaining the purpose of the television viewing survey and the procedures the children should follow for keeping the daily logs. Younger children who cannot write the names of the programs independently will need to ask their parents to help them complete their surveys.

4. Have students fill out the daily viewing survey.

5. After completing the week's survey, determine the total number of hours of each child's television viewing; average the number of television hours watched by the total class; determine the number of hours spent by each child in viewing specific types of television; average the number of television hours spent watching specific types of television shows for the total class. For example:

_____ Grade Television Viewing

a. Average number of hours watched each week = _____

b. Average number of hours (minutes) spent in watching each kind of television program.

cartoons _____	detective shows _____
news _____	police shows _____
game shows _____	westerns _____
mysteries _____	science shows _____
comedy _____	stories about families _____
science fiction _____	animal programs _____
music _____	educational TV _____
sports _____	other _____
specials _____	_____

c. Television shows watched by the greatest number in the class.

1st = _____

2nd = _____

3rd = _____

4th = _____

5th = _____

6. Finally, compare the number of hours actually spent in viewing specific types of programs with the information obtained on the television interest inventory. Do the stated interests on the inventory match the viewing habits of the children? If they do not, discuss possible reasons for these discrepancies.

USING A GUIDE FOR SELECTIVE VIEWING

TYPE		TERM	
CLASS	☑	STA	☐
GROUP	☐	LTA	☑
IND	☐	LC	☐

Purpose:
1. To understand that planning can help a viewer find programs of interest or merit
2. To understand that television viewing should be selective
3. To locate specific information using a television guide

Materials:
Weekly television guide from the local Sunday newspaper or *TV Guide* magazine; mimeographed viewing suggestions and scheduling worksheet

Grade level:
Second grade through middle school

Procedures:
1. Introduce the television guide to the children. Discuss the purposes for printing and reading a television guide. "What information can you learn from the television guide? Why would you want to use the guide?"

2. Look at the different sections of the television guide. "Is there a table of contents? How would the table of contents help us locate information? How is the television guide arranged?" Ask children to find the table of contents. Using the table of contents, ask them to find the programs scheduled for Tuesday, etc. After they find a specific day, ask questions demanding that they locate information on the schedule for that day. "At what time do the television stations start broadcasting? What is the first program shown in our area? What is the last program shown in our area? How does the television guide indicate the number of the television channel?" (Find an example of this number.) "How many different channels are listed in the television guide?" (Have students find examples of each channel.) "How is the daily television guide divided so that it is easier to find programs?" (The day is divided into half-hour time segments starting at 6:00, and continuing until the stations go off the air.) Ask specific questions that require students

to use both the television station number and the time period. For example: "What programs are on at 8:30 on Tuesday evening? On what channel is each program? Find a comedy show listed on Tuesday evening. Find a science program about the planet Mars. When could you watch a news program on Tuesday?" Have the children ask each other questions about the time or subject matter for specific programs.

3. Ask the students if any information in the television guide will help them find programs of special interest or special merit. Discuss sections such as those describing recommended programs for the week, special sports programs, special children's programs, etc. Discuss how this information can help a family choose the best television programs to watch during the week.

4. Discuss the fact that many people fear children watch too many poorly-selected programs. Develop with the children a list of positive reasons for watching television and a list of negative results of too much television viewing; for example:

Watching Television is Good Because:

a. TV provides entertainment
b. TV shows us pictures of places we have never been
c. We can learn about new subjects on TV
d. We can learn about what is happening in the world
e. We can see and hear famous people
f. We can talk about what we see on television

Watching Too Much Television Is Bad Because:

a. If we do not spend enough time studying, our grades will not be good
b. We may not have time to read if we watch television all the time
c. We will not do things with our families, such as play games, go on trips, and talk
d. Some programs are too violent
e. We will not play outside with our friends and family

5. With the class, develop several recommendations for appropriate television viewing that allows opportunities to see the best shows, but still allows plenty of time for activities with family and friends, as well as time for homework and other chores.

Our Television Viewing Suggestions

Do: a. Select good shows your whole family wants to watch
b. Read the TV guide and plan your viewing
c. Turn the TV off when you are not watching a selected show

    d. Learn more about a TV subject by reading a book about it
    e. Talk about the good programs you see with your family
    f. Read a book about your favorite TV character

Don't: a. Leave the TV on when there is not a personally selected program
    b. Become a TV addict
    c. Always watch TV alone
    d. Watch TV when you are studying
    e. Choose TV instead of a book, game, or other family activity

6. After selecting several television viewing suggestions, have the students discuss their television viewing recommendations with their parents. (Compose a class letter explaining the purpose of this activity and asking for parental cooperation.) Then, ask them to develop a TV viewing schedule with their parents for the week This schedule should allow them to see special programs of interest, but still leave time for school work, sports, playing with friends, etc. These television scheduling forms may be mimeographed and presented to each child.

My Special Television Schedule for the Week

Name _____

Title of Program	Day	Time	Station
_____	____	____	_____
_____	____	____	_____
_____	____	____	_____
_____	____	____	_____
_____	____	____	_____
_____	____	____	_____

_____
Parent's Signature

7. During class discussion, talk about the children's impressions of and reactions to some of the television programs selected by a majority of the class. Allow individual children to tell why they and their families chose a certain program. Did they have special interests? Had they read a book about the story? Had they visited a special location? If they could have chosen just one television program to watch during that week, which one would they have chosen? Why?

USING TELEVISION TO MOTIVATE READING—PART I

TYPE		TERM	
CLASS	☑	STA	☐
GROUP	☑	LTA	☑
IND	☐	LC	☐

Purpose:

1. To enjoy listening to television-related stories

2. To enjoy reading television-related stories

3. To compare a television presentation to a book presentation

4. To create a dramatic presentation of a television production and related stories

5. To produce creative writing after seeing a television production and reading related stories

Materials:

Television-related picture books, such as *Winnie-the-Pooh,* the Dr. Seuss stories, *Rikki-Tikki-Tavi, Charlie Brown,* books about Sesame Street characters; box cut to show a roll story; roll of paper for the story; puppet theater and materials for puppets

Grade level:

Lower elementary

Procedures:

1. This activity may be used with any book-related television special or series; the teacher needs to be aware of television programs to be shown in the area.

2. Create an attractive display of television-related stories or a display of books relating to a specific television program. As part of the display, design a bulletin board with spaces the children can fill in after seeing the television presentation and reading the story. A bulletin board might be developed prior to a television production of Winnie-the-Pooh.

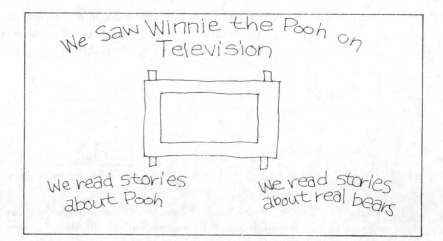

3. Introduce the book display table and the bulletin board to the children. Show them that the handmade television screen does not have anything drawn on the roll of paper. Ask them what they think is missing. Explain to the class that they will make their own television show and draw pictures to fill in the rest of the bulletin board, after the television production and after they read or listen to other stories about Winnie-the-Pooh.

4. Ask children to watch the television presentation of the book. Tell them to watch carefully so they can make their own television shows the following day.

5. After the television production, discuss the story with the children. Allow them to describe the characters, the settings, the action, and their reactions to the program. After they have all had an opportunity to respond, ask them to relate the sequence of the story; what happened first, second, etc. Divide the children into groups, and assign each group a portion of the story to illustrate. Divide the roll of paper into sections so that each group has a manageable length of paper to work with. Measure and mark the space for each picture. Have each group determine what illustrations they will draw.

After the sections are completed, tape them together to form a continuous roll story. Place the roll in the box, and allow children to retell the story using the roll story.

6. Read aloud the picture book or story that was shown on television. Discuss differences and similarities between the two presentations—setting, characters, illustrations, descriptions, dialogue, etc. Ask the children what they consider the advantages of each type of presentation.

Why I Like to Watch the TV Story	Why I Like to Read the Book
1. The animals and people look alive.	1. I can read the book when I want to.
2. I like the colors and music.	2. I can learn more about the people in the story.
3. The TV shows me what characters look like.	3. I can use my imagination and think about what the story looks like.
4. I don't have to ask anyone for help with words.	4. I can ask someone to read the story to me.
5. I like the action on TV.	5. I can read the story to my little brother. This makes me feel good.

7. Read aloud, and allow children to read other stories about the television presentation. For example, there are numerous Winnie-the-Pooh stories other than those that have been shown on television. Allow groups of children to select their favorite Pooh stories. Make puppets of the characters and present the story to the rest of the class. A dismantled television set can become a puppet theater for television tie-ins—when the back and inside of the set are removed, the shell forms a box with an opening in the front. Children enjoy acting out and viewing their own television

shows. One class of first graders named its own classroom television station and set the dial on that number.

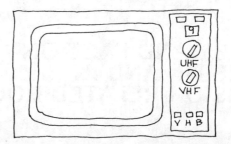

8. After the children have seen the TV show, listened to oral presentations of books, and read related stories, give them an opportunity to write creative stories. Several motivational methods may be used. For example, you can read a portion of a story they have not read. Stop at an exciting place, and allow the children to finish the story. Or, you can ask them to pretend they are going to meet one of the main characters and have an adventure together—Where will they go? Who will they meet? Will they have problems? What will they do? Share their finished stories orally with a group of children.

ACTIVITY 8-5:
FANTASY AND FACT ON TELEVISION AND IN TELEVISION-RELATED BOOKS

TYPE		TERM	
CLASS	☑	STA	☐
GROUP	☑	LTA	☑
IND	☐	LC	☐

Purpose:
1. To identify characteristics of television and television-related books that are fantasy and those that are factual

2. To compare factual presentations with fantasy

3. To motivate reading for evaluation of fantasy and factual writing and viewing

4. To motivate factual reading and writing following an enjoyable television story

Materials:
Television-related picture story books (e.g., Winnie-the-Pooh); factual picture books and magazines depicting real bears, rabbits, tigers, pigs, owls, etc.; film of real animals, or a zoo trip to see real animals.

Grade level:
Lower elementary

Procedures:
1. This activity is an extension of the previous activity, in which children read television-related stories. The example, Winnie-the-Pooh is a fantasy, and can be used to stimulate an interest in real animals and in the realization that fantasy stories are quite different from factual stories.

2. Provide factual picture books about the animal seen in the television fantasy. Ask the children if they think real animals could do all the things the animals in the television show could do. Ask them to think about the television show, the books they read, and their own creative dramas and stories. "Which parts were real and which parts were make believe?" Ask them to think about a real pet they have at home. "How is that pet different from the animals in our story? Why can the television show and the stories show animals talking, living in their own furnished houses, and

wearing clothes?" Ask the children to list the animals they saw and read about in their stories. Explain to the children that they will be learning more about the exciting real lives of these animals. Have them compile a list of questions they would like to have answered about each animal. Put their questions on a chart.

WHAT I WOULD LIKE TO KNOW ABOUT REAL BEARS	WHAT I WOULD LIKE TO KNOW ABOUT REAL TIGERS
1. Where do real bears live?	1. Where do real tigers live?
2. What do real bears eat—do they like honey?	2. What do real tigers eat?
3. How big are real bears?	3. Do tigers climb trees?
4. Are real bears friendly like Pooh?	4. How big are real tigers?
	5. Would I want a real tiger for a pet?

3. Discuss with the children how they might find answers to their questions. Discuss information found in books about real animals, television shows about real animals (Animals, Animals, Animals; National Geographic; Wild Kingdom, etc.), and from observing real animals in a zoo or on a farm. Show the available books to the students. Allow each child to choose an animal as a subject for further reading and research.

4. Create a bulletin board showing the fantasy and real worlds of the animals:

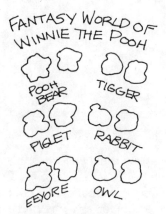

FANTASY WORLD OF WINNIE THE POOH

POOH BEAR   TIGGER

PIGLET   RABBIT

EEYORE   OWL

THE HUNDRED ACRE WOODS

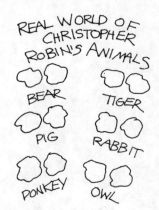

REAL WORLD OF CHRISTOPHER ROBIN'S ANIMALS

BEAR   TIGER

PIG   RABBIT

DONKEY   OWL

THE FOREST, THE JUNGLE, AND THE FARM

5. Write factual paragraphs about the specific animal. Place the factual paragraphs and the fantasy stories on a table below the fantasy and real-world bulletin board. Include examples of related books on this table.

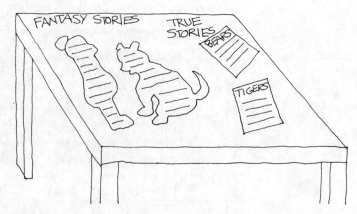

ACTIVITY 8-6:
USING TELEVISION TO
MOTIVATE READING—PART II

TYPE		TERM	
CLASS	☑	STA	☐
GROUP	☑	LTA	☑
IND	☐	LC	☐

Purpose:

1. To enjoy reading television-related stories

2. To compare strengths and weaknesses of a television presentation to the same story in book form

3. To compare the setting, main idea, character development, writing style, and illustrations of television presentations and the same stories in book form

4. To create an original drama after seeing a television presentation

Materials:

Books from which various television series originated, such as *Little House on the Prairie*; books written as a result of a television series; books that will be forthcoming specials, such as *Charlotte's Web, Heidi, Treasure Island, Tom Sawyer,* and *Robin Hood* are repeated yearly as specials, or may appear as short series on educational television

Grade level:

Middle and upper elementary

Procedures:

1. Create a library display of television-related books. Introduce the books to the students, and describe the connection between the book and the television program. (In some cases, a television show is an adaptation of a book; some books are written because of interest in a television series.)

2. Assign the viewing of a book-related television program. Before viewing the show, discuss with students any comparisons they could make between the television presentation and the book, and list items they can look for.

```
THINGS TO LOOK FOR:        TELEVISION     BOOK
  1. Where did the story    _____   _____
     take place?            _____   _____
  2. Did this setting seem  _____   _____
     real to me? Why or why _____   _____
     not?                   _____   _____
  3. Who was the main       _____   _____
     character in the story? _____   _____
  4. Who were the support-  _____   _____
     ing characters in the  _____   _____
     story?                 _____   _____
  5. Did these characters   _____   _____
     seem real to me? Why   _____   _____
     or why not?            _____   _____
  6. What was the main      _____   _____
     idea of the story?     _____   _____
  7. How was the dialogue   _____   _____
     presented?             _____   _____
  8. What did I like best   _____   _____
     about this presenta-   _____   _____
     tion?                  _____   _____
  9. What did I like least  _____   _____
     about this presentation? _____ _____
```

3. After viewing the television story, discuss the "Things to Look For."
   What were the particular strengths and weaknesses of this presentation?

4. Make comparisons between the television presentation and the
   book. Allow students to read the book and answer the same questions they discussed after the television presentation. Find examples in the book of setting, characters, and dialogue. "Are there
   differences in interpretation? Do we know more about the character, setting, or plot after reading the book? Are there differences
   in picture interpretation?"

5. Allow students to divide into groups and choose a television-
   related book. After they read the book, ask the students to present
   a book report as if it were a television presentation. Present the
   report to the rest of the class or to a group of classmates. Encourage students to use any techniques that are effectively used
   on television (costumes, music, sound effects).

ACTIVITY 8-7:
IDENTIFYING COMMERCIALS ON CHILDREN'S TV SHOWS

TYPE		TERM	
CLASS	☑	STA	☑
GROUP	☑	LTA	☐
IND	☐	LC	☐

Purpose:

1. To identify products advertised during programs designed specifically for children

2. To understand that companies advertise different products, depending on audience

Materials:

Tapes of commercials played on several children's programs; mimeographed worksheets for listing products advertised during specific time periods

Grade level:

Lower and middle elementary

Procedures:

1. Tape record the commercials shown during a Saturday morning cartoon show designed specifically for children.

2. Discuss with children the expenses connected with paying actors, directors, film crews, etc. Ask them to think about how the television networks pay for the shows they see. Through discussion, develop the understanding that networks charge advertisers so much money per minute for commercial time. These commercials pay for the production, allowing the networks to present the programs to the viewer without charge.

3. Continue the discussion by talking about what the children believe the advertisers receive in return for their money. "If you were going to spend thousands of dollars for a short commercial, what would you want in return?" Discuss the products advertisers want us to buy.

4. Play tape recordings of the commercials heard during Saturday morning cartoons. Before playing the tape, ask the children, "Who is the audience for Saturday morning cartoons? Who are

the advertisers trying to persuade? What kinds of products would this audience want to buy?" Ask the children to listen to a tape of the advertisements heard during a half-hour cartoon show on Saturday morning. Ask them to listen for the products sold, who is talking during the commercial (the main characters), and what persuasive words they hear on the commercials. Develop a chart of this information:

COMMERCIALS HEARD ON SATURDAY CARTOONS, CHANNEL _____, 9:00–9:30		
Products Advertised	Main Characters	Persuasive Words
1. breakfast cereal	Animated cartoon	mm-mm, delicious
2. a toy	Two boys playing with toy	high speed, great action
3._____	_____	_____
4._____	_____	_____
5._____	_____	_____
6._____	_____	_____

5. After compiling the chart, discuss why these specific products might be included in a children's show, why the advertisers would use animated cartoons and children in the commercials, and why some of the persuasive words might appeal to children.

6. Assign children (with parental permission) to listen to various segments of the Saturday morning cartoon shows. Divide the assignment to include the major networks seen in your area; for example:

	ABC John	CBS Mary	NBC Susan
8:00–8:30	_____	_____	_____
8:30–9:00	_____	_____	_____
9:00–9:30	_____	_____	_____

9:30–10:00	_____	_____	_____
10:00–10:30	_____	_____	_____
10:30–11:00	_____	_____	_____
11:00–11:30	_____	_____	_____
11:30–12:00	_____	_____	_____

7. Provide each child with a mimeographed worksheet for listing the commercials viewed for their assignment. This worksheet should look something like this:

Commercials Heard on _____
(Program)

Saturday Morning at _____
(Time)

On Channel _____
(Network and number)

My Name Is _____

	Product Advertised	Main Characters	Persuasive Words
1.	_____	_____	_____
2.	_____	_____	_____
3.	_____	_____	_____
4.	_____	_____	_____
5.	_____	_____	_____
6.	_____	_____	_____

8. After the assignment in #7, have the children tabulate the number of different products advertised on Saturday cartoons, and the frequency of such advertising. For example:

Kinds of Products Advertised	Number of Advertisements
breakfast cereals	_____
candy	_____
fast food stores	_____
toys, games	_____
bicycles	_____
soda	_____
etc.	_____

9. Have children tabulate the main characters in the ads or the kind of ad presentation. For example:

Who Presented the Ad	Number of Advertisements
animal cartoon	_____
people cartoon	_____
live animals	_____
children	_____
sports heroes	_____
famous actors	_____
etc.	_____

10. Finally, have children list the persuasive vocabulary words they heard. Discuss the meaning of each word. "Do you believe all of these words really describe that product? Why or why not?"

11. Create a bulletin board that illustrates Saturday morning commercials for children. Have the children draw pictures of some of the commercials. Include on the bulletin board some of the facts learned from the commercial survey, and tapes of some of the commercials.

ACTIVITY 8-8:
THE POWER OF PERSUASION— A UNIT OF STUDY

TYPE		TERM	
CLASS	☑	STA	☐
GROUP	☑	LTA	☑
IND	☐	LC	☐

Purpose:

1. To identify propaganda techniques used in commercials shown during children's television programs

2. To critically evaluate propaganda techniques used in television commercials

3. To write original television commercials

4. To dramatize television commercials

Materials:

Transparencies illustrating each type of propaganda technique; tapes of commercials heard during Saturday morning cartoon shows; video tapes of commercials seen during Saturday morning cartoons; worksheet for surveying propaganda techniques found in commercials; questions for team participation; lists of statements that use propaganda techniques and statements that do not

Grade level:

Middle and upper elementary

Procedures:

1. These activities would be a logical extension of the previous activity, in which children identified the products advertised, the type of presentation, and the persuasive words in Saturday morning commercials.

2. Ask the children: "Have you ever had an experience in which you sent for something advertised on television or bought something at a store that was advertised on television?" (Sending for a toy advertised by a cereal sponsor, or buying games, toys, or cereals are examples.) "Did the toy or the item always do what the advertisement led you to believe it could do? Were you ever disappointed because you believe you would get something better than you actually received? What made you believe the product was some-

thing you really wanted or needed?" Allow each child to share his experience with the class.

3. Writers and producers of television commercials use various approaches to persuade the viewer to buy products. Inductively lead children into identification of specific propaganda techniques:

Bandwagon technique:

a. Place the following statements on the chalkboard or on a transparency (fill in the blanks with current names and places):

All the kids on our block chew _____ gum.

Every boy and girl wants this new game for Christmas.

Don't eat any more dull meals, join the gang at the _____.

Everyone who wants to win the race wears _____ shoes.

---

b. Read each statement with the children, and ask if there are similarities among all of the statements. "What is each statement trying to lead us to believe?" (Everyone is doing something, and we should too.) "What are some key words that help persuade us everyone is doing something?"

All the kids
Every boy and girl
Join the gang
Everyone

c. Ask the group if anyone knows what this type of persuasive technique is called. If no one knows, introduce the term "bandwagon." Discuss the reasons why "bandwagon" is a good term for this kind of advertising. Ask the students if they see any bias or falsehood in this kind of advertising. "Does everyone really do what the ad suggests? Even if they did, should you do it too?"

d. Ask students to supply other examples of statements that use the bandwagon approach. Ask them to suggest commercials they think use this approach.

e. Listen to or view tapes of several television commercials that use the bandwagon technique. Ask children to identify which part of the commercials uses bandwagon statements or pictures. "Are these statements all true? Why or why not?"

f. Ask students to draw a picture illustrating a bandwagon commercial. (These pictures may be used to develop a bulletin board or a book on propaganda techniques.) Ask them to write their own definitions of "bandwagon" under their pictures.

Everyone is doing or buying something.
You should do it too.

Testimonials:

a. Place the following statements on the chalkboard or on a transparency (fill in the blanks with current names and products):

_____ _____ the great Olympic swimmer eats _____ for breakfast every morning.

_____ _____ the tennis pro wears _____ tennis shoes.

_____ _____ the child film star uses _____ tooth paste.

_____ _____ gets his energy by eating a _____ bar between meals.

_____ _____ rides a _____ motorcycle.

b. Read these statements with the children and ask them to identify what technique is used in each statement to persuade them to buy something. "What is the advertiser trying to make us believe by telling us that so-and-so eats Greebie cereal for breakfast? Do you believe eating this cereal would make you a great swimmer? Why or why not? Why would the advertiser for tennis shoes choose so-and-so to sell his product? What does this suggest to us? Why do you believe so-and-so might be asked to do a toothpaste commercial? What is the advertiser suggesting might happen if we also use that toothpaste?" Continue asking similar questions about each statement. Stress the connection between the well-known personality, the type of product, and the intended implication to the consumer. Discuss what facts may have been left out of the statements. "Would we need to know all these facts before we could decide about the worthiness of the product?"

c. Ask the students if anyone knows the name for this persuasive advertising technique. Introduce the term, "testimonial." Ask the students to give you a definition for the term "testimonial." (A respected or well-known person tries to influence the buyer by saying he uses something. It is often suggested that we will have some of the same benefits if we also use the product).
d. List testimonials suggested by the class.
e. Listen to or view tapes of several television commercials that use a testimonial approach. Ask the students to identify the person giving the testimonial, to identify the relationship (if any) between the product and the person, and to identify the benefit suggested by the commercial.
f. Ask the students to draw a picture of a testimonial commercial to add to the bulletin board or book on propaganda. Have them write a definition for "testimonial" under their pictures.

Testimonial
A well-known person tries to persuade the buyer by saying that he or she uses the product.

Glittering Generalities:
a. Place the following statements on the chalkboard or transparency:

> For the greatest time of your life visit the _____ amusement park.
> For a wow taste chew _____ gum.
> Don't eat at another ho-hum restaurant, eat at _____, the most magical place in town.
> Have hours of excitement with your friends after you buy the new fantastic _____ game by _____.

b. Read the statements with the children and ask if they see any similarities among the statements. "What words are used to try to persuade us to buy a product or to visit some place?" List these terms, or have the children underline them in each statement:
    greatest time of your life
    a wow taste
    most magical place in town

hours of excitement
fantastic

c. Ask the students to close their eyes and visualize each statement as you read it. Allow students to share their imagined pictures for each statement. Ask them if anyone knows the name for this persuasive technique. If they do not, tell them the term is "glittering generalities." Discuss the meaning of this term, and why advertisers might use these terms. Ask the students to give you a list of other words they would also call "glittering generalities." Finally, ask them to provide a definition for the term "glittering generalities." (These are terms that cause the listener to accept something because of the association with the words. The exact meaning is not always clear.)

d. Ask the students to list any commercials they can think of that use "glittering generalities."

e. Listen to or view tapes of television commercials that use "glittering generalities." Ask the students to identify these terms, and to describe what they would expect the product to be after they heard the commercials. Discuss with the students their feelings about the accuracy of each of these terms. If possible, have them try some of the products and decide whether the term is appropriate.

f. Ask the students to illustrate the "glittering generality" persuasive technique for the bulletin board or for their booklets. Write a definition for the term below the picture.

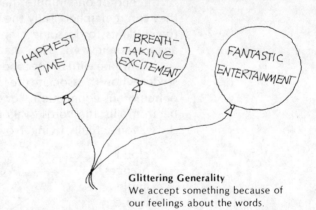

Glittering Generality
We accept something because of
our feelings about the words.

Persuading with Humor: Many commercials shown during children's programs use visual or sound techniques to create humor. Cartoons, jingles, exaggerated incidents, or preposterous situations appeal to the viewer's sense of humor. (Certain humorous symbols are readily associated with specific products—a clown advertising a fast-food chain, or a dancing cat singing the praises of a brand of cat food.)

a. Select several humorous advertisements from magazines. Ask the students to look at them and tell you what approach the advertisers are using. Ask children to identify the humorous or exaggerated incident in each ad. "How do you feel when you look at these advertisements? Why do you think the advertiser might want you to feel that way?"

b. Ask the students to list several T.V. commercials that use humor to sell a product. "How does each commercial show humor?"

c. Listen to or view tapes of several television commercials that rely on humor to persuade the viewer to buy a product. Ask the students to identify the type of humor.

d. You can experiment with your class to demonstrate how successfully some types of humor or exaggeration help a person to retain information. Memory authorities often suggest that, to remember a list of items or people's names, one should associate the item with something funny, or place it in exaggerated circumstances.

For this experiment, provide the class with two lists of items to remember. Present the first list of items, and give students one minute to memorize them:

cat	wagon
boy	lamp
tree	chair
fence	horse
car	football

At the end of one minute, have them write as many items as they can remember. Tally the number of items retained. Allow the students to do something else for awhile, then test them again on their words. How many items do they remember now?

Continue with the second experiment. This time, show the students how to associate the items on a list with an exaggerated or humorous connection. For example, if they want to remember from a list the words "wagon" and "fly," they could visualize the wagon actually flying. Now, if we added the words

cloud
oranges
apples
house
face
plant
man
tub

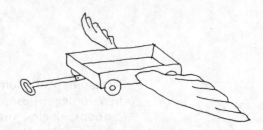

We could visualize our list of words as a wagon flying near a cloud of oranges and apples, which is over a house with a smiling face, next to a man planted in a tub.

After they have rapidly made their associations and visualized their results, ask them to list the items in this second group of ten words. Have them tally the number of words they remembered. Compare the number of words remembered in the two approaches. If more of the children remember the second list, why do they think memories improved? Do they also remember commercials for a longer time if they are humorous or exaggerated? Later in the day, ask the children again to visualize their second word list, and write down the words they remember. Are they still able to remember most of the words, even though considerable time has passed?

e. Have the students illustrate a humorous commercial for the bulletin board or the commercial booklet. Write a definition for a humorous commercial under the picture. For example:

The cheapest flight to Hawaii takes you into the beautiful clouds.

4. Now that the children have identified and experienced many of the persuasive techniques used in commericals, they can survey propaganda techniques in children's programming. (Other propaganda techniques, such as name calling, plain folks, snob appeal, and transfer, can also be introduced with older children. The procedures would be similar to those already introduced, but most examples would come from commercials aimed at adults.) Give the children a mimeographed sheet for surveying television com-

mercials during a specific time. (Divide the class so the networks and different time periods are surveyed.) A mimeographed commercial survey might resemble the following:

```
PERSUASION TECHNIQUES USED
        IN COMMERCIALS

Commercials seen from _____ to _____
                      (beginning time)  (end time)

on _____. Channel _____
      (date)

        Name of surveyor _____


        Name              Propaganda          Key
      of product          techniques         words
  1. _____        _____        _____
  2. _____        _____        _____
  3. _____        _____        _____
  4. _____        _____        _____
  5. _____        _____        _____
  6. _____        _____        _____
  7. _____        _____        _____
  8. _____        _____        _____
  9. _____        _____        _____
 10. _____        _____        _____
```

Discuss the results of the survey and tabulate the findings. Ask questions such as, "What types of persuasive techniques are most widely used with programs that children watch? What does this mean to us as viewers? Did you believe everything you heard and saw on the commercials? Which commercials did you feel were the most accurate? Why? Which commercials did you feel might not be telling the whole truth? Why? How can we check the accuracy of the commercial before we buy a product? If you watch television with a younger brother or sister, what could you tell them about commercials?

5. Mock Television Game Show—Divide the class into teams. On slips of paper write questions about the propaganda devices they have studied, and examples of different kinds of propaganda to identify. Allow the teams to take turns selecting the items from a container. Give one point for each correct answer. Examples of items could include:

What is the definition for a "bandwagon" commercial?	What is the definition for a "testimonial"?
Define a "glittering generality."	Why does a sponsor use humor in a commercial?
Name three terms often used in "glittering generalities."	Name three terms often used in "bandwagon" commercials.
Name three people who might do a testimonial commercial for athletic socks.	Name three famous dogs who might do testimonials for a dog food commercial.
What kind of a commercial is this? "Most people prefer Swiggley Hair Shampoo. Try it and you'll know why."	What kind of a commercial is this? "Swift Eagle, the fastest runner in the world, always wears Blue Dot Tennis Shoes."
What kind of a commercial is this? "Let your dreams come true. Visit the fabulous 10 Flags Over the Hudson."	

6. Reinforcement Worksheet—On a worksheet, list statements that use propaganda techniques and statements that do not. Have the students read the randomly organized statements, underline those they think use propaganda techniques, and identify the techniques used.

IDENTIFYING PROPAGANDA TECHNIQUES

Some of these statements use propaganda devices to persuade us to do something. Some of the statements do not. Underline the sentences that use propaganda devices. If you underline the sentence, write the name of the propaganda device it uses.

_____1. Dr. and Mrs. Jerald Norris are leaving Sunday for a three-week tour of England and Scotland.

_____2. The newly-crowned Miss America says her beautiful smile is due to Dazzle toothpaste. She wants you to have this beautiful smile, too.

_____3. Jo-Jo the clown flips with joy every time he takes a bite of a foot-long hot dog.

_____4. The new cars were shown for the first time today. Studies show these cars get better mileage than last year's models.

_____5. The members of the Saturday Jogging Club all buy their jogging shorts at the Coaches' Corner.

_____6. The falls at the State Park drops over a 400-foot gorge. It will be used to generate electricity.

_____7. Stay at the new, elegant State Falls Park Hotel. The gourmet dining room will thrill you with its fabulous new menu.

7. As a culminating activity for a unit of study on propaganda techniques, divide the class into small groups. Ask each group to develop a television commercial. They may use as many propaganda devices as they wish. If possible, videotape each commercial and play them back to the class.

ACTIVITY 8-9:
IDENTIFYING PERSUASIVE TECHNIQUES

TYPE		TERM	
CLASS	☑	STA	☑
GROUP	☑	LTA	☐
IND	☐	LC	☐

Purpose:
1. To identify commercials designed to sway public opinion (Public Interest Commercials)
2. To identify visual and auditory techniques commercial writers use to attract attention.
3. To stimulate creative writing of public interest commercials

Materials:
Tapes of commercials illustrating public interest concerns; television —live or videotaped public interest commercial; worksheet for surveying public interest commercials

Grade level:
Middle and upper elementary

Procedures:
1. Discuss with children the fact that television commercials use various techniques to persuade us to buy something, or to act in a certain way, for the good of the company that aims the ad at us. Their purpose is to reach as many people as possible. Sometimes, however, television tries to influence us to do something for our own good or safety. Ask the children to think of examples of television commercials that do not try to make us buy something, but that try to get us to act in a certain way for our own good; for example, spot ads about vaccinations, safe driving in school zones, prevention of forest fires, pollution, and zip codes. "Why do you think these commercials are called public interest commercials? Who do you think would want to sponsor these commercials?"

2. The writers and producers of public interest commercials hope to attract our attention and persuade us to do something. Play a tape recording of several public interest commercials. Ask the children to identify the techniques the commercial writer uses to attract

our attention. List the auditory techniques illustrated in the commercial:

This Attracted Our Listening Attention

Music
Jingles, rhymes
Persuasive words:
   "Protect our children"
   "Save the forest for these families"
A famous personality's voice
Sound effects: a fire burning, a horn, an ambulance

3. Television commercials not only use sound to attract our attention, they also use sight. Discuss the following: "Do you remember seeing these commercials on television? Would you like to listen to the tape of these commercials, or would you rather see them on television? Why? What advantages do sponsors of commercials have when the commercials are shown?"

4. Play a public interest television commercial or a videotape of several commercials. Ask the children to identify the visual techniques the commercial uses to attract attention. List the visual techniques:

This Attracted Our Visual Attention

Colors
Patterns
Cartoons
Dancing animals
Puppets
Famous personalities
Beautiful scenery
Picture of a disaster
Children

5. Assign students the task of viewing public interest television commercials during a specific time period. Divide the task so all the networks will be surveyed. Ask the students to identify the purpose of the public interest commercial, the sponsor, and the visual and auditory techniques used to attract the viewer's attention. The following worksheet will help students in this survey:

SURVEY OF PUBLIC INTEREST COMMERCIALS

Channel _____   Time _____

Day _____   Name _____

Public interest commercial subject:

_____

What does the sponsor want me to do? _____

_____

What might happen if I do not do it? _____

_____

Who sponsors the commercial? _____

_____

What visual techniques are used to attract my attention? _____

_____

What sound techniques are used to attract my attention? _____

_____

Draw a picture illustrating this commercial.

6. Divide the class into smaller interest groups and allow each group to select a subject of public or school interest. Ask each group to write and present a public interest commercial to the rest of the class, using the visual and sound techniques found in commercial advertising.

FANTASIA— A WALT DISNEY UNIT

TYPE		TERM	
CLASS	☑	STA	☐
GROUP	☐	LTA	☑
IND	☐	LC	☐

Purpose:

1. To listen for specific details

2. To develop sequential ordering skills

3. To interpret familiar animals and musical selections through art

4. To produce creative writing motivated by familiar animal characters and Disney comic strip titles

5. To stimulate creative movement with music from Fantasia

6. To develop appreciative listening

7. To create a film

8. To engage in group investigation, interaction, and oral reporting

9. To stimulate critical evaluation of a cartoon, Disney book, and original version of a story

10. To interpret a story orally through creative dramatization

11. To analyze good and evil characters

12. To stimulate reading for enjoyment

Materials:

1. Comic strips and pictures depicting Walt Disney cartoon characters: Mickey Mouse, Minnie Mouse, Donald Duck, Pluto, Goofy

2. Picture books with Walt Disney illustrations: *Winnie the Pooh, Dumbo, Walt Disney Treasury of Children's Classics, Peter Pan,* etc.

3. Stories and books filmed by Disney (the original version, as well as any Walt Disney version available): *Robin Hood, Snow White, Bambi, The Jungle Book, Cinderella, Lady and the Tramp, Pinocchio, Peter Pan, Sleeping Beauty,* etc.

4. References on the life of Walt Disney:
   Disney's Wonderful World of Knowledge (Danbury Press, 1973).

Montgomery, Elizabeth Rider. *Walt Disney: Master of Make Believe* (Garrard, 1970).

Finch, Christopher. *The Art of Walt Disney* (Abrams, 1970).

5. References on filmmaking:
Andersen, Yvonne. *Teaching Film Animation to Children* (Van Nostrand Reinhold Co., 1970).

Ferguson, Robert. *How to Make Movies: A Practical Guide to Filmmaking* (Viking Press, 1969).

Helfman, Harry. *Making Your Own Movies* (William Morrow and Co., 1970).

Lidstone, John and Don McIntosh. *Children As Filmmakers* (Van Nostrand Reinhold Co., 1970).

National Geographic, August, 1963. (Disney's filmmaking technique)

National Geographic World, Nov. 1977. (The Disney studio)

Norton, Donna. "Language Arts and the Media," in *The Effective Teaching of Language Arts* (Charles E. Merrill, 1980).

Rynew, Arden. *Filmmaking for Children.* (Pflaum/Standard, 1971).

6. 100-foot roll of 16-mm white leader, colored permanent-ink felt tip pens, transparency markers, 16-mm film projector

7. Record of Fantasia

8. Art supplies

Grade level: Any grade; younger children must have stories read to them, rather than reading many of their own selections. With younger children, the movement and creative drama activities can be expanded. Older children can create a more detailed film, research the various studio departments, and critically evaluate differences between films, Disney-adapted picture books, and the original stories. (I have made films with children as young as first grade, and there is no upper limit to this activity.)

Procedures: Many of these activities can be developed into an interest-center format. Other activities require small-group or large-group interaction with teacher leadership.

1. Listening for Specific Details and Motivation for the Unit—Provide several references on the life and accomplishments of Walt Disney. Disney's experiences suggest numerous language arts-related learning activities. Compile a tape that provides some background information on Disney. The dialogue for this tape might be similar to the following:

Mickey Mouse, Donald Duck, and Pluto are some of the most lovable animals in the world. After listening to this tape, you will know more about the father of these cartoon stars, the creator of films like *Peter Pan* and *That Darn Cat,* and the developer of Disneyland and Disney World. As you listen to this tape, I want you to think about the answers to the following questions: (1) Where do you think Walt Disney might have seen the models for his early animal cartoons? (2) How old is the character, Mickey Mouse? When did he first appear? (3) In what other form, beside film cartoons, can you see Mickey Mouse and Donald Duck? (4) How do we know that Walt Disney enjoyed nature and wanted to preserve it for others to enjoy? (5) How do we know that Disney films are enjoyed throughout the world?

Walt Disney, the originator of Mickey Mouse, was born in Chicago, Illinois, on December 5, 1901. Disney began drawing pictures of animals when he was a young boy. When he was 6, he drew these animal pictures on the walls of his family's farm house. Later, in Kansas City, Missouri, Disney distributed newspapers for his father. He always liked show business and, with a friend who was also named Walt, put on a vaudeville show called "The Two Walts."

One of his early jobs was with the Kansas City Film Ad company. He made one-minute commercial cartoons that were shown in local movie theaters. After years of effort and experimentation, Disney produced the first sound cartoon, "Steamboat Willie." This cartoon was shown in 1928 at the Colony Theater in New York City. The hero of the cartoon was the now famous Mickey Mouse. "Steamboat Willie" was such a success that Disney was able to start his own studio, and to experiment with animation and music.

In 1932, Disney showed the first animated color cartoon. This cartoon was a silly symphony called "Flowers and Trees." The cartoon won an Academy Award for Disney. In 1937, Disney produced his first full-length cartoon, "Snow White and the Seven Dwarfs." Since then, he has produced other fairy tales, such as "Pinocchio," "Peter Pan," and "Bambi."

During the 1930s, the Disney cartoon appeared in newspaper comic strips. The first comic strip was black and white, and was titled, "The Audacious Exploits of Mickey Mouse on the Island of Mystery." The first Disney color comics were printed in the Sunday papers in 1932. This comic strip, "Mickey Mouse and the Dogcatcher," was also about the adventures of the famous mouse.

The full-length cartoon, "Fantasia," combined classical music and animated images. Disney enjoyed experimenting with such new techniques. In the 1950s, Disney started a new series of true life advanture films. These films showed the beauty of nature in *The Living Desert, White Wilderness, The African Lion,* and *The Vanishing Prairie.*

In 1955, Disney opened the amusement park that has attracted millions of visitors. Disneyland recreates fairy tales and episodes from America's past and future. It was so popular that, in 1971, Disney opened the larger Disney World in Florida.

Disney studio creations are shown at movie theaters and on television. They are also popular in other countries; they have been produced in seventeen languages.

2. Listening Comprehension—After they listen to the tape or the accompanying dialogue, have the students answer the thought-organization questions at the beginning of the tape.

3. Sequencing—To reinforce sequential ordering, have students place the major events from Disney's experiences onto a time line, then draw illustrations to show the accomplishments in each time period.

4. Art Interpretation, Oral Discussion—When Disney was a young boy, he liked to draw pictures of animals. He even drew animals on the walls of his farmhouse.
   a. Discuss with children: Many of Disney's early cartoons look like they might have been modeled after animals one might see on a farm; for example, Slicker the rat, Kat Nipp the cat, Mortimer Mouse, Bucky Bug, Tanglefoot the horse, Mr. Gloomy the dog, Max Hare, and Toby Tortoise. (If possible, show illustrations of these cartoon characters.)
   b. Discuss with children the animals they see frequently; for example, pets such as cats, dogs, hamsters, goldfish; wildlife, such as birds, crickets, insects, and bugs; farm animals; and zoo animals (depending upon the location of the school).
   c. Suggest that each child pretend he is a young Walt Disney. Ask them to draw cartoon characters illustrating their own animals. Have them name their cartoon animals, then put the pictures together in a cartoon booklet or on a bulletin board.

5. Creative Writing—After the students have drawn their own cartoon characters, have them look at their characters and think about an adventure that might happen to those characters. Have them write and illustrate a creative story.

6. Art Interpretation, Creative Writing—Disney cartoons first appeared in the comic sections of the newspaper in the 1930s.
   a. Ask children to look at the comic strip sections of newspapers and at comic books that show Disney characters. Show them how a cartoonist writes dialogue directly onto the picture in a bubble, or balloon.
   b. Read several comic strips, and discuss the action and the pictures.
   c. Remind the children that the first Disney comic strip was called "The Audacious Exploits of Mickey Mouse on the Island of Mystery." Discuss the meaning of "audacious ex-

ploits" with the children. "What kind of adventures would be fearless, bold, and brave? What might happen on the Island of Mystery?" The second Disney cartoon was "Mickey Mouse and the Dogcatcher." Discuss the occupation of dogcatcher with the children. "What kinds of adventures could Mickey Mouse have in a comic strip of this title?"

d. Allow children to choose one of the Disney titles for a cartoon. Have them draw their own cartoon, using the selected title. Then write the corresponding story in dialogue format. Display the cartoons for everyone to read on the bulletin board.

7. Creative Movement, Appreciative Listening—Disney used music to bring life to animation effectively. "Fantasia" combined classical music and animated images. "Fantasia" contains eight different sequences, each accompanied by a different composition. Select one or several of the following compositions. Describe the animated subject for the selection. Play the composition as children interpret the music creatively through their own movements.

a. "Toccata and Fugue in D Minor" (Bach) This section shows abstract images moving to the music.

b. "The Nutcracker Suite" (Tchaikovsky) Dancing plants and animals present a ballet.

c. "The Sorcerer's Apprentice" (Dukas) Mickey Mouse interacts with the magic brooms.

d. "The Rite of Spring" (Stravinsky) This segment depicts the creation of the world and the disappearance of the dinosaurs.

e. "The Pastoral Symphony" (Beethoven) Fauns and centaurs dance, while Pegasus, the winged horse, flies.

f. "The Dance of the Hours" (Ponchielli) Ostriches, elephants, hippopotamuses, and crocodiles dance a ballet.

g. "A Night On Bald Mountain" (Mussorgsky) Demons, witches, and ghosts dance to this music.

h. "Ave Marie" (Schubert) A procession of devoted followers walk through a forest that resembles a cathedral.

8. Art Interpretation, Appreciative Listening—Walt Disney effectively combined animated images with music in the film "Fantasia." Play any of the above selections from "Fantasia"; allow children to draw their own artistic interpretations as they listen to the music.

9. Media Interpretation (making a film without a camera)—the film "Fantasia" shows colored, abstract lines, objects, and animated characters moving to music. Children of all ages can make colorful films by drawing directly on 16-mm white leader.

a. Place a protective covering on the floor or on several tables joined together to provide a long work space.

b. Unroll the film (100-foot roll of 16-mm white leader) onto the protective covering. The dull emulsion side should face the child.

c. Measure the film into even sections so that each child has an equal portion of film to draw on (i.e., four feet, if you have twenty-five students in the class). Mark the sections with paper clips so that each child knows which is his portion of the film.

d. Divide the class into groups so a manageable number are drawing in the work area.

e. Demonstrate to the group how they should draw lines and other designs directly onto the film with colored, permanent-ink marking pens or transparency markers. If they wish to draw an individual object that moves, they must draw the object over and over again, varying the position of the object slightly.

f. After the drawings are finished, roll the film onto the reel, project it through a 16-mm projector, and add musical background to emphasize the gaily-colored film.

10. Reference Skills, Group Discussion, Oral Reporting—Completion of the first simple film drawn directly on the white leader may motivate interest in learning about film production in the Disney Studios. After viewing a Disney cartoon feature on television, in a theater, or at school, students can investigate and experiment with some of the processes cartoonists use to create a film. Such a study can motivate art, creative writing, and an understanding of this medium as a communication process. A question and a startling statement may provide a good introduction: "We have all watched and enjoyed the film so-and-so. Does anyone have any idea how many pictures were drawn to complete the film?" (Allow children to guess, and record the numbers.) "A full-length cartoon takes about 250,000 frames. But a great deal of work goes into the production before the pictures are transferred to film." Introduce each department in a film studio; then encourage children to choose a specific department and investigate in groups the responsibilities of and techniques used by each department. After the investigations, have each group report its findings to the class.

a. *Story Board Department.* In this department, story ideas are drawn on sheets of paper, pinned to a story board (similar to a bulletin board), and the writers experiment with ideas until the desired action and sequence is achieved.

b. *Sound Department* This department synchronizes musical background with action and dialogue, and chooses other appropriate sound effects.

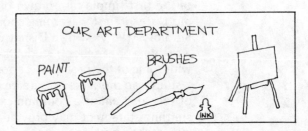

c. *Art Department.* The art department works with the ideas developed by the story board department, and draws the scenic background for the cartoons.

d. *Animation Department.* The animator draws lifelike characters that show movement and expression. Each frame must correspond with the action and dialogue. The artist draws lines to show expression, emotion, and movement.

e. *Inking and Coloring Department.* The penciled cartoon figures from the animation department are copied, in ink, onto transparent celluloid sheets and filled in with color.

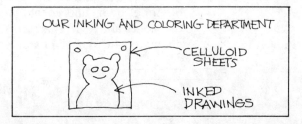

f. *Film Department.* The director, camera operator, and scriptwriter put the story on film. The sheets of celluloid from the inking and coloring department are arranged over the backgrounds, and photographed from above. The director then checks the sound track, sound effects, etc., to determine whether the film is syncronized. The final version is printed and distributed to theaters.

11. Critical Evaluation (Comparison of Cartoon Version and Original Story), Motivating Reading—Ask students to choose a book or story that Disney has created on film. The story should, if possible, be one they have recently seen on television or in a movie theater. Next, have them read the Disney-illustrated version of the story, and, finally, the original version. Have them compare, either orally or in writing, the film, Disney-book, and original versions. For example, "What do you think is the best feature of each version—pictures, story, plot, character development? Were there any changes between the original story and the animated version of the Disney book version—characters, plot, setting? Were any characters added to or dropped from the original story? From your study of the animation process, do you see any reason for these changes? Was the book version more real to you after you saw the film version? Why or why not?"

12. Creative Dramatization—After reading several stories produced by the Disney Studios, have students select a story they would like to dramatize, divide the class into those specific groups, and prepare the story for presentation to the rest of the class.

13. Critical Thinking, Character Analysis—Walt Disney created both good and evil characters in his full-length features and in his shorter cartoons. Have the students choose a story with both good and evil characters, draw illustrations of these characters, describe them, find vocabulary terms in the story that describe the good and evil characters, and find examples of dialogue characteristic of each character.

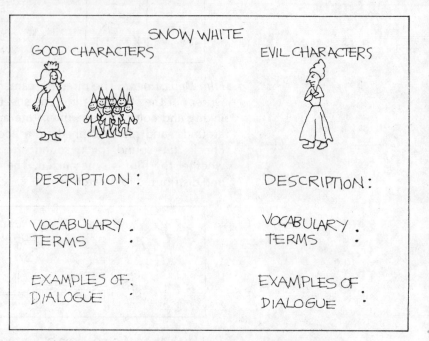

14. A "Fantasia Festival" might be a culminating activity for this unit of study. The class can invite parents and/or other classes to see their work and listen to talks by the studio-department interest groups. The Fantasia Festival might include:
   a. Displays of Disney books
   b. Art displays of creative cartoons and Fantasia pictures
   c. Displays of their own creative stories and creative interpretations of "The Audacious Exploits of Mickey Mouse on the Island of Mystery" and "Mickey Mouse and the Dogcatcher"
   d. Interest groups set up as booths to describe the responsibilities and demonstrate the techniques of each studio department

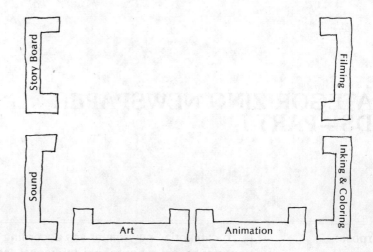

e. A listening table, with phonograph and earphones for individual enjoyment of Fantasia music
f. Showing of the film made during the unit
g. A creative movement activity to accompany music, or several creative drama activities

ACTIVITY 8-11:
CATEGORIZING NEWSPAPER ADS—PART I

TYPE		TERM	
CLASS	☐	STA	☑
GROUP	☑	LTA	☐
IND	☑	LC	☐

Purpose:

1. To categorize newspaper ads according to food, clothing, transportation, toys, household appliances, etc.

Materials:

Ads from newspapers and magazines illustrating food, clothing, transportation, toys, appliances, etc.; newspapers and magazines; envelopes for sorting pictures

Grade level:

Lower elementary

Procedures:

1. This activity can reinforce a lesson on categorizing. Provide a number of advertisements showing pictures of foods, toys, clothing, cars, boats, etc.

2. Look at each picture and discuss what is illustrated. Discuss the similarities among any of the pictures: "How are these pictures different? Could we group some of these pictures together so we would not have so many different piles?" (Discuss different ways of grouping—size, color, use, price, etc.)

3. Assist children in choosing appropriate categories and placing advertisements under appropriate headings.

FOOD ADVERTISEMENTS

CLOTHING ADVERTISEMENTS

4. Provide additional advertisements and ask children to find illustrations for each category.

5. Try more refined categorization under each heading. For example, look at the group of clothing advertisements. "Are there better descriptions for these items than just 'clothing'? What use is made for each article of clothing advertised? Who wears each article of clothing? When is each article of clothing worn?" Ask students to suggest different categories, then group all the advertisements appropriately. For example, categorize according to who wears the clothing, according to season of the year, or according to where people wear the clothing.

CLOTHES WORN BY GIRLS  CLOTHES WORN BY BOYS

CLOTHES WORN BY MEN CLOTHES WORN BY WOMEN

CLOTHES WORN IN SUMMER  CLOTHES WORN IN WINTER

CLOTHES WORN TO CHURCH  CLOTHES WORN TO SCHOOL

6. For an individual reinforcement activity provide large envelopes labeled with specific categories, and advertisements for the child to sort and place into the appropriate envelopes.

ACTIVITY 8-12:
CATEGORIZING NEWSPAPER
ADS—PART II

TYPE		TERM	
CLASS	☐	STA	☑
GROUP	☑	LTA	☐
IND	☑	LC	☐

Purpose:
1. To categorize newspaper advertisments according to the kind of store where the item is purchased

Materials:
Advertisements showing items that can be purchased in a grocery store, a drug store, a shoe store, a clothing store, a hardware store, a furniture store, a toy store, a nursery, a pet store, a jewelry store; newspapers and magazines

Grade level:
Second and third grades; students must have had experiences with different types of stores

Procedures:
1. Discuss the different types of stores we can go to buy things. What kinds of stores are available in a city or at a shopping center?

2. List the kinds of stores available in your city or town.

3. Find advertisements for items that can be purchased in each kind of store, and categorize them under appropriate headings. "Some items may be found under more than one category. Why? Use the ads to help you decide which store might be the best place to buy the item. Why did you make your decision?"

FOOD STORE   DRUGSTORE

THE PARTS OF A NEWSPAPER

TYPE		TERM	
CLASS	☑	STA	☑
GROUP	☑	LTA	☐
IND	☐	LC	☐

Purpose:

1. To name major sections of the newspaper

2. To identify the primary purpose for reading each section of the newspaper

3. To identify the proposed audience for each section of the newspaper

4. To locate newspaper features using the index

Materials: Duplicate copies of a local newspaper; copies of several different newspapers

Grade level: Middle and upper elementary

Procedures:

1. Ask each child to bring a copy of a local newspaper, or obtain copies from other sources.

2. As a group activity, introduce the various sections of the newspaper.
   a. Identify and underline the name of the newspaper. "Is there any reason for that particular name? Does the newspaper use any technique to make the name more visual? Why would the newspaper want to be visual? This top portion which contains the name of the newspaper is called a 'masthead.' Why do you think that might be an appropriate title?" (Find the term in a dictionary.) "Why do you think the term is used by newspapers? What information do you gain by looking quickly at the masthead of your newspaper?" (Name of paper, date, location, edition.) On a large sheet of newsprint, paste the masthead from your newspaper. Label this portion "masthead."

(Masthead)

The Daily Chronicle

DATE   LOCATION   EDITION

b. Look at the front page of the newspaper. Ask the students to read the front page for one minute. Instruct them to acquire as much information as they can in that minute. Now, have them cover or fold the paper so they cannot see it. Lead a brainstorming session in which as much information as possible is written on the chalkboard. Ask the students how they learned so much information in one minute. (Some students will try to read an article, while other students will scan the headlines. Learning to scan the headlines is the point you want to stress.) "What attracted your attention as you tried to identify the contents of the front page?" (Headlines and pictures.) "How does the newspaper indicate that one story may be more important than another story?" (Size of headline.) "Which story do you think is the most important on the front page of your paper? Where is that story located?" (The top story on the page.) "What two ways did your newspaper use to indicate the importance of the story?" (Size of headline and location of story.) Ask the students to look again at their list of information on the chalkboard and the headlines in the newspaper. "What kinds of stories are included on the front page?" (Important news stories from around the world or the United States). "What does the headline tell us about the story?" (The main idea of the story.) "Look at the headlines again. Which stories would you want to read? Why? What words attracted your attention? Why is the front page of the paper so important?" Cut out the headlines from the front page of the paper and place them on the newsprint sheet containing the masthead. Label the headlines.

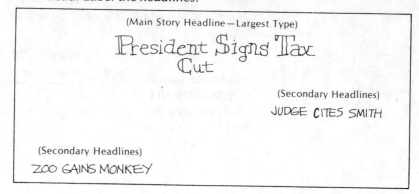

(Main Story Headline—Largest Type)

President Signs Tax Cut

(Secondary Headlines)

JUDGE CITES SMITH

(Secondary Headlines)

ZOO GAINS MONKEY

c. Ask the students what parts of the newspaper they like to read. When a student mentions a section, ask the class to find that section. During this first experience, observe the techniques students use to locate information. Do they browse through the paper page by page, or do they use the index? Ask the students to look carefully at the front page. "Is there anything on the front page that would help you find the comics or the television section?" Help them identify and locate the index. While looking at the index, discuss the fact that newspapers are divided into sections. Ask the students to locate the section numbers in the newspaper. "Where are section numbers found?" (Top right-hand corner of each page.) Provide an opportunity for students to identify the number and location of sections in their newspapers. Using the index, allow students to identify specific features located in the newspaper. While one student names a feature, the remainder of the class can locate the item. This activity can be used as a game, with teams of students competing.

	Team 1	Team 2	Team 3	Team 4
Obituaries	_____	_____	_____	_____
Horoscope	_____	_____	_____	_____
Classified Ads	_____	_____	_____	_____
Comics	_____	_____	_____	_____
Sports Section	_____	_____	_____	_____
Weather	_____	_____	_____	_____
Television	_____	_____	_____	_____
Editorials	_____	_____	_____	_____

d. Continue your introduction to the newspaper by looking at each section of the paper listed in the index. "What information is found in each section? Why would you want to read that section?" Cut out examples of articles in each section of the paper. Make a newsprint page for each section of the newspaper.

3. Reinforcement Game—After introducing them to the newspaper, divide the class into teams. Have the teams write specific types of articles on slips of paper. These slips are then drawn, and the teams, using the index and their knowledge of feature locations, compete to see which team will be first to find each story or feature.

	Team 1	Team 2	Team 3	Team 4
An editorial cartoon	_____	_____	_____	_____
A report of the NFL football game	_____	_____	_____	_____
The 7 P.M. TV show on Channel 3	_____	_____	_____	_____

A house listed for sale   ———— ———— ———— ————
Forecast for today's weather ———— ———— ———— ————
A hero in the comics   ———— ———— ———— ————
A letter to the editor   ———— ———— ———— ————
A recipe for children   ———— ———— ———— ————
The temperature in Moscow ———— ———— ———— ————
Report from the New York
 Stock Exchange   ———— ———— ———— ————
The movie at the _____   ———— ———— ———— ————
A pet for sale   ———— ———— ———— ————
The latest hair style   ———— ———— ———— ————
A lost poodle   ———— ———— ———— ————

ACTIVITY 8-14:
SIGNIFICANCE OF NEWSPAPERS AND PERIODICAL NAMES

TYPE		TERM	
CLASS	☑	STA	☑
GROUP	☑	LTA	☐
IND	☐	LC	☐

Purpose:

1. To expand vocabulary
2. To study inferred meaning from newspaper and magazine names
3. To study audience appeal and newspaper and magazine names

Materials:

Titles of many newspapers in the United States and other parts of the world; copies of newspapers, if possible; copies of a variety of magazines; dictionaries

Grade level:

Middle and upper elementary

Procedures:

1. Look at a number of the newspapers the class is reading and studying.
2. Discuss the fact that newspapers use many different names. Have children offer reasons they think a newspaper might choose a specific name.
3. List the names of some major newspapers. Discuss the significance of the name. Use a dictionary to learn the meaning of each title. Why is it appropriate for a newspaper?
4. Create a bulletin board showing the titles of U.S. and foreign newspapers. On the bulletin board, illustrate the meanings of the newspaper names and provide a written meaning for each title. Here are some examples of newspaper names:

Los Angeles Times	Arkansas Gazette
New York Times	Indianapolis Star
Chicago Tribune	Desert News—Salt Lake City
Milwaukee Journal	Minneapolis Star

Denver Post	Gulfport Daily Herald
Idaho Statesman	Star Telegram—Fort Worth
Des Moines Register	Wall Street Journal

Foreign Newspapers

London Times—England	Guardian—Rangoon, Burma
Manchester Guardian—England	Daily Mail—London
Ottawa Citizen—Ottawa, Canada	Pravda—Russia (means truth)
Globe and Mail—Toronto, Canada	Izvestia—Russia (means news)

5. Discuss the fact that magazines use many different names. Look at several magazines, and discuss the meaning of the names, the appropriateness of the names for the subject matter, and the appeal of the names for the desired audiences.

6. Ask students to select a magazine, investigate the subject matter, the appropriateness of the title, and the appeal of the title for the desired audience. Put this information on a poster. Here are some examples of magazine names:

Fortune	American Home
Business Week	House Beautiful
Time	Changing Times
Newsweek	Life
U.S. News and World Report	Seventeen
Ladies Home Journal	

7. Choose a name for a classroom newspaper or magazine. Why would that name be appropriate?

ACTIVITY 8-15:
RELATING PARTS OF A NEWSPAPER TO A BOOK OR STORY

TYPE		TERM	
CLASS	☑	STA	☐
GROUP	☑	LTA	☑
IND	☑	LC	☐

Purpose:
1. To reinforce study of parts of a newspaper
2. To stimulate book reporting
3. To stimulate creative writing

Materials:
William Pene du Bois's *The 21 Balloons;* sections of the newspaper—editorial, news, women's section, home, sports, entertainment, weather, etc.

Grade level:
Middle and upper elementary (This activity is developed around a specific book, but would be equally appropriate for many other books or stories.)

Procedures:
1. After studying different parts of a newspaper, the class can try many creative writing activities that use a newspaper format. Read the Newbery Award winner, *The 21 Balloons*.

2. Students can select the newspaper approach they would like to use for reporting information from this book. Suggestions include:
   a. Write a front-page news story describing Professor William Sherman's unusual voyage in his balloon.
   b. Write a front-page news story relating the true incidents of the volcanic explosion on the Island of Krakatoa in Java. Include a worthy headline for this disaster, such as:

   "Volcanic Matter Thrown 23 Miles in the Air"
   "Most Terrible Volcanic Explosion in History"
   "Ocean Bed Sinks 900 Feet"
   "50 to 135 Foot Tidal Waves Sweep Coasts"
   "Explosion Heard 3000 Miles Away"
   "36,000 Perish in Holocaust"

c. Write a feature article for the home section of the newspaper. Describe a room in the Moroccan House of Marvels. Illustrate your article.

d. Write an editorial expressing an opinion about "The Gourmet Government," "The Selection of Citizens for Krakatoa," or "Secrecy and Diamonds."

e. Write a feature article for the fashion section of the newspaper. Illustrate the fashions worn by the citizens of Krakatoa in the 1880s.

f. Write a feature article for the travel section of the newspaper. Describe and illustrate the wonders of visiting a tropical island in the Pacific Ocean.

g. Write a feature science article describing the scientific reasons for the eruption of the volcano on Krakatoa, or write an article describing the history of ballooning.

h. Write a story for the recreation section of the paper describing the Airy-Go-Round, or write a story about a good place to eat.

i. Write an article for the sports page, describing ballooning as a sport.

j. Design advertisements for the paper that relate to the book, such as: a furniture ad for a fantastic invention; a restaurant ad for one of the family restaurants; or a travel ad selling a voyage in a balloon.

3. Choose a title for the newspaper. Combine the articles for the newspaper and duplicate the newspaper so all students have their own copies.

ACTIVITY 8-16:
HEADLINES SHOW THE MAIN IDEA

TYPE		TERM	
CLASS	☐	STA	☑
GROUP	☑	LTA	☐
IND	☑	LC	☐

Purpose:

1. To understand that a headline shows the main idea of a story
2. To practice writing headlines
3. To learn to identify the main idea of a fairy tale

Materials:

List of headlines describing familiar folk stories; collection of familiar folktales

Grade level:

Lower and middle elementary

Procedures:

1. Provide a list of headlines that a newspaper might write to introduce familiar folk or fairy tales:
   Goat Destroys Troll (Three Billy Goats Gruff)
   Pigs Finally Defeat Wolf (Three Little Pigs)
   Prince Overcomes 100-Year Curse (Sleeping Beauty)
   Cinderwench Hit of the Ball (Cinderella)
   Animals Terrify Criminals, Capture Jewels (Bremen Town Musicians)
   Cat Wins Kingdom for Poor Master (Puss and Boots)
   Ruler Parades in Underwear (Emperor's New Clothes)
   Old Lamp Has Unbelievable Powers (Aladdin and the Wonderful Lamp)
   Space Travel Possible with Beanstalk (Jack and the Beanstalk)

2. Ask children to identify fairy tales represented by the headlines.

3. Ask children to write their own headlines for a group of fairy stories. Use, perhaps, Rumpelstiltskin, Tom Thumb, The Three Bears, Henny Penny, The Gingerbread Boy, Hansel and Gretel, Little Red Riding Hood, Dick Whittington and His Cat, Thumbelina, and Fat Cat.

4. Allow children to read their headlines to a group so the group can identify the story described by the headline.

ACTIVITY 8-17:
NEWSPAPERS HELP
US TO SHOP FOR FOOD

TYPE		TERM	
CLASS	☐	STA	☑
GROUP	☑	LTA	☐
IND	☐	LC	☐

Purpose:

1. To learn the art of comparative shopping using newspaper advertising

Materials:

List of groceries illustrating food needs of a family for one day; grocery store newspaper ads from all available newspapers for one day

Grade level:

Middle and upper elementary

Procedures:

1. Divide the class into groups and ask each group to plan a one-day menu for a family of four. The menu should include items from the basic food groups:

Breakfast	*Lunch*	*Dinner*
Milk	Sandwich (kind)	Meat (kind)
Cereal (brand name)	Soup (kind)	Vegetables (kinds)
Bread	Fruit (kind)	Salad (kind)
Orange Juice	Milk	Dessert (kind)

2. After planning the menu, write a grocery list for that day.

3. Next, search the newspaper ads for the items on the grocery list. Write the cost of each item under the appropriate store; for example:

Shopping List   Price in Stores with Grocery Ads

Shopping List	A&P	Eagle	Piggly Wiggly	Safeway
Bread (loaf)	_____	_____	_____	_____
Orange juice (6 oz)	_____	_____	_____	_____
Cereal (kind)	_____	_____	_____	_____
Milk (gallon)	_____	_____	_____	_____
Tuna fish (6½ oz)	_____	_____	_____	_____

```
Tomato soup (11 oz)  _____  _____  _____  _____
Four apples          _____  _____  _____  _____
Chicken              _____  _____  _____  _____
Frozen peas          _____  _____  _____  _____
Potatoes             _____  _____  _____  _____
Lettuce              _____  _____  _____  _____
Ice cream (1 qt)     _____  _____  _____  _____
```

4. Compare the costs of the items. Would it be better to shop in one store? Would it be cheaper to shop in several stores? What are the differences between the cheapest and most expensive listings for one item? Are store brands less expensive than name brands?

5. Finally, ask the groups to compare their grocery list with other items advertised in the paper. Could they plan an equally good, but less expensive, menu if they took advantage of sale items? For example, "Is there meat advertised that would be a better buy than chicken, or a fruit that would be preferable to apples?" Some additional questions to consider are: "What are the advantages of comparison shopping? Are there any disadvantages? Why do grocery stores advertise specials for the week? When is a special a good buy, and when do you think it is not a good buy?"

ACTIVITY 8-18:
NEWSPAPERS HELP US
DO MORE SHOPPING

TYPE		TERM	
CLASS	☐	STA	☑
GROUP	☑	LTA	☐
IND	☐	LC	☐

Purpose:

1. To learn the art of comparative shopping using newspaper advertising

2. To compare values using *Consumer Reports*

Materials:

Newspaper advertisements showing large and small appliances, bicycles, etc.; current issue of *Consumer Reports Buying Guide*; Catalogues from Sears, Ward's, Penney's, etc.

Grade level:

Middle and upper elementary

Procedures:

1. Have students select a small appliance, such as a toaster, an iron, or an electric blender. Find ads in newspapers that advertise the item. Try to find ads from a department store, a discount store, and a small appliance store. Compare the cost of the item from the different stores. "Which would be the best buy?" Now, find the small appliance in several catalogues. "How do the prices compare with the newspaper ads? Is the lowest-priced item still the better buy?"

2. Discuss the concept of quality and price with children. "The ads do not always help us make any decisions on quality. Is the cheapest item always the best buy? One way to learn about quality is to find the item in a publication such as *Consumer Reports*." Show the publication, and discuss the information it offers.

3. Locate the chosen small appliances in *Consumer Reports*. Read the various ratings. "Is the lowest-priced appliance still the best buy? Why or why not?"

4. Ask the students to select an item they would like to have (e.g., a bicycle, a phonograph, a camera). They have worked very hard,

saved their allowances, and earned money through other kinds of odd jobs. Now they want to buy the item that will give them the very best value. Using the newspaper ads, catalogues, and *Consumer Reports,* ask them to select the brand name and location for purchasing their "best buy" merchandise.

ACTIVITY 8-19:
ADVERTISERS TRY TO APPEAL TO A SPECIFIC POPULATION

TYPE		TERM	
CLASS	☐	STA	☑
GROUP	☑	LTA	☐
IND	☐	LC	☐

Purpose:
1. To identify advertisements designed to appeal to a specific population
2. To find words that might appeal to a specific population
3. To write advertisements designed for a specific population

Materials:
Ads from newspapers and magazines that appeal to different age groups and segments of the population; magazines aimed at specific segments of the population

Grade level:
Middle and upper elementary

Procedures:
1. Discuss the following: "Do all of the people who read advertisements want to buy the same things? How do you think advertisers reach the people who are most likely to buy their products? Are there any differences between readers that allow the advertisers to write a more appealing ad? Who are the groups that advertisers wish to reach?" (Children, sportsmen, teenagers, men, women, homeowners, campers, car owners, farmers, ranchers, boat owners, hobbyists.) "How can each of these groups be reached most efficiently? What are some items each group might want to buy? What would they want to know about the item? What might make the item more appealing to this buyer?"

2. Supply newspapers and magazines. Have students search for advertisements that appeal to specific populations. Find an advertisement designed to appeal to each of the following: a home owner; a child; a car buyer; a man; a teenager; a hobbyist; a sportsman; a woman. Label each advertisement according to its appeal.

3. Underline any words in the advertisement that might have special appeal to that population.

4. Supply several magazines written for a specific population; for example, *Sports Illustrated, Field and Stream, Motorboating and Sailing, Modern Photography, McCall's, Fortune, Business Week, Popular Mechanics, Architectural Digest, Daisy* (Girl Scout magazine). Have the group look at the ads in the magazines, identify the advertisers, and discuss the relationship between the advertisements and the content of the magazines. Students may divide into groups and create a chart for each type of magazine. For example:

MAGAZINE: *BUSINESS WEEK*

Articles in Magazine

1. Economics
2. Finance
3. Government
4. International Outlook

5. Management
6. Marketing
7. Accounting
8. Corporate Strategies

Advertisers in Magazine

1. Las Vegas Convention Center
2. Diners Club
3. 3M— data recording products
4. Western—temporary business help services
5. Lyon Office Products—office furniture

6. Digital Computer
7. Xerox Compact Copier
8. Swissair
9. Hewlett Packard Computers
10. RCA American Communications

Examples of advertisements with key words underlined:

850,000 <u>square feet</u> 4 <u>exhibit halls</u> 50 <u>meeting rooms</u> boost <u>attendance</u> and <u>profits</u>	<u>double</u> <u>sales</u> and production	<u>reduce</u> <u>costs</u> $5,000 per month $60,000 <u>annual</u> <u>savings</u>

PEOPLE WHO PROBABLY READ *BUSINESS WEEK* :

1. People who work for large businesses.
2. People in business management.
3. People who make buying decisions for businesses.
4. People who own their own businesses.
5. White-collar workers (the ads show businessmen and women in suits).
6. People who earn high salaries (they fly to Europe; they are looking for investments).

5. Select a particular population, consider its needs, and write an advertisement to sell something to that group. Make your ads as appealing as possible.

CRITICAL READING—
FACT vs. FICTION

TYPE		TERM	
CLASS	☐	STA	☐
GROUP	☑	LTA	☑
IND	☐	LC	☐

Purpose:
1. To define the difference between fact and fiction
2. To identify factual sections of the newspaper
3. To identify fictional sections of the newspaper
4. To identify factual magazine articles
5. To identify fictional magazine articles

Materials: Examples of factual and fictional materials; newspaper articles that illustrate fact and fiction (*My Weekly Reader,* etc.); magazine articles that illustrate fact and fiction (*Jack and Jill, Highlights for Children,* etc.); dictionary and thesaurus

Grade level: Lower and middle elementary

Procedures:
1. Discuss with children their viewpoint of what is fact and what is fiction. Make a list of characteristics for fact and fiction.

2. Ask the group to find the words "fact" and "fiction" in their classroom dictionary and thesaurus. Write a definition, and synonyms, for "fact" and "fiction" on the chalkboard. Compare this list with the children's previous list. "Are the two lists similar? Did we give an accurate meaning for fact and fiction? What new information do we have now?"

Fact	Fiction
Meaning: Something that has happened or is true. Synonyms: truth, reality, certainty, accuracy	Meaning: Making up of imaginary happenings. Something that did not happen. Synonyms: story, tale, yarn, invention, fantasy, falsehood, lie, fib

3. Some articles containing fact or fiction are easy to identify. Ask, "How do we know for sure which of these two articles is fact and which is fiction?" Then read articles such as these:

Man's Best Friend

Dogs have been helping man for thousands of years. Early man tamed and trained dogs to go hunting and protect their camps. Later, dogs were trained to guard and herd flocks of sheep. The Egyptians may have been the earliest people to keep dogs as pets. If you are looking for a dog today, you have six different groups of dogs to choose from. First, there are the sporting dogs, like the pointers and spaniels used for hunting birds. The second kind is the hound, including bassetts and elkhounds, which are often used for hunting fur-bearing animals such as raccoons or squirrels. The third group includes the working dogs, such as German shepherds and huskies. Terriers are the fourth group of dogs. They are very good at catching rats. The fifth kind of dog is the toy dog, including chihuahuas and the smallest poodles. The final group is the nonsporting dog, such as the standard poodle. At one time, these dogs were used for hunting, but now they are owned as house pets.

The Three Poodle Puppies

Three poodle puppies named Raja, Tooto, and Samantha lived in a pretty house on the edge of a large woods. They were happy puppies, and spent their days chasing butterflies in the meadow, eating their mother's delicious dinners, and sleeping in their own baskets by the fireplace. This ideal life continued until one day when mother poodle walked out to the meadow and said, "Raja, Tooto, and Samantha, you are big dogs now, and you must learn a trade so you can get a job." Mother poodle told Raja, "You are very good with your hands. You will help your father carve toys for boys and girls." Then she turned to Tooto and said, "Tooto, you jump so high when you chase butterflies and land so gracefully on your feet, that we will send you to Madam Fifi to learn to be a ballerina." Finally, she turned to Samantha and said, "Samantha, you like to bring home little animals, so we will send you to the Woods Veterinary College so you can take care of the woodland animals when they are hurt or sick."

The next morning, Raja, Tooto, and Samantha dressed in their very best clothes, said "Goodbye" to their mother, and started out to learn their new jobs. As time passed, they learned to be a very good wood carver, ballerina, and veterinarian. But they never forgot those happy days spent chasing butterflies.

4. Have the students identify which story is fact and which is fiction. Compare the two stories with the list of information compiled about fact and fiction. "When did you decide the second story was fiction? What things in the story could not happen? How can you be positive the first story is fact?"

Fact	Fiction
"Mans Best Friend"	"Three Poodle Puppies"
1. Listed information about dogs that can be checked.	1. Mother poodles can't talk.
2. Named six real groupings of dogs that can be checked.	2. Poodles cannot carve toys or go to school.
	3. Poodles do not wear clothes.

5. The above two stories are easy to identify as fact or fiction. Other stories and articles, however, are not as easy to classify. Children often have difficulty telling the difference between stories that actually happened and stories that did not happen, but that seem lifelike. Read several realistic selections to children, and discuss the differences and how to identify them.

6. Allow students to look through newspapers and magazines (include *My Weekly Reader,* and children's magazines such as *Jack and Jill* and *Highlights* for the younger elementary child). Select articles that really happened and others that did not really happen. Create a bulletin board of fact and fiction. Draw pictures to illustrate the stories and articles.

7. Motivate children to write or dictate both factual and fictional stories about a specific subject. For example, bring into the class a small animal, such as a baby chick, rabbit, kitten, or hamster. Allow the children to look at the animal, touch it, and observe its habits. Discuss the care of the animal, why people would own it, its characteristics, and any personal experiences the children have had with the animal. Now, have them write a factual account of the animal. These compositions can be written inside a large drawing of the animal. Next, have the children think of an imaginary experience their animal might have. "Does your animal have a secret wish? What would it want to do? Where would it want to go? What special things can it do? Who are its friends? Does it have any problems? If you could talk to it, what would you talk about?" Write these fantasy stories inside a fanciful representation of the animal, or write them in the format of a comic strip, using bubbles for speech.

FACT
THINGS THAT HAPPEN
AND ARE TRUE.

FICTION
THINGS THAT DID NOT
HAPPEN AND THINGS
THAT COULD NOT HAPPEN.

CHILDREN IN THE NEWS

REAL — SEVEN YEAR OLD WINS RACE. / BROWNIE SCOUTS CAMP AT STATE PARK — TRUTH

COMICS

TALE — FANTASY

SCIENCE DISCOVERIES

ACCURACY — SPACE FLIGHT DISCOVERIES

CHILDREN'S CREATIVE STORIES

INVENTION — IMAGINATION

LET'S EXPERIMENT

MAKE A WIND-MILL / FUN WITH WATER

A HALLOWEEN PLAY

THE "TALL TALE" CHICK

CRITICAL READING— FACT vs. OPINION

TYPE		TERM	
CLASS	☐	STA	☐
GROUP	☑	LTA	☑
IND	☐	LC	☐

Purpose:

1. To define the difference between fact and opinion

2. To identify factual sections of the newspaper

3. To identify opinion sections of the newspaper

4. To identify vocabulary terms related to factual writing and to opinion

Grade level: Middle and upper elementary

Procedures:

1. Read the following three statements, or write them on cards for students to read independently.

    a. The Model-T Ford was built in 1908 by Henry Ford. In 1912, the Model-T was the first car to be mass-produced. Mass production reduced the price of cars, and allowed more people to buy them. There have been many changes since these early cars. In 1915, tops and windshields became standard equipment on cars. Rearview mirrors, stop lights, and windshield wipers were added in 1916. Four-wheel brakes were added in 1923, and automobile heaters were introduced in 1926. Car radios were added in 1929. The first automatic transmission was placed in a car in 1937.

    b. The automobile may be one of the most dangerous machines invented by man. Fumes from gasoline engines cause damage to plants, animals, and people. Bands of highways cover the green grass with cement and destroy the forests. Billboards block out the beauty of the countryside. The automobile kills many pedestrians and drivers every year. It would be better to go back to the simpler life people lived before this dangerous invention.

    c. The automobile affects all of our lives. It may be one of man's greatest helpers. Instead of walking or riding in a horse-drawn carriage, you can now use the car to buy groceries, take a trip, or go to work. Distances that would once have taken hours are now covered in minutes. Cars also provide many jobs. Men and women work in factories to build cars. They also work on highway crews to build roads for the cars. The oil industry provides many jobs so that cars can travel. People would not live well without the car for transportation.

2. After they read the three paragraphs, discuss their differences. "Which statements are factual? Why do you believe it is factual? How can you check to make sure the statements are factual? Why are the other two paragraphs not factual?" (Help students identify the final two paragraphs as someone's opinion.) "Are these two paragraphs similar in the opinion expressed?" (Help students develop the understanding that the second paragraph has a negative opinion, or bias, and the third paragraph has a positive opinion.)

3. The same article may contain both fact and opinion. Ask students to underline facts that can be checked in the above paragraphs with red pen or pencil; circle statements that are someone's belief with a blue pen or pencil.

4. Now have students look through various sections of the newspaper. Ask them to locate factual articles and opinion articles. Underline factual statements with red, and circle opinion statements with blue. Place the predominately factual articles in one group, and the predominately opinion articles in another group. Compile a list of the types of newspaper articles that are usually factual, and those that are usually opinion.

5. Create a bulletin board of factual vs. opinion newspaper articles.

	Fact		Opinion
	Statements can be checked for proof.		Statements include beliefs.
World News	Local and State News	Editorials	Editorial Cartoons
			Letters to the Editor
Obituaries	Birth		
Sports News	TV	Horoscope	Advice Columns

6. Choose a subject to write about as a factual news article and as an article containing considerable personal opinion. Possible subjects are a little league baseball game, the Girl Scout cookie sale, the school lunch program, and Saturday morning children's television.

ACTIVITY 8-22:
NEWSPAPER AND MAGAZINE READING HABITS

TYPE		TERM	
CLASS	☐	STA	☐
GROUP	☑	LTA	☑
IND	☐	LC	☐

Purpose:

1. To identify the most-read parts of the newspaper
2. To identify the reasons adults read certain sections of the newspaper
3. To identify the most popular magazines
4. To develop a questionnaire for evaluating newspaper and magazine reading preferences of peers
5. To administer a questionnaire to peers and tabulate results

Materials:

Articles describing research on adult reading habits; teacher-written paper relating these facts, or charts illustrating reading habits of adults; examples of questionnaires for administering to students

Grade level:

Accelerated upper elementary

Procedures:

1. Supply copies of journal or newspaper articles on reading habits of adults.

2. Place some basic information on charts. For example, Amiel Sharon reported the following results of a national survey of 5076 adults (*Reading Research Quarterly*, volume 9, 1974):

WHAT PARTS OF THE NEWSPAPER DO ADULTS READ EACH DAY?

Part	Percent of Readers
Main News	66
Local News	55
Women's or Society Section	37
Editorials	38
Comics	36

Sports	36
Regular Advertisements	35
Classified Ads	29
TV Listings	27
Financial News	22
Movie and Book Reviews	16
Magazine Section	12

WHAT PARTS OF THE NEWSPAPER ARE CONSIDERED THE MOST IMPORTANT

Part	Percent of Readers
Main News	43
Local News	33

WHAT ARE THE REASONS THAT ADULTS GIVE FOR READING THE NEWSPAPER?

First: Obtain general information
    a. to find out what is happening.
    b. to have something to do.
Second: Obtain specific information
    a. what new jobs are available
    b. learn about new styles in clothes
    c. learn new recipes

WHAT MAGAZINES ARE READ BY MANY ADULTS? HOW MUCH TIME DO THEY SPEND READING THEM EACH DAY?

Kind of Magazine	Percent of Population	Minutes per Day
General Interest:		
Reader's Digest	11	17
News and Editorial:		
Newsweek, Time, National Observer	6	29
Homemaking:		
Good Housekeeping McCall's	6	21
Media:		
TV Guide, Modern Screen	4	11

Sports and Recreation:		
Sports Illustrated	4	29
Field and Stream		
Home and Garden:		
House and Garden	3	20
House Beautiful		
Science Magazines:		
Scientific American	3	27
National Geographic		
Automotive and Mechanical:		
Motor Trends	2	17
Popular Mechanics		

3. Discuss the information obtained from reading the articles and looking at the charts. "What parts of the newspaper do more adults read each day? What parts of the newspaper are not as popular? Why do you think this may be true? Do you think the reasons people give for reading are accurate? Why do you read a newspaper?" Look at the magazines adults read. "Why do you think *Reader's Digest* is so popular? Why might *Reader's Digest* be read by more people than *Scientific American*? Do you believe there are any differences between people who read *Reader's Digest* and *Scientific American*? What do you think these differences are?"

4. Ask the students if they think these adult-reading habits are similar to those of their parents, and also of their classmates. Discuss methods they could use to discover similarities. Compile a list of questions they could ask their parents and classmates; for example:

---

1. Do you read a newspaper almost every day? (or on Sunday)
2. If you do, how much time did you spend reading the newspaper yesterday? (or Sunday)
3. What parts of the newspaper did you read?
    World News _____
    Local News _____
    Editorials _____
    Sports Section _____
    Comics _____
    Fashion _____
    Financial Business _____
    TV _____
    (add any other sections that are part of your newspaper) _____

---

4. What part of the newspaper did you read first, second, third, etc.?
5. Why did you read each part of the newspaper?
6. What do you believe is the most important part of the newspaper?
7. What magazines do you subscribe to each month?
8. What other magazines do you read each month?
9. What is your favorite magazine?
10. How much time do you spend reading magazines each day?

5. After compiling a questionnaire, ask the students to interview their parents and classmates. Have them tabulate their findings, and compare them with the adult-reading habits reported on the charts.

6. Discuss with the group the procedures for gathering information through observation. Have them tabulate the time they see their parents, classmates, and themselves reading specific parts of the newspaper and specific magazines.

Notes:

Chapter 2

1. Walter Loban, *Language Development: Kindergarten through Grade Twelve* (Urbana, Ill.: National Council of Teachers of English, 1976), p. 1.
2. Fran Everett Tanner, *Basic Drama Projects* (Pocatello, Id.: Clark Publishing Co., 1979), pp. 1–119.
3. Robert B. Ruddell, "Developing Comprehension Abilities: Implications From Research For An Instructional Framework," in *What Research Has to Say About Reading Instruction,* S. Jay Samuels, ed. (Newark, Del.: International Reading Association, 1978), pp. 114–15.
4. Fran Everett Tanner, *Creative Communication* (Pocatello, Id.: Clark Publishing Co., 1979), pp. 279–80.
5. George Strauss and Leonard Sayles, *Personnel, The Human Problems of Management* (Englewood Cliffs, N.J.: Prentice-Hall, 1972), pp. 226–40.
6. Benjamin Capps, *The Indians* (New York: Time-Life Books, 1973), p. 31.

Chapter 3

1. Thomas G. Devine, "Listening: What Do We Know After Fifty Years of Research and Theorizing," *Journal of Reading* 21 (Jan. 1978): 296–304.
2. Paul T. Rankin, "Listening Ability: Its Importance, Measurement, and Development," *Chicago Schools Journal* 12 (Jan. 1930): 178.
3. Susanna Davis, "A Record of Clothing From Early Plymouth," *Highlights for Children* (Nov. 1975): 35.
4. Francelia Butler, *Sharing Literature With Children* (New York: David McKay Co., 1977), p. 93.

Chapter 4

1. Roach Van Allen and Claryce Allen, *Language Experiences in Reading* (Chicago: Encyclopedia Britannica Press, 1970).
2. Russell Stauffer, *The Language Experience Approach to the Teaching of Reading* (New York: Harper & Row, 1970).
3. Richard J. Smith, Wayne Otto, and Lee Hansen, *The School Reading Program* (Boston: Houghton Mifflin Co., 1977), pp. 375–403.

Chapter 5

1. Donald H. Graves, "Let's Get Rid of the Welfare Mess in the Teaching of Writing," *Language Arts* 53 (Sept. 1976): 645–51.
2. Beatrice A. Furner, "Creative Writing Through Creative Dramatics," *Language Arts* 50 (March 1973): 405–408.
3. Alan J. McCormack, "Science, Wonderblob and the Idea Machines," *Instructor* (Jan. 1979): 111–112, 114, 116.
4. Robert E. Moore, *So You Want to Be a Writer* (San Francisco: Boyd and Fraser Publishing Co., 1974) pp. 43–44.
5. Gerald Simons, *Barbarian Europe* (New York: Time–Life Books, 1968), p. 159.

Chapter 6

1. National Council of Teachers of English, Commission on Composition, "Composition: A Position Statement," *Elementary English* 52 (Feb. 1975): 194–196.
2. William Fagan, "Transformation and Comprehension," *Reading Teacher* (Nov. 1971): 69–72.
3. Carol Chomsky, "Reading, Writing and Phonology," *Harvard Educational Review* (May, 1970): 287–309.

Chapter 7

1. James A. Smith, and Dorothy M. Park, *Word Music and Word Magic* (Boston: Allyn & Bacon, 1977), p. 31.

Chapter 8

1. Rozanne Weissman, "How TV Affects Your Children," *Family Weekly* (Jan. 28, 1979), p. 17.

Index

405